Raising
Great Kids

Chicken Soup for the Soul: Raising Great Kids
Inspiring Stories about Sharing Values from Generation to Generation
Amy Newmark, Dr. Milton Boniuk. Foreword by David Leebron.

Published by CSS Boniuk, an imprint of Chicken Soup for the Soul Publishing, LLC.
www.chickensoup.com.

The publisher gratefully acknowledges the many publishers and individuals who granted Chicken Soup for the Soul permission to reprint the cited material.

Front cover photo courtesy of istockphoto.com/andresr (©andresr)
Back cover and interior art courtesy of istockphoto.com/johnwoodcock (©Jonathan Woodcock)
Photo of Amy Newmark courtesy of Susan Morrow at SwickPix.

Design by Brian Taylor, Pneuma Books, LLC

Distributed to the booktrade by Simon & Schuster. SAN: 200-2442

Publisher's Cataloging-In-Publication Data
(Prepared by The Donohue Group, Inc.)

Chicken soup for the soul : raising great kids : inspiring stories about
   sharing values from generation to generation / [compiled by] Amy
   Newmark [and] Dr. Milton Boniuk ; foreword by David W. Leebron.

   pages ; cm

ISBN: 978-1-942649-04-5

   1. Child rearing--Literary collections. 2. Child rearing--Anecdotes.
3. Parenting--Literary collections. 4. Parenting--Anecdotes. 5.
Children--Conduct of life--Literary collections. 6. Children--Conduct of
life--Anecdotes. 7. Anecdotes. I. Newmark, Amy. II. Boniuk, Milton.
III. Leebron, David W. IV. Title: Raising great kids : inspiring stories
about sharing values from generation to generation

HQ769 .C45 2015
649.1   2015944627

PRINTED IN THE UNITED STATES OF AMERICA
on acid∞free paper

25 24 23 22 21 20 19 18 17 16 15   01 02 03 04 05 06 07 08 09 10 11

Raising
Great Kids

Inspiring Stories about
Sharing Values from
Generation to Generation

Amy Newmark & Dr. Milton Boniuk
Foreword by David W. Leebron

Chicken Soup for the Soul Publishing, LLC
Cos Cob, CT

The Boniuk Foundation
www.theboniukfoundation.org

Chicken Soup for the Soul

For moments that become stories™
www.chickensoup.com

Contents

❶
~Be a Role Model~

❷
~Make Time for Togetherness~

❸
~Be an Advocate for Acceptance~

❹
~Encourage Independence and Responsibility~

❺

~Be Kind to Strangers~

❻

~Stay Positive~

❼
~Use the Power of Forgiveness~

❽
~Think Outside the Box~

❾

~Learn from the Next Generation~

Foreword

From the very first time we hold *our* child (by which I mean any child we have undertaken the responsibility of parenting) we are typically struck by two thoughts: the awesomeness of that responsibility and, especially if it is a first child, how unprepared we feel for that task. It is indeed an awesome responsibility, and although it is a responsibility primarily to that child, it is also a broader social responsibility. We want our children not only to be successful people, but good people with good values who contribute to the betterment of our world and the lives of others. As a college educator, I know that behind every great student stands a parent and others, including teachers, who have nurtured in that child the values and behaviors that make those parents and us proud. How can we learn to be the parents we aspire to be?

One way is, of course, learning from the experiences of others, and one of the best ways to do that has always been through stories. The stories in this volume reflect many aspects of successful parenting. These include demonstrating through our own actions the values and behaviors we seek to instill, spending time with our children and truly listening to them, and giving them the space and appropriate autonomy to learn from their own decisions. We must be creative and flexible in our thinking, and learn from others, including our own children.

Families come in many configurations, from single parents raising children largely on their own to multi-generational extended families where parenting roles are widely shared. Grandparents and other relatives often play key roles, as heritage and values are passed across generations. For that reason, you will find numerous stories in this collection about the opportunity and responsibility that grandparents have as well, although in some families these roles will be played by other relatives or longtime family friends. Because these roles and relationships are typically quite different from those of a parent, children may sometimes find it easier to listen and value advice they receive from these sources.

Dr. Milton Boniuk is a father and grandfather and a man who believes strongly in the ability that all of us have to raise great kids, sharing our values with them and setting them up for wonderful, happy, productive futures. The stories in this volume were selected by him and the team listed in his introduction, and published with the support of The Boniuk Foundation. Dr. Boniuk and his wife Laurie are two of the most remarkable people I have met. They have generously devoted substantial resources to fostering religious tolerance in particular, but also improving the education of our children to instill broad values of tolerance and appreciation for diversity of all kinds. They believe that the education of our children is the foundation of a better society.

This work takes place not only as in this publication through the efforts of The Boniuk Foundation, but also through an allied endeavor at Rice University, The Boniuk Institute for the Study and Advancement of Religious Tolerance. The mission of the institute, founded in 2013, is "to understand and promote religious tolerance by using innovative methods" to undertake research, produce educational programming, and foster dialogue. It identifies religious *intolerance* as one of the root causes of war, discrimination, and violence in our world, and is committed to undertake those educational and research activities that will begin to eliminate such intolerance. (You can find more information at www.boniuk.rice.edu.)

While the goal of this volume is considerably broader, and it addresses many of the goals and techniques of successful parenting, almost all of them also affect the degree to which we practice and foster tolerant and, indeed, welcoming attitudes toward the differences we see in others. The Boniuks sincerely hope, as do so many of us, that through such efforts we can raise new generations that will end the hatred and violence that have ruined so many lives. This volume of stories can provide some of the inspiration and guidance needed to raise truly great kids who will do their part to achieve these goals in their own lives, and in the lives of others.

~David W. Leebron
President, Rice University

Introduction

Many people will agree that raising children can be one of the most difficult jobs we face in our lifetime. Nevertheless, it is one of the most rewarding jobs there can be, as nothing is better than watching a young person develop into a happy, healthy, productive adult. It is also a huge responsibility. Parents and grandparents are helping to create the next generation of our society — and the next generation of parents.

Parents and grandparents are the first and most important role models for children. Tolerance, respect, compassion and other good values start at home, in healthy, strong relationships between the generations.

My wife Laurie and I were very fortunate to have spent a lot of time with our three oldest grandsons. We spent many weekends at our ranch, which is less than one hour from our home in Houston. We took them on vacations and cruises individually, together, and with their parents. This worked well for everybody — children, parents, and grandparents.

Having good relations with siblings, parents, grandparents, in-laws, stepparents and stepchildren produces a great environment and allows for healthy emotional, academic, and other forms of development. That is why the stories in this new Chicken Soup for the Soul collection provide great advice on how to have those conversations and how to form meaningful relationships with the children in our families.

An important part of raising children is setting expectations. What do you expect from your children and grandchildren in the way of behavior? How will you let them know when you are pleased and when you are not? The family disciplinarian can be either parent, or a combination of parents and grandparents. It seems that some children who do well academically, and who are very polite with strangers, end up being confrontational and have a poor relationship with their parents. This book is meant to help create those good relationships, with open dialogue that goes in both directions between children, parents, and grandparents.

I am the child of immigrants. I have always been impressed by how immigrant parents to Canada and the United States produced so many brilliant, motivated children. These children had the support and encouragement of their parents, many of whom had limited education and were unable to speak English fluently. Although in many families, it was customary to choose the same career as one's parent—it was viewed as a sign of respect for that parent and a happy family upbringing—choosing a different career does not necessarily imply a strained relationship with one or both parents. It may also indicate a desire to pursue an independent career because of special talent or special academic, artistic, musical or other accomplishments.

It's interesting that in the case of the children of immigrants, sometimes the first generation children did well but subsequent generations did not do as well for a number of reasons. One of those reasons may be the way some children are raised today.

In a *New York Times* Op-Ed piece on April 24, 2015, David Brooks wrote about the two defining features he sees in childrearing today. The first is that "children are now praised to an unprecedented degree," by parents who may be overly concerned about boosting their kids' self-esteem, and the second is that "children are honed to an unprecedented degree," by parents who are more anxious than ever about their kids getting into good colleges and onto good career paths. Parents glow when their children study hard, practice hard, win first place, or get into prestigious colleges. These children tell their parents things that will elicit praise and hide the parts of their lives that won't. They can be model students but suffer in the long run if they come to resent their parents, and then feel less worthy as adults. Brooks points out that parental love is meant to be unconditional support that cannot be bought and cannot be earned. The author Jane Haddam summed it up when she said, "In my day, we didn't have self-esteem, we had self-respect, and no more of it than we had earned."

We all want our children and grandchildren to become self-reliant, resilient, and responsible adults, ones who respect others, reject stereotypes, and demonstrate compassion. We also want to have honest, open, caring relationships with our children and grandchildren. I believe that the stories we have chosen for this book will help you accomplish just that.

You'll read about being a role model for children and grandchildren, demonstrating the values you hope they will make their own. You'll find a chapter about the importance of making time for togetherness, as a family and individually with each child. You'll read stories about the value of listening to the next generation and learning from them, too. You'll meet parents and grandparents who are advocates for acceptance, and who encourage independence and responsibility in their younger family members. And you'll be impressed by how children are influenced by parents and grandparents who are kind to strangers, who use the power of forgiveness to repair relationships and move forward, and who use positive thinking to make better lives. You'll read tales of gratitude and giving, sportsmanship and honor, and you'll pick up some wonderful parenting tips — easy changes you can make in your own family that will make a big difference.

I am very grateful to Bill Rouhana, CEO, and Amy Newmark, Publisher, of Chicken Soup for the Soul, for allowing us to develop these books and educational programs with them. Bill and Amy share our commitment and dedication to these projects.

I would like to acknowledge the assistance of the following individuals who helped select the stories for inclusion in this book: my wife Laurie, my son David Boniuk and his wife Kelli, my grandsons Justin Sable and Ryan Sable, Yan Digilov, Dr. Silvia Orengo-Nania and her daughter Julia Nania, her nieces Anna Hanel and Marisa Rao, Lee Pelton, a sophomore at Rice University, and Gaby Barrios, Natalie

Danckers, and Anjale Raghuran, all seniors at Rice University.

I would also like to thank David Leebron, president of Rice University, for his continued support. I also thank the following members of the advisory board of The Boniuk Institute at Rice University for their unwavering support: Charley Landgraf, member of the board of trustees and current chairman of the advisory board; Malcolm Gillis, former president of Rice; and Bill Barnett and James Crownover, former chairmen of the board at Rice University.

~Dr. Milton Boniuk

Chapter 1

Raising Great Kids

Be a Role Model

Back to the Bank

To bring up a child in the way he should go — travel that way yourself.
~Josh Billings

"Why are we going back to the bank?" I asked my mother. The five of us — my mother, three brothers, and I — had just returned home from a morning of running errands. Packages were mailed, utility bills were paid and cash withdrawn from the bank. Trapped in the car with my younger brothers all morning was torture anyway, and besides that, it was a hot, humid day and the car's torn seats were itchy and uncomfortable. Our little house, with the white bed linens hanging from the clothesline in the back yard, was a welcomed sight.

As a reward for good behavior all morning, my mother had promised to take us to our aunt's pool for an afternoon of swimming. My brothers and I had bolted from the old black station wagon toward the house when we were brought to a halt by our mother's voice. "Everyone back in the car," she said. "We are going back to the bank."

I had only two things on my twelve-year-old mind — lunch and swimming. Although my aunt and uncle lived down the street, it was rare that we were invited over for a swim. Since pools in this part of the country were a novelty, this was an opportunity not to be missed. I couldn't wait to get in the water to work on what I called my water ballet moves and maybe get up some courage to dive off the diving board. All we had to do was eat a quick sandwich, wrestle on our bathing suits, grab our beach towels and go. And now, we had to get back in the car?

We lived in a small, rural town in New England. We drove nearly an hour on narrow, curved roads and routes to the services and businesses we had visited in the morning. I calculated the timeline in my head. This could take at least two hours, not counting the time in the bank. I pleaded with my mother. "Can't we go back tomorrow? We can't go today. Please? We want to go swim. Please?" My mother replied calmly, "We are going back to the bank."

My mother herded us back into the hot, stuffy car. She brought some snacks—apples, cheese, and a rare treat—chilled bottles of Coca-Cola. I would have none of it. I sat in the back seat with my arms crossed tightly against my chest. I stared out the window, seeing nothing. I resisted the urge to physically communicate to my tired, noisy brothers how much their whining irritated me. My mother was driving and singing along to a Chet Atkins song, as if on a leisurely Sunday drive on a spring day.

My mother parked the station wagon in front of the bank. The bank was a grand two-story building constructed of granite blocks. Four tall columns flanked the brass-framed, glass door entrance. The brood tumbled out of the car and up the granite stairs. The polished stone floors and vaulted, painted and gilded ceiling echoed our noisy entrance into the bank. I stayed close to my mother's side as we approached the tellers' windows and then my mother paused. She looked from one teller to the next, and then with assurance she approached a teller standing behind the window at the end of the long, marble and mahogany counter.

The teller was a pretty and petite woman who looked nervous and tense. My mother told the young woman that she was the customer who had come to the bank in the morning and this woman had given my mother the cash she had withdrawn. Talking to this young woman in a kind, soft voice, my mother explained that she had returned to the bank to correct an error that had occurred earlier.

A worried look quickly replaced the teller's smile. My mother reached into her purse with the broken clasp and pulled something out. Then, I saw my mother slide a one-hundred-dollar bill over the marble countertop to the teller. "You gave me one hundred dollars too much," my mother said.

Trying to hold back the tears, the teller leaned forward and whispered, "I'm so sorry. I'm worried and upset and I have made several errors. I was told this morning that if I made one more error, I would lose my job. You see, my husband left me this week. I have two small children to support. Thank you so much for returning this money. I can't thank you enough. Not many people would have returned this money. Thank you so much." My mother simply said, "You're welcome." And gently patting the teller's hand, she said, "Good luck to you."

We filed out of the grandiose bank and into our dirty, rundown station wagon. It was raining now. Any hope of swimming today, or for the rest of the summer for that matter, was lost. As my mother drove the country roads for the second time that day, she said little. She treated this event as business as usual, nothing special. But I knew that something important had happened on that disappointing, swim-less day, though I could not have told you what it was at the time.

But fifty years later, I can tell you what happened on that one summer day. I had been taught, by my mother's humble act, the lessons of honesty, integrity and kindness. Throughout my life, whenever I have been faced with the inevitable what-is-the-right-thing-to-do dilemma, the choice has been made easy thanks to my mother. I simply recall my mother's voice and hear her say, "We are going back to the bank."

~Elizabeth Greenhill

The Greatest Lesson Never Spoken

Leaders don't create followers, they create more leaders.
~Tom Peters

Sometimes, the greatest lessons taught by our fathers are those that they never so much as mention.

Growing up, I understood my father only as a man known for his business accomplishments: a leader of convention, an attorney and small business owner whose law firm had earned a respected reputation; and who had worked alongside important state officials, unions, and municipalities for decades.

In my youth, I understood my father, the attorney, to be an indistinguishable part of who my father was as a dad at home. I connected his distinguished, structured style of teaching my siblings and me as no different from the way in which he would formulate an argument in court.

He would often teach us lessons like, "You cannot judge your actions on the basis of what others do or don't do," and "The ways the world works cannot be separated into black and white." I concluded that these parenting lessons were nothing more than results of his years of experience with the complexities of practicing law. In many ways, they were.

But, all the while, my father was teaching me a great lesson that

I would not come to realize for decades. Remarkably, this lesson was never so much as spoken. I've only come to understand it now, after having realized that I inherited this quality from him as much as I have any physical characteristic or personality trait. The unspoken lesson that my father taught me was by his quiet example as a constant, selfless giver.

A product of my dad's immigrant family's impoverished history and the family's general "lack" of everything throughout most of his young life, my father became a quiet giver, one who sought to provide beyond his means and at his inconvenience to both family, friends and strangers alike. In his career, giving took the form of upstanding moral integrity and public service as an attorney.

Much of his giving, I've realized, has been often without reason and without purpose. But thankfully, it has also been without limitation.

As if to counterbalance the utter deficit of material and emotional comfort that he had growing up, my father has strived to provide a surplus of both forms of comforts to his family and friends: to always open his home to others without question; to grant the foremost opportunities for his children through the best schooling and college education that he could afford; to provide an unquestionable amount of moral support and encouragement; to provide the means to alleviate any possible financial burden that might fall upon us; and truly, to allow us the means to follow our hearts and pursue our most sincere passions in life.

After years of witnessing his quiet but persistent giving, something dawned upon me: my own will to give beyond my means and at my inconvenience was a trait I inherited from my father, like any other. My father's quiet example was a subtle side to him that I had felt and witnessed all of my life. But because this side to him was never advertised, discussed, or iterated, I emulated his example without so much as ever realizing it. And so it became as much a part of me as any other inherited quality.

My father, I now realize, has not been just a leader of convention as an attorney. He is also — and, perhaps, more importantly — a quiet leader who teaches by loving example. Whether he knew it or not, his quiet leadership was an integral component of his fatherhood and influenced his children perhaps more notably than any spoken lesson that I can recall.

The dualistic nature of his fatherhood is an integral component of teaching by example: on the one hand, to lead by traditional fatherly example, and on the other, by being a living example of an individual who his children naturally want to emulate.

Sons inherit much from their fathers. Physical characteristics, like body type and eye color, are easy to recognize. Personality traits, like one's sense of humor, can be measured in laughter. But a quiet life lesson like the one taught by my father to be a constant giver and to give beyond one's means and at one's inconvenience — a lesson that was never spoken, and taught only by quiet example — can only be measured by the extent that others feel it, and oftentimes, never realize it.

~Dave Ursillo, Jr.

Speak Up

*Don't be afraid to stand up for yourself, you should speak up
even if you don't get the answer you were looking for; it's the fact
that you said something that matters.*
~Author Unknown

o, I don't want to go to school anymore. Anyway, I can't find my backpack," I protested.

My mom looked at me, puzzled. "What's going on? Why don't you want to go to school?"

"I can't find my backpack. Besides, I don't like school anymore! Can you teach me here at home, please?"

My mom remained adamant. "What is the real reason you don't want to go to school? Is someone bothering you?"

"No! I just don't like school anymore, and I can't go to school without my backpack. That's where I have my homework."

Earlier that morning I had sneaked into the back yard and, attempting to hide my backpack, I'd thrown it on the roof. My mom walked straight into the back yard and pointed up to the roof.

"Maria, isn't that your backpack?"

My heart sank. How did she know it was up there? My brilliant plan had backfired.

At the beginning of the school year I had been so happy to start second grade. I had a few friends and we were always playing and talking about school and planning new adventures for our weekends. I had my routine. Every day after school I would take off my uniform and get it ready for the next day. I had a jump rope that I took to school and only my friends and I could use it. School was fun. After school I would tell my mom all about my day and everything that had happened.

But now I didn't want to go back. And Mom was trying to get to the root of the problem. I finally gave in and told her, "I don't want to go to school anymore because the teacher pinches me on my arm and sometimes on my back."

Very calmly Mom said, "Okay, let's go; I'm going to have a talk with her." At that moment I regretted telling my mom about the pinching. I pleaded with her to forget what I'd said.

I had the whole scenario down in my mind. I could see it. After the meeting my teacher was going to slap me and continue to pinch me and separate me from my friends. I was terrified, but my mom grabbed me by the hand and took me to school.

We arrived late. My teacher came to the door and said, "Good morning. What is going on?" I did not respond; I was paralyzed with fear.

Mom took charge by saying, "Good morning. I am Maria's mother, and I'm here because my daughter does not want to come to school anymore. She says you pinch her arm and her back."

My teacher glared at me with a piercing gaze that sent chills down my spine. She proceeded by saying, "What a little liar you are, Maria. When have I ever done those things to you?"

I wished the floor under me would open and swallow me. I wanted to disappear, but my mother courageously said, "I don't think Maria has a reason to lie, but let me tell you something. My daughter does not come to school to be punished; she comes to school to learn. And if there is a problem with her behavior, you can send me a note. I need to make sure you understand that if this punishment continues I'm going to have a meeting with the principal, and if that does not give me good results, I will go to the district. Do you understand my concern?"

The teacher changed her tone and said, "I'm sorry for this misunderstanding. It will never happen again."

My mother gave me a hug and a kiss and left. As I walked inside the classroom I heard a tender sweet voice directing me to my seat. It was my teacher saying, "Maria, take your seat. We are reading page 22."

After that magical day my life at school changed. My teacher treated me decently, and I was not afraid to go to school anymore. She never pinched me or anyone else in my class that year.

That day I learned you don't have to be a victim, and that when you speak up people listen. Even though this incident happened many years ago, that day my mom became my hero. This experience gave me the courage to speak up throughout my adult life whenever I encounter an injustice, which is something I've passed on to my children.

~Maria Calderon Sandoval

My Mother, The Patriot

He loves his country best who strives to make it best.
~Robert G. Ingersoll

ain, wind, cold sleet on my face… I will never forget standing there, chilled to the bone in my slicker and boots, handing out fliers to weary voters entering the red school doors that I passed through on a daily basis. Today these doors represented change and American principles.

Next to me, also being beaten by the weather, was my mother. Looking up at her, I saw her friendly smile as she was meeting, greeting and conversing with our neighbors and residents of the local community. As the rain ran down her face, dripping from her eyelashes, she never stopped working, promoting and talking political issues that her favored candidates represented. I didn't understand any of the conversations; I just knew they were important, and that the whole process was patriotic.

Surrounding us were the local politicians extending handshakes to the hopeful people who wanted better for the community. Among them stood the principal of my school, who was running for an office of some distinction to improve educational policies. I also saw the neighborhood attorney, the local storeowner, the insurance man who visited our house to sell his policies to my dad; even our local doctor was there. There were also friends of my father, husbands of my mother's friends, men with hopes to better their lives, and the rest of us living in a neighborhood that was falling apart and facing ruin from economic changes. I was young, the only child there, but I loved being part of making change and doing something that would make a difference.

Now an adult, as I handed out fliers this past presidential election, I reflected on why I was standing in the rain in my slicker and boots once again. The image of my mother — a daughter of immigrants, a child abandoned by her mother and later orphaned by her father, a victim of the depression, a mother so loyal to America that she made her children stand and salute when the President addressed the nation on TV, and a citizen who totally appreciated living in America — came to mind. The image of my mother, a stay-at-home mom trying to keep America strong in the only way she knew how, trying to protect her children, her home, and her community, flashed by. Why, I was just like her! She instilled patriotism in me at a young age, by setting an example, by showing love for her country and by working for what she thought was right.

Thank you, Mom, for giving me this passion, this drive, this enthusiasm, this willingness to do whatever I can to maintain the values that my country represents. Thank you for passing on to me the appreciation of being born in America, and the determination to do whatever I can to help preserve freedom for my children and my grandchildren. Thank you for making me a patriot, too.

~Terrilynne Walker

Where's Your Notebook?

One father is more than one hundred schoolmasters.
~George Herbert

I was thirteen years old when Dad called my two younger brothers and me into the game room of our house. I was excited! I thought we were going to play pool or pinball or maybe even watch movies together, just us guys! "Bring a notebook and something to write with," my dad bellowed before we reached the game room. My brothers and I stopped dead in our tracks and stared at each other in horror! His request was unusual, and our excitement turned to dread as we became well aware that games or movies were not the reason we were pulled away from watching *Fat Albert*. This felt more official and tedious, like schoolwork, chores or worse, a family meeting.

As we each retrieved a notebook and pencil, we continued to ponder the reason for this summons. We ruled out a family meeting because Mom was still out shopping. We entered the game room to find three metal folding chairs facing a huge blackboard. Dad instructed us to sit in the chairs and NOT on the cushioned sofa just inches from us.

"I want your full attention. That is why I have you sitting in these chairs," he stated, businesslike.

Immediately we began to pout and whine.

"Where's Mom, aren't we gonna wait for Mom?" my youngest brother asked.

"Is this gonna take long?" my other brother sighed.

I silently squirmed in the uncomfortable metal chair.

"Your mother won't be back for hours, and if you must know, she has nothing to do with this," he said calmly. "And how long this takes depends entirely upon each of you. The more you participate, the more you'll learn, and the faster we can move on and be done. Understood?"

"Yes, sir," we responded unenthusiastically.

"Now," my father began, "we are going to have a weekly meeting with just us guys. We will have these meetings every Saturday morning, but if you have school or sports activities on Saturday morning, we'll reschedule for Sundays after church. I'm going to teach you what I have learned about life. It is my responsibility, before God, to prepare you to be strong, proud, African American men who will be assets to the community and to the world at large. It is a responsibility I take very seriously."

I just had to jump in, "You're going to teach us everything about life?"

"Everything I can."

"But that will take forever."

"Maybe." He turned to begin writing on the blackboard. "Maybe."

For the next five years, rain or shine, in sickness or in health, Dad taught us about life once a week. He instructed us on a wide variety of subjects — personal hygiene, puberty, etiquette, the importance of education, racism, dating, respect for women, respect for those in authority, respect for our elders, Christian salvation, a good work ethic, what it means to be an adult, what to look for in a wife, landscaping, minor home repairs, auto repairs, budgeting, investing, civic duties and the list goes on. We begrudgingly filled notebook after notebook after notebook.

As I approached my eighteenth birthday, the weekly lessons became monthly lessons and then every other month, until they slowly drifted away. My brothers and I were older, we had girlfriends, school activities, sports activities and job responsibilities that became extremely difficult to schedule around. I'm not sure when it happened, but the importance of our weekly lessons and notebooks began to pale in comparison to our busy teenage lives. Soon the classes and the notebooks were mere memories.

It's been years now since we had those classes with Dad in the game room. We are grown with careers and wives of our own. At every challenge in life, my brothers and I have frantically looked in attics, basements and storage sheds for our notebooks. We can't find them anywhere.

At least once a month one of us has a situation where we need to call home and ask Dad for his advice or guidance. We hesitantly pick up the phone to call him, knowing good and well he's going to laugh and say, "Where's your notebook?"

~John W. Stewart, Jr.

Neighbor from Hell

*Today, give a stranger one of your smiles. It might be the only
sunshine he sees all day.*
~H. Jackson Brown, Jr., P.S. I Love You

She was determined to make our lives miserable from the moment we met. Edna Strom looked to be in her late seventies. She had a perpetual squint. Her lips curled sourly, as if she had mistaken a bottle of vinegar for soda.

We'd barely moved one stick of furniture into the lower duplex we'd rented next door to her converted two-story home when Mrs. Strom hobbled onto her upstairs front gallery. She glared down at my twelve-year-old son David and then at me, announcing, "You make sure you keep that child out of my yard!"

Since our buildings shared a communal six-foot-high privacy fence that separated our lots, I couldn't understand her concern or hostility. Nevertheless, I replied curtly, "Don't worry!" as I ducked into my entryway with the box I was carrying.

That encounter set the tone for weeks. The next day, while my son was laughing on the phone, we were stunned to hear a loud pounding from the other side of his bedroom wall, which connected our dwellings and ran the entire length of both houses.

"Stop that racket right this minute!"

Mrs. Strom's furious voice filtered right into the kitchen I was painting. I rushed towards David to find him sitting on the bed, eyes wide with shock, his conversation forgotten.

"Mom, I was just laughing!" he protested.

"I know, honey," I soothed, gulping back my own growing anger. "Listen, let's just let this go until we're a little more settled in. I'll deal with it in a few days if it continues, okay?" I promised.

"Okay," he agreed reluctantly.

That same afternoon, he and a friend went out front to play pitch and catch. Within minutes, they both returned, their expressions clearly indicating that they were upset about something.

"What happened?" I sighed, certain our neighbor had struck again.

"She yelled at us from her balcony to go play in the back yard," David complained.

I handed each of the kids a soda, instructing them go out back. Then, I marched out the front door to confront the cranky old woman. This was our home too and I was going to nip this problem in the bud. There was no way she was going to continue scolding my child, especially since he'd done nothing wrong, nor been excessively loud.

I found her sitting ramrod straight in a rocking chair on her front porch, peering out into the street. Her summer dress was crisply ironed, her polished shoes gleamed, and every hair was in place. She wore a pearl necklace with matching earrings. When she saw me approach, she narrowed her eyes, pursing her lips even tighter.

"Is something wrong?" I asked her.

"My boy is coming to visit," she informed me haughtily. "I didn't want to get hit by your son's baseball while I wait for him."

"I'm sure he was being careful," I told her stonily. "He's not a bad kid, ma'am. In the future, if there's a problem, please come to me so we can solve it instead of shouting at him."

Not waiting for an answer, I turned and went back into the house. As I entered the common foyer, I almost bumped into the upstairs tenant who was checking her mail.

"I see you've met Edna Strom." She smiled. "Pay her no mind. She sits out there every day the minute the weather turns warm and waits for her son to visit. He only comes when he needs money. Even then, he's loud, rude and obnoxious, treating her like dirt!"

The apple doesn't fall far from the tree, I almost muttered, but bit my tongue. "Is she always that crabby?" I asked instead.

"Always. Just ignore her. Everyone does."

Edna didn't let up on her tyrannical behavior. She hammered on the walls if we so much as dropped a pot cover or raised our stereo or television to a decibel above a whisper. Even adjusting the ring of our phone to accommodate her couldn't please the woman. We could almost feel her scowl sear into us as she kept her ever-present vigil on the balcony in the pathetic hope that her son might drop in.

Two months later, we were finally settled in and decided to have a cookout for friends and family. I prepared for the event, ignoring the persistent banging whenever I closed a cupboard or refrigerator door a little too hard. By that time, Mrs. Strom was becoming background noise.

The day of the barbecue, as people arrived, I noticed that Edna wasn't at her usual post. Her son had dropped in two days earlier and was every bit as vocal and insufferable as I'd been told, belittling his mother and demanding money. I assumed she wouldn't expect him again anytime soon and was taking a break from her lookout.

As the last guest arrived, we moved to the back yard. I was serving appetizers when a movement from her upstairs window caught my eye. I looked up to see her observing a laughing group of my visitors. Unaware that she could be seen, her usual bitter demeanor was absent. Instead, a combination of sad, wistful loneliness seemed to suffuse her features, and I felt a growing sympathy tug at my heart.

Seconds later, I was ringing her bell. She opened the door, shocked to see me.

"Can I help you?" she asked coldly, and I smiled.

"Mrs. Strom, I was wondering if you'd like to join us since we're neighbors. I'm sure my family and friends would love to meet you."

"Well, I — that is — I — I'm not really dressed to — "

I noticed then that she was clothed more casually than I'd ever seen her.

"You look fine," I assured her. "Everyone is in jeans or shorts. You'll fit right in. Please come."

For the first time ever, I saw her smile, catching a glimpse of the beauty that must have been hers when she was younger.

"Well, if you're sure," she said shyly, patting her hair nervously and straightening her blouse. "I have a fresh cheesecake I can bring—my late husband's favorite. I made it this morning."

"Why, that would be wonderful," I gushed. "Come, let's go."

My husband and son hid their shock, welcoming our neighbor with warm smiles when I escorted her into our yard on my arm.

"Everyone," I called out, "I'd like you to meet my friend and neighbor, Edna Strom."

We never heard a harsh word from her again. In fact, we became close friends, forgiving and forgetting our rocky beginning, and embracing our friendship instead. She no longer sat on her balcony waiting tirelessly for her son's sporadic visits. She was far too busy teaching me her favorite recipes, and joining us for family occasions where she was received with love and respect until she died peacefully five years later in her sleep. Only a week before, she had hugged me tightly and thanked me for being the daughter she never had. I mourned her like I would a beloved relative, grateful that I looked past the thorns to see the fragile flower within.

~Marya Morin

Everlasting Lessons

A grandfather is someone with silver in his hair and gold in
his heart.
~Author Unknown

While the women of our family slept in pre-dawn darkness, Granddad and I grabbed buckets and rods and slipped into his brown Zephyr station wagon. Rumbling up and down the hills of our Pittsburgh neighborhood, we were off on an adventure just for the guys. We sat side by side on the front seat as the music of Granddad's oldies filled the car. When we pulled up to a creek behind a gas station, soft light spread across the sky. We were there. I stepped out and waited for the magic to start.

Wearing a trucker hat and overalls, Granddad transformed into a master fisherman. His face glowed as he dipped his worn bucket into the green water and slowly pulled it up. Like a kid in awe of a magician, I gazed wide-eyed at the hundreds of minnows that swam inside.

Back then I was just a nine-year-old boy happy to be spending time with Grandpa. But years later, memories like that one would mean much more. They were lessons in living and manhood. They were touchstones that anchored me in values and faith. And one day, those moments with Granddad would save me from myself.

Some boys look to their fathers for direction. I had my mom's dad. Where my father's presence was scarce, my Granddad was my rock.

He imparted wisdom like he sowed seeds in his garden. He planted the knowledge and waited for it to sprout.

Any time we spent together was an opportunity to teach. He schooled me in the importance of learning new things. "You can play anytime," he would say in the accent that revealed traces of his West Virginia childhood. "Crack open a book and learn something." As I watched him work on car engines in the yard, he would tell me how important it was to learn a trade: "That's something no one can take away." When I would trail him around our backyard garden and help him tend to the tomatoes and green beans, he would tell me about enjoying God's blessings.

Then Granddad got sick. His pecan-colored skin turned pale. His hair, always dyed jet black, showed its true silver. I watched his body weaken and his fight for living slip away. Ten days before my fourteenth birthday, my Granddad died of prostate cancer. Losing him was like losing my compass. Everywhere I turned, I was lost. Not only did I no longer have a father figure in my life, I felt abandoned and alone. Suddenly, I was left to be a man on my own. Or at least that's what I thought.

I turned my back on the lessons Granddad taught me and started making bad choices. I stopped going to church. My birthdays, because they fell right after yearly anniversaries of Granddad's death, were painful reminders he was gone. So I stopped celebrating them.

One day, I looked at myself in the mirror and saw someone I didn't know. My eyes looked cold and hard. My heart was ice. I knew I was at a turning point. I could keep following the path I was on and end up defeated or dead. Or I could choose the road to hope. Right then, my grandma said something that shook me to the bone: "Your Granddad would be heartsick to see you like this." Softly at first and then louder, I could hear his voice in my ears: "Learn a trade. Crack open a book. Be a man who makes his family proud." The lessons Granddad taught me as a child returned to lead me when I needed them most.

Turning things around was a process. I stopped hanging out. I started learning an automotive trade. Slowly, purposefully, I started to find my way.

Today, I'm a husband and father. I own my home and work hard six days a week as a detailer at a car dealership. I dream of one day owning my own business. I know Granddad would be proud.

I go to his grave sometimes and thank him for filling me with lessons that live on like his memory in my heart. At my house, I have a picture of Granddad. His eyes crinkle with joy as he smiles. It's my reminder to be the kind of man he was.

~Kevin Price as told to Kelly Starling Lyons

"You Didn't Quit, Mommy, So Neither Did I"

*Don't worry that children never listen to you; worry that they
are always watching you.*
~Robert Fulghum

I truly thought that I might die that day. Had I not seen three bears and a few wolves over the last couple of days near the road, I might have just laid down and called it quits. What in the world was I thinking, dragging my bike up to Yellowstone and thinking I could ride from West Yellowstone to Old Faithful — in the snow, no less! A year ago I would never have believed it.

I don't know what made me decide to change my life. One day in March, I just woke up tired of being fat. I was tired of feeling like my weight defined my whole existence. I wanted to play with my children and to be the kind of mother of whom they could be proud. I convinced my husband that our family could stand to get a little healthier and just like that it began.

I threw myself into discovering better ways to eat. I got all of the sugar and junk food out of the house and replaced it with fresh fruits and vegetables. For the first time in my life, I started to exercise every day. At first it was absolute torture. I kept the phone right by me, just in case I had a heart attack on my stationary bike. I told everyone I knew that I was getting healthy — my pride ensuring that because everyone would be watching, I would try harder. Amazingly, just like it is supposed to, the weight started to come off.

The change spread through my whole family. My husband, who hadn't cycled in years, bought a new road bike and soon convinced me to join him. By June, he had signed me up to do a twenty-two mile charity ride with him. I was scared to death, but I ended up having a fantastic time. It felt so empowering to be in good enough shape to not only finish the ride, but to finish before more than half of the people riding.

Soon I was getting up to ride my bike early every morning. On Saturdays, my husband and I would get a babysitter and ride for a couple of hours. Imagine that! The girl who hated walking a quarter of a mile to school was trading date night at the IHOP for hours on a bike.

By August, I was sixty pounds lighter and in better shape than I had ever been. I coached my daughter's soccer team and ran around doing drills with them. They got winded before I did. I could tell that my daughter was proud of me, and that was inspiration to keep going. Later that month, I completed a sixty-eight mile ride in a little less than five hours total time. Completing that ride was a dream come true and I thought that I could now do anything. Then came Yellowstone….

Had everything gone perfectly, it wouldn't have been so bad. However, besides the weather, I wasn't feeling well and had not eaten properly for such an effort. We had planned this trip for more than two months, though, and I wasn't about to give up so easily. The first few miles were beautiful. Ten miles in, I started sucking wind. Fifteen miles and my legs felt like they were made of lead. By twenty miles, my lungs were burning and I felt like there was nothing left in the tank.

That's when I turned around and saw my three children cheering me on in the van behind me. I knew then that I couldn't quit. I tell my children all the time that just because something is hard doesn't mean that you stop doing it. I had to live what I'd been preaching.

That thought and a lot of prayer got me up that mountain and to the end of the ride. It took everything I had and then some, but I made it.

The importance of that ride was apparent after only a week. My eight-year-old daughter Emalee wanted to ride in a twelve mile breast cancer awareness ride. We told her it would not be easy, but we thought that she could do it. That day was cold as well. She was the youngest rider and I was already proud of her for even trying. About four miles into the ride, she started feeling the cold. The chill was making her muscles cramp a little and she began to struggle. By six miles, she had tears running down her face.

It broke my heart to see her suffering like that. I told her that she didn't have to finish, that we could stop and call someone to pick us up. She said that she wouldn't quit. I told her how I had wanted to quit the week before, but that prayer and perseverance had gotten me to the end and I knew that she could do it too.

I don't remember much more of that ride — I was too busy praying for my little girl and trying to keep her safe and inspired. The look on her face as she pulled into the finish was priceless. She threw her arms around me and said "You didn't quit, Mommy, so neither did I." Everything I'd been through for the last seven months was worth it for that one moment when I realized that my daughter wanted to be like me, and for once, that was okay!

~Kimberlee Garrett

Tools for Life

A child enters your home and for the next twenty years makes
so much noise you can hardly stand it. The child departs,
leaving the house so silent you think you are going mad.
~John Andrew Holmes

I t was December when my father had to live the moment every dad dreads—times two. I, with my bachelor's degree in hand, was officially and permanently leaving the nest for Connecticut. My sister, clutching her master's degree, was heading off to New Jersey to start her new life.

And to make matters even worse, there was a long-time boyfriend waiting for each of us. Not only was my father losing both of his girls at once, he was losing them to other men. He had us hostage for the holidays, but after that, all bets were off. The clock was ticking.

So that's the year he gave my sister and me the best presents we ever received.

A pony? No, I'd given up on that dream years ago when he bought me a stuffed horse instead. A car? Nope, my father insisted the old Buick he'd procured from our elderly neighbor was "a great car!"

Sitting underneath the tree on Christmas morning were two identical gifts my brother, muscles straining, pushed in front of his sisters. Large, slightly lumpy, and heavy enough to make me question what I'd do with a box of rocks.

"This is from your father," my mother said, eager to re-distribute the credit. With slightly nervous glances cast each other's way (my father does not do his own shopping), my sister and I tore open the paper to reveal... toolboxes.

Just what every little-girl-at-heart wants for Christmas.

"Open it, open it!" our very own Santa announced gleefully, clapping his hands.

So we did.

Hammers. Wrenches. Nails. Duct tape. Tire gauge. Tape measure. Screws.

The fun just kept coming, and he couldn't have looked prouder.

We couldn't have been more confused.

Like your average girls, we dutifully ooh-ed and ah-ed over our loot and kept our eyes glued to the clearly denoted GAP box under the tree.

"He did that all by himself, you know," Mom confided to us later when all of the crumpled wrapping paper had found a home on the floor and presents lay scattered about. "It took him hours to pick all of that out."

Suddenly, it was clear—tightly packed into those cumbersome, clunky toolboxes were all of a father's lessons and love. He may have been passing us on to other men, but his girls were going to be able to take care of themselves—and always remember who it was in their lives that first built a foundation and always picked up the pieces and hammered them back together.

Yes, my father gave me a tire gauge for Christmas, along with the forethought to avoid problems before they happen.

A spare key holder—and the knowledge that everybody's human and forgets their keys sometimes.

A hammer—and the strength to know that girls can swing them, too.

Nails—and countless memories to hang on the walls.

A toolbox—and all of the love and support to get through the good and the bad in life. No matter what's bent out of shape or broken.

Thanks, Dad. For all of the tools you've given me.

~Caitlin Q. Bailey

Money!

God only looks to the pure, not to the full hands.
~Laberius

 ur family was Christmas shopping in the clothing department of a large department store, when our nine-year-old son, Bradley, shouted, "Money!" Rolled up with a rubber band was a substantial amount of cash, apparently dropped unknowingly by its owner. The money had rolled under a display table and it was by sheer luck that my son saw it at all.

He was so excited about his find that my husband and I hated to rain on his parade with a gentle reminder, "Somewhere, someone else is very sad about losing this much money," his dad told him.

I added, "Yes, and the person who lost it may have saved for a long time and is frantically looking for it now."

After a short discussion of who might have lost it we asked him, "How would you feel if you had lost the money?"

"I think I'd be sad and maybe even sick to my stomach," he admitted.

I asked, "Do you think your should keep the money or turn it in to the store manager?"

It wasn't an easy decision for a nine-year-old. He frowned. "Turn it in."

When the lady behind the desk at Lost and Found asked, "How can I help you?" I nudged Bradley forward to speak for himself. "But,

Mom, what if no one ever comes to claim it?" he asked.

I gave him a smile and stepped forward to explain about the lost money. "Do you think if the money isn't claimed it could be given to our son, who found it?"

The desk clerk had watched Bradley struggle with changing his mind and readily agreed.

We left his name and address and the clerk wrote a quick note. Then using the rubber band she attached the note to the money and placed it in a lock-box.

When we retold this incident to others, many called us naive. "Surely the store manager or some other employee will keep that money," people would say. In fact, the general consensus was that we were "fools" to encourage our son to turn the money in. His neighborhood friends teased Bradley, chanting, "Do gooder! Do gooder! You're nuts!"

He just shrugged it off and said, "It wasn't my money." His dad and I were so proud of him.

Two years later a letter came in the mail addressed to Bradley. It was from the department store, which was now going out of business. The letter stated that they had found a roll of money in their vault with Bradley's name and address on it. A notation said it should be sent to him if not claimed. Attached to the letter was a check made out to Bradley with a note from the manager:

Dear Bradley,

I do admire you so much for making such a grown up decision at age nine. I remember your struggle and know it wasn't easy. It took a person of strong character to turn in that money. There are many adults who would struggle with such a decision. The money was never claimed and so I am pleased to honor your request. The money is now yours!

She made a smiley face with the words "enjoy" and "have a ball" under it.

It would be a wonderful story if it ended right here, but there's more.

Twenty years later Bradley had a son born prematurely. Little Nathan only weighed two pounds and suffered a stroke when two days old. My son was laid off, job searching, and short of money. Times were bad all around for him and his young wife. Bradley left the ICU and went to the hospital chapel and prayed for his son's life. On his way back to ICU, he stopped at a vending machine for a cheap snack. He deposited his coins and retrieved his selection, then coins began to pour out like a slot machine paying off a jackpot! Bradley collected the coins in his shirttail and marveled at his luck. Just when he was thinking about counting his loot he remembered his childhood experience. He knew what he had to do. He had just prayed for a miracle for his son. He knew however, this was not the miracle he needed. Perhaps it was a test from above.

"Well, God," he prayed, "I figure I need all the points I can get right about now. My son's life hangs in the balance and the outcome is in Your hands. This isn't my money. You've seen me through till now and I'm counting on You. Please, God, Give me a strong, healthy son."

Then he walked over to the nurses' desk carrying his shirttail filled with coins and emptied them on the counter. "Can you return this to the vendor, Ma'am?" he asked.

The wide-eyed nurse was astounded. "Are you sure you don't want to just keep this? Most people would."

Bradley just grinned. "I don't know how much money is here… but I'm certain that my reward will be much greater by far."

He was correct…

That was six years ago. Little Nathan is now healthy and happily in kindergarten and the joy of our lives… God's ultimate payoff!

~Christine M. Smith

My Bruin Banner

We make our decisions and then our decisions turn around
and make us.
~R. W. Boreham

I was primed to spend five beautiful, sunny California days on the campus of the greatest collegiate basketball program ever. For the second year in a row, I was coaching at the UCLA Bruin Basketball Summer Camp. The program is an overnight camp so we sleep in the dorms and have non-stop basketball from 7 a.m. – 11 p.m. For five days, I would be a surrogate Bruin.

The first day of camp we created teams and kept those teams for the remainder of the week. Every day we ran practices with our teams and then played in games against the other high school teams. I was fortunate to get some great kids who were competitive, played hard, and were eager to please to gain my approval. We won every game all week and ended up in the championship game on the last day of camp. The last game is played in Pauley Pavilion on the Nell and John Wooden court in front of the whole camp and all the parents.

Before the game started, I paused to look at all the championship banners and to think of all the greats who had played there. Now I was getting to coach in a championship game in "Basketball's Mecca." It was just a summer camp game, but the UCLA legacy of excellence made this a true championship game for me.

The score was close the whole game. Since every camper pays over

$500 for this camp, we are given a substitution pattern we are supposed to follow so everyone gets equal playing time. It came down to our last substitution, and the coach of the other team still had not taken out his best player. He was flat-out cheating. One of the other coaches noticed what he was doing and came over to my huddle and said, "Steve, if he is going to cheat, then you can, too. Keep your best guy on the floor."

I said, "No, I don't need to cheat. That's not me."

The final four minutes started and my best player was sitting right next to me. He had heard what the coach had told me and he was willing to go back in. I quickly explained to him that it would not be the right thing to do and that it is important to always do the right thing. The other team took the lead, but I still had my peace of mind and character intact. I looked down at the university's blue ink logo that spelled out Wooden on the court and I was reminded how Coach Wooden talked about having faith that things will work out as they should as long as we do what we should.

The final buzzer sounded and my team won by two points. We did it! We had won and we won the right way. I could envision them raising our banner to the rafters to add to the lofty Bruin collection.

Since there had been so many high school players in camp, it was broken up into two sections, so one more championship game followed ours. One of the coaches in that game was the coach who had come up to me during my game telling me to keep my best players in. I knew he was just trying to defend me as he was upset about what the other coach was doing. Once his game started I didn't think anything of our conversation. His team won the game by one point in overtime. UCLA coach Ben Howland gave a speech to all the parents and awards were handed out and camp was over. Many of the parents of my players came and had me pose for pictures with their sons. I felt like I was famous. My team just won a championship game in Pauley Pavilion and now I was posing for pictures. Could it get any better?

A little later that same coach who won his game came up to me and said he wanted to thank me. I asked why. He said that during his game he was tempted to cheat and keep his best player in during overtime. However, the fact that I had chosen not to inspired him and gave him the strength to do the right thing as well. I was blown away. I was just being me; I was not consciously trying to influence another coach. I was twenty-one years old and my example had been a positive influence on a man in his late forties who had been coaching for more years than I had been alive. It was a brief moment shared between two people that no one else knew about. It was my most profound moment of camp.

This moment served to reinforce my beliefs that staying true to myself, never compromising my character, and choosing to always do the right thing was still important and necessary, not just for my well-being, but for that of my fellow human beings as well. It taught me just how powerful positive examples are to leadership and how people are always watching, "taking notes." We never know when the choices we make will have an effect on the choices of those around us and, exponentially, those we have never dreamed of. Remember, it does not matter how old you are, you can still be a formidable leader.

They might not be raising a banner at UCLA for my team's accomplishments at summer camp, but my fellow coach and I experienced a championship thrill like the players represented by the banners in the rafters; not because both our teams went undefeated, but because of the choices we made.

Choices create the champions. You never know when you might change a life. It can happen on a hot summer's day inside a basketball gym through the quick decision you make while you have your team in a huddle. I am proud of what my team did that week at camp. I am pleased that I could mirror UCLA's basketball tradition for the five days I got to be a Bruin. I think Coach Wooden would approve, too, of the manner in which I conducted myself on his court. Every time I return to UCLA to watch a game or observe a practice, I always look up in the rafters, imagine my banner hanging up there, and am reminded of the lives that were elevated along with it.

~Steven Schultz
Boys' Head Basketball Coach, Fountain Valley High School,
Fountain Valley, CA

Her Turn

Your life does not get better by chance, it gets better by change.
~Jim Rohn

The first time I met them, I was nervous. I didn't know what to expect but I desperately wanted their approval. The prospect of meeting my future in-laws was enough to make me seriously doubt my qualifications. Would they like me? Would they measure me against the possibility of better offers for their grandson? Would they secretly wish for someone else, or would they actually welcome me into the family? Instead of sizing me up and down, Jack pulled me in for a great big hug and Joan handed me a beautiful afghan — handmade, with special colors and patterns chosen just for me.

I have to admit; at first their gestures were a little foreign to me. Not having spent much time with my own grandparents growing up, I didn't quite know how to respond to their generosity. The time and energy Joan had poured into my blanket both honored and inspired me. No one had ever given me a gift like that and I was humbled by the weight of the warmth it offered. Each stitch symbolized a moment of time she had spent thinking of me, and every intricate design embodied another gesture of unexpected kindness.

Jack and Joan were no strangers to welcoming others into their family. After raising five children of their own, they adopted another little boy — their grandson, my future husband. Selflessly putting aside plans for retirement, they took on another generation of PTA meetings, slumber parties, Boy Scouts, and private school tuition.

The kitchen table became another neighborhood hangout, and the stove rarely cooled between indulgent homemade feasts. Love wafted through the air in the form of lingering aromas of fried chicken, biscuits and gravy, and Joan's infamous coffee-glazed doughnuts. I've been told several stories of late night doughnut feeds that would have provided enough nourishment for a small country.

While they'd only say, "He was no trouble at all," I'm forever indebted to them for their years of servitude and self-sacrifice. Their lessons of love shaped my husband into the man he is now. Together, the two of them showed him what a home founded on grace and unlimited acceptance looks like. They taught him to have integrity and helped him create unending memories of laughter and adventure. Their faith provided an anchor of hope and their patience formed a foundation of gentle leadership that guides our marriage today.

Over thirty years ago, they stepped into a difficult situation, and altered history. With no regard for themselves, they created a potential that will reach generations to come. When they chose to take in their grandson, they chose to adopt me as well. When they changed his life, they forever transformed mine too. I couldn't be more thankful for the example they have given us. They have shown us what it looks like to stand firm in conviction, persevere with patience, and commit in spite of uncertainty. I'm always moved by their gracious understanding and constant support, and our children and grandchildren will be blessed because of a decision Jack and Joan made decades before they existed.

This last year Jack lost his battle with heart disease and medical complications, and left Joan to carry on without him. The house is empty now, and Joan is alone for the first time in her life — without the responsibility of caring for children, grandchildren, or an ailing husband. Her tears are many and her heartache is raw and unbearable at times. Still, she remains steadfast in expectation and confident in hope. Somehow, her care and concern for her family continues, as she prays blessings and guidance over all of us. She daily seeks to wrap her tenderness and attention around us, and never ceases to offer encouragement and support when we need it most.

Although we could never come close to repaying the depth of her compassion and affection, it's her turn to be adopted now. It's her turn to be pulled in and comforted; and like the afghans she has meticulously stitched for others, it's her turn to be wrapped in the safety and security of those who cherish her. When the chill of love lost pierces her heart, it's her turn to be taken in and consoled. Jack's departure is an experience that can't be mended this side of Heaven, but my fervent prayer is that her years of unconditional love and moments of immeasurable pain will be met by a blanket of peace that wraps around her soul and gently begins to heal her heart.

Thank you Joan, for adopting your grandson, for welcoming me into the family, and for faithfully standing beside us. But, now, it's our turn to return the favor.

~Kara Johnson

A Quiet Hero

There are times when silence has the loudest voice.
~Leroy Brownlow

ne of the most important lessons I learned from my stepfather is that true heroism is silent and sober. Heroes take journeys, fight wars, and battle incredible odds, but they never seek praise.

My stepfather used to keep a large wooden locker in the tool shed behind our garage. The locker, a big, heavy chest with an iron handle on each end, was painted battleship gray. His name, Ernest McKenzie, was stenciled on the lid. The locker was old and splintered in places, and padlocked with a tarnished brass lock, the key to which was kept on a ring in the house. I saw him open the box only once when a friend came to visit. He lifted the lid of the chest and pulled out a dusty photo album filled with pictures from the war.

Ernie had fought in World War II. His visitor was an old Navy buddy. They had served on the same ship together. They laughed over photographs and drank beer as I stood outside and listened. I don't recall much of what was said, but I do remember the man calling my stepfather "Duck" and commenting on what a strong swimmer he was.

"You're the one who saved us, Duck," the man kept saying over and over. "You kept us alive out there." And I think they cried together, or maybe it was just drunken giggles. I'm not sure. That was the only time I ever saw my stepfather open the footlocker. That was 1961 and I was twelve years old.

Ernie had served four years in the United States Navy during the war. Despite his years of service, our house was entirely devoid of memorabilia. A visitor would have no idea about my stepfather's military career were it not evident in his walk and demeanor. Civilians might miss even these clues. I knew that my stepfather had served in the Navy, but I did not find out what a highly decorated sailor he was until several months after his death.

I was cleaning up the yard and stepped into the tool shed for a rake. That's when I spotted the footlocker. I went back into the house, found the key, and took it out to the shed. Quietly, and with an archaeologist's caution, I unlatched the lock and lifted the lid of the locker. An amazing smell rushed out, deeply sweet, of mothballs and cedar. The smell also belonged to the contents of the chest, to the history inside.

The first thing I saw was a tray full of medals and wooden plaques commemorating different things my stepfather had done during the war. There was a Purple Heart, a Bronze Star and a Silver Star. There was a plaque for being on the commissioning crew of a ship, and another one for serving on a ship that was sunk by a Japanese submarine.

Underneath the top tray I found uniforms — dress blues neatly pressed and folded. I found a shoeshine kit and a white sailor hat with my stepfather's name stenciled on the inside brim. There were newspaper clippings and a book in the trunk as well. The book was a thin U.S.S. Indianapolis cruise book, dated 1943. I flipped through the black-and-white photos, looking for pictures of Ernie. The photos were mostly headshots of similar-looking young men in dress blues and white hats. I found pictures of my stepfather standing in front of an anti-aircraft gun, on the mess deck with his buddies, and sitting on his bunk. He was still youthful and very masculine, stern-looking but not weary.

Underneath his uniforms, wrapped in a white handkerchief, were his dog tags. His name was pressed into the thin aluminum.

Under the dog tags I found more uniforms. Dungarees this time, work clothes with "McKenzie" stenciled on the pockets. There was also a pair of black work shoes, a blue web belt, and several more sailor hats.

That afternoon I discovered that my stepfather had been a Gunnery Petty Officer in World War II, and had two ships sunk out from under him: A light cruiser, the *U.S.S. Bismarck Sea*, and a heavy cruiser, the *U.S.S. Indianapolis.*

Two Japanese torpedoes sunk the *Indianapolis* shortly after transporting components of the atomic bomb to the island of Tinian. The ship sunk within minutes, along with 300 of its crew. My stepfather was one of the lucky ones who made it into the water. The *Indianapolis* had been observing radio silence during that time. No one other than the crew of the Japanese submarine knew of its location. When they were rescued four days later, only 317 men were still alive. The rest died of exhaustion, exposure, and wounds inflicted when the ship was hit. Many others were victims of shark attacks. The sharks fed nonstop, day and night, darting into the men with speed and fury. The water around the dwindling crew remained a constant crimson.

All during my childhood, my stepfather never talked about that harrowing ordeal. Occasionally, if we were alone, he would speak of some aspect of his years in the Navy, such as how it was to live on board a ship or how a five-inch gun battery was operated, but that was it. Ernie never once bragged about surviving the sinking of the *Indianapolis*, or how he had saved the lives of other sailors. Had it not been for that footlocker, I would have never known.

Through my stepfather I learned that the greatest heroes are those who find the courage to serve others and face overwhelming obstacles, yet expect nothing in return, not even praise.

~Timothy Martin

Chapter 2

Raising Great Kids

Make Time for Togetherness

Never Too Busy

*As each day passes, you must spend your time, your energy
and your efforts on one thing or another. Choose then, to
invest yourself in something that truly matters.*
~Ralph S. Marston, Jr.

M y mom's life was a busy one. Raising four kids
on her own was a full-time job in itself, but she
also worked outside the home. Remarkably, she
always seemed to find a little bit of extra time for
us despite her schedule.

She would bundle us up and take us over to my aunt's in the evening when she worked as a waitress in a small diner. We would just
be finished with school and have to hurry so my mom would be on
time for work. I thought when this began that she would pass us over
to our aunt and hurry off as soon as we made it through the front gate,
but that didn't happen. Instead we would sit on the porch, my mom
in her waitress uniform, and we would rock in my aunt's big wooden
swing and talk about what happened that day.

"I learned how to add numbers up to the hundreds," my sister
Sandy would say.

"That's wonderful," my mom would reply, hugging her tight.

"I learned how to write my name!" Larry, my younger brother,
would shout.

My mom would get a piece of paper and a pencil out of her purse and hand it to my brother. "Show me how you do it," she'd ask softly.

"Do you have enough time to hear what I did today?" I'd ask her.

Mom would smile at me and nod. "I'm never too busy for something important like that!"

She'd sit and listen as I described whatever wonderful adventure I'd had at school that day. Then she'd give us all a hug, wish us good night, and hurry off down the street. No matter how much of a hurry she must have been in, she always treated what we had to share with her as if it were the most important thing in the world.

There always seemed to be time for us. If my mom came home after a very long day from her two office jobs, I knew we would open the door to her smiling face. She would take just a few minutes to catch her breath, and then we'd gather in the kitchen and talk to her about everything under the sun while we helped her make dinner. She never seemed too tired to ask us questions and she was really interested in what was important to us, even though I know she must have been exhausted from work.

She gave us the gift of time again and again throughout the years. She would appear at the school play in which I had a part, even though I knew she would have to make up the time at work. She would smile at us when we came down during the summer to the office where she worked and asked if she had time to have lunch with us.

"I can't think of anyone I'd rather have lunch with," she'd say, and then we'd take the sandwiches we'd brought along with us down to the river that flowed through the city, sit on the grass and have a wonderful lunch. I never thought about all the things she could have done for herself, the break from activity she might have enjoyed, because she actually did love to give us any time she could.

Later on in her life, when she came to live with us following her retirement, my mom gave the gift of time to my children too. They would run around excitedly, asking their grandma if she would play with them, or read them a story, or go for a walk with them. By then my mom had health problems but she would always nod and sit down and read to them or tell them stories about when she was a little girl. Those moments were a tremendous gift that my children still talk about and treasure.

In the last few years of her life, I would take her to lunch or sit with her on the porch, and we would talk, reminisce about the past, dream of the future, and just enjoy being with each other. My mom would listen as I shared all of my hopes, my fears, and my dreams for my family, and she would always hang on every word. I would look at her and ask her if she minded me taking up so much of her free time.

"Nonsense," she'd tell me. Then she'd give me a wink and say, "I'm never too busy to spend time with you. It's one of the greatest joys of my life."

I will always remember those wonderful words, and the loving heart behind them. It is a gift my mom gave to me for which I will forever be grateful. In this oh-so-busy world of ours, and in a life filled with challenges, she always had time to share her joy with me.

~John P. Buentello

The Constant

*Love is the condition in which the happiness of another person
is essential to your own.*
~Robert Heinlein

My parents divorced when I was seven years old. My dad moved out of our house and into his own place and we began our memorable routine of weekly visitations on Wednesday nights and sleepovers every other weekend. It was the characteristic and predictable court-appointed agreement for divorced families. My dad's idea of visitations and parenting, however, was vastly different from the Court's. He made a promise on the day his divorce was final that would change the course of my life forever.

My dad promised that he would be more than just a "weekend dad" who fulfilled his obligatory parental duties with limited visits. He wanted more than anything to be a significant presence in my life even though we were not living under the same roof. To this day, I am so grateful to him for overcoming the many obstacles that face divorced dads and cementing an unbreakable bond with me, his youngest daughter.

Throughout my life my dad made me a priority and everybody knew it. He would stop by my house every day, usually after school, to chat for a minute and tell me how much he loved and missed me. I waited on most days with eager anticipation for his shiny, yellow

1976 Stingray Corvette to turn the corner of our block and meander slowly toward my house. When I spotted my dad with the T-tops off and the windows down, I just knew my day was going to get better. Sometimes he would take me for a ride and sometimes we would just sit in the car and talk for a few minutes in the driveway while he learned about what went on in my day.

I felt like the luckiest girl in the world to have someone so interested in what was happening in my life. If he could not see me in person he would call on the phone. For the next eleven years until I left for college, I talked to my dad every single day.

During the weekends that I spent at his house I can remember him grilling the best pork chops I've ever tasted. He made scrambled eggs for breakfast every morning and cooked pot roast to perfection on Sundays. He always let me help because everything we did, we did together. He rarely accepted any party or dinner invitations on our weekends together because he cherished our time alone as much as I did. We played catch or Frisbee in the yard and rode bikes or took walks to find secret treasures. My fondest memory of those weekends, however, was when my dad would turn on the stove after dinner and I would hear the slow crackle and smell the unmistakable aroma of Jiffy Pop popcorn. I can remember like yesterday the excitement I felt as the tinfoil pouch began to rise and steam poured out from the sides of the pan. My dad would shake and jiggle and pop those kernels to absolute perfection every time.

My adolescence was a typically confusing time, but the bond I had with my dad was the constant in an otherwise chaotic life. After the divorce, and during all of the tumultuous times that the divorce brought to our family (remarriages, stepfamilies, bitter ex-spouses etc.), he always listened patiently. He never discounted the sometimes complex feelings of a young girl. He just listened. And he remained the only reliable, stable presence in my life. I could count on my dad to take me to every doctor or orthodontist appointment, watch every softball game, attend every conference and be present at every significant life event. He always lived up to his promise. I cannot say that about anyone else.

All of my life lessons I learned from my dad. He taught me that you must keep your word. Period. He taught me to be kind, fair and just. He taught me to take the high road, give 110% and never let 'em see you sweat. He taught me that success is a journey, not a destination. But most importantly, he taught me by example.

Conventional wisdom says that to be successful you should simply develop the traits you admire in other successful people. As I figured out what to do with my life and how I wanted to live I didn't have to look too far for inspiration. My dad is, by far, the most successful person I know. Ever since I was a little girl, I have admired his sense of humor, determination and integrity. He taught me that my only limitations were those that I imposed on myself. I will always be thankful for having such an encouraging and loving teacher in my father; something that many young women of divorced families never get to experience with their own fathers.

Even though I recognized and appreciated my dad's love, it wasn't until I had my own children that I realized the profundity of our bond. The closeness we share has always transcended space and time, but I am even more in awe of our relationship because now I can fully appreciate his sense of purpose. To comprehend my dad's unconditional love for me I need look no further than my own children. When I look deep into their adoring eyes and promise to love them forever and ever, I see the reflection of pure happiness and joy staring back at me. I know my dad must have seen that same blissful reflection in my eyes.

The confidence and security I possess today as a person and a parent is directly related to the man who vowed so many years ago to be more than just a "weekend dad." He made good on his promise in more ways than I can convey in one story. However, I am most thankful for the father who took in his arms a scared, confused and angry seven-year-old and whispered in her ear, "I love you and I will never leave you."

~Kimberlee Murray

Somebody to Turn the Rope

Kids spell love T-I-M-E.
~John Crudele

Growing up with seven brothers and sisters, there was always someone to play with. Sometimes though, when my older brothers were scattered throughout the neighborhood with their friends, there weren't quite enough kids at home to play some of our favorite games. Many times one of my sisters or I would run into the house calling, "Mama, Mama, we need somebody to turn the rope." Mama would put down her broom or turn off her iron and come outside for a game of jump rope.

One evening, my younger sister and I went to Mama, our faces forlorn and our eyes pleading. My sister held our worn jump rope in her hands. I coaxed her to make the plea because she was younger, cuter and harder to ignore.

"Mama, we can't play jump rope by ourselves. It takes two people to turn the rope, and at least one jumper." She gave Mama her most beguiling smile. "Will you play with us, Mama? You can jump, can't you?"

Mama leaned on her mop and gave me a knowing grin. She was on to my ploy. I managed a weak smile and ducked my head guiltily.

"Of course I can jump," Mama said, putting the mop back in the bucket. After that, Mama frequently joined in when we played jump rope. To my chagrin, she was a better jumper than I was.

Games were always more fun when Mama played with us. Neighbors would shake their heads and smile when they saw Mama playing hopscotch, jump rope, leapfrog or softball with us. She was a small woman, so from a distance she looked like just another kid. She always seemed to have as much fun as we did.

Once a neighbor questioned Mama's willingness to drop whatever she was doing and play with us. Mama smiled and said, "I was an only child and I was very shy. I seldom had playmates. I guess I'm making up for what I missed when I was growing up." She looked around at her bevy of kids who were hanging onto her words. "I can't imagine why anybody would rather shine their floors than play with their kids. My house will always need cleaning, but someday all of these kids will be gone."

We were the only kids in the neighborhood who had a mother who came outside to play with us. She joined in our games with as much enthusiasm as we did. When we divided into teams to play ball, we always had to pick a number to decide which side got Mama. Mama would smile as we fought for her since she always got chosen last when she was a girl. I am so grateful that I grew up with a mother who put our childish wishes ahead of her many chores. In her wisdom, she knew that having fun was more important than having a perfectly clean house.

I can honestly say, when looking back, that I can't recall if our kitchen floor was clean or whether there were crumbs in the corners. I don't remember whether our bathroom fixtures gleamed or whether there was a faint ring around the tub. I don't know if our clothes were always starched and ironed or whether we wore them wrinkled to school. But I do recall very vividly how Mama looked as she jumped rope, her ponytail bouncing up and down. I can hear her voice chanting, "Miss Mary Mack, Mack, Mack, all dressed in black, black, black; with silver buttons all down her back, back, back," as she smiled happily. She gave us such wonderful memories that we still talk about them today as middle-aged adults.

Mama is growing old now. Her steps are slow and halting. Her memory is fading. Her shoulders are bent. But when I look into her warm blue eyes, I still see the young mother who thought that happy children were more important than a spotless house.

~Elizabeth Atwater

Just Say It!

If you were going to die soon and had only one phone call you
could make, who would you call and what would you say?
And why are you waiting?
~Stephen Levine

O ne night, after reading one of the hundreds of parenting books I've read, I was feeling a little guilty because
the book had described some parenting strategies I
hadn't used in a while. The main strategy was to talk
with your child and use those three magic words: "I love you." It had
stressed over and over that children need to know unconditionally
and unequivocally that you really love them.

I went upstairs to my son's bedroom and knocked on the door. As
I knocked, all I could hear were his drums. I knew he was there but
he wasn't answering. So I opened the door and, sure enough, there
he was sitting with his earphones on, listening to a tape and playing
his drums. After I leaned over to get his attention, I said to him, "Tim,
have you got a second?"

He said, "Oh sure, Dad. I'm always good for one." We proceeded
to sit down and after about 15 minutes and a lot of small talk and stut-
tering, I just looked at him and said,

"Tim, I really love the way you play drums."

He said, "Oh, thanks, Dad, I appreciate it."

I walked out the door and said, "See you later!" As I was walking downstairs, it dawned on me that I went up there with a certain message and had not delivered it. I felt it was really important to get back up there and have another chance to say those three magic words.

Again I climbed the stairs, knocked on the door and opened it. "You got a second, Tim?"

"Sure, Dad. I'm always good for a second or two. What do you need?"

"Son, the first time I came up here to share a message with you, something else came out. It really wasn't what I wanted to share with you. Tim, do you remember when you were learning how to drive, it caused me a lot of problems? I wrote three words and slipped them under your pillow in hopes that would take care of it. I'd done my part as a parent and expressed my love to my son." Finally after a little small talk, I looked at Tim and said, "What I want you to know is that we love you."

He looked at me and said, "Oh, thanks, Dad. That's you and Mom?"

I said, "Yeah, that's both of us, we just don't express it enough."

He said, "Thanks, that means a lot. I know you do."

I turned around and walked out the door. As I was walking downstairs, I started thinking, "I can't believe this. I've already been up there twice — I know what the message is and yet something else comes out of my mouth."

I decided I'm going back there now and let Tim know exactly how I feel. He's going to hear it directly from me. I don't care if he is six feet tall! So back I go, knock on the door and he yells "Wait a minute. Don't tell me who it is. Could that be you, Dad?"

I said, "How'd you know that?" and he responded, "I've known you ever since you were a parent, Dad."

Then I said "Son, have you got just one more second?"

"You know I'm good for one, so come on in. I suppose you didn't tell me what you wanted to tell me?"

I said, "How'd you know that?"

"I've known you ever since I was in diapers."

I said, "Well, here it is, Tim, what I've been holding back on. I just want to express to you how special you are to our family. It's not what you do, and it's not what you've done, like all the things you're doing with the junior high kids in town. It's who you are as a person. I love you and I just wanted you to know I love you, and I don't know why I hold back on something so important."

He looked at me and he said, "Hey, Dad, I know you do and it's really special hearing you say it to me. Thanks so much for your thoughts, as well as the intent." As I was walking out the door, he said, "Oh, hey, Dad. Have you got another second?"

I started thinking, "Oh no. What's he going to say to me?" I said, "Oh sure. I'm always good for one."

I don't know where kids get this—I'm sure it couldn't be from their parents, but he said, "Dad, I just want to ask you one question."

I said, "What's that?"

He looked at me and said, "Dad, have you been to a workshop or something like that?"

I'm thinking, "Oh no, like any other 18-year-old, he's got my number," and I said,

"No, I was reading a book, and it said how important it is to tell your kids how you really feel about them."

"Hey, thanks for taking the time. Talk to you later, Dad."

I think what Tim taught me, more than anything else that night, is that the only way you can understand the real meaning and purpose of love is to be willing to pay the price. You have to go out there and risk sharing it.

~Gene Bedley

An Invitation Not an Interruption

Everywhere is walking distance if you have the time.
~Steven Wright

had four children in five years... on purpose. Two of my sons were born so close together there was only one inch and one pound difference between them for their first five years. People would often ask if they were twins, and they'd say yes, but they were born a year apart.

We lived on a farm so, besides the four children, I had horses, sheep, goats, cattle and chickens to take care of. When four children are born so close together, they often feel they are part of a herd or a flock. It isn't always easy to spend special time with them individually. So, every evening after dinner, I would take each of my children on a fifteen-minute walk.

One at a time, I would take them through the grove of oak trees, or down to the rocky creek, or up the hill. In bad weather, we'd just walk up and down the long dirt driveway. We'd talk about anything, everything, nothing. We'd tell jokes, sing a song, make up poems and talk about the family. After fifteen minutes, we'd go back to the house, and I'd take the next kid out for his walk. It took an hour of my time, but for me, it was the best hour of the day. There were very few days we skipped our walks.

When my children asked me to do something with them, I would stop whatever I was doing and look at them, really look at them, and listen to them. And, if possible, I would do what they asked.

Could I stop washing dishes to play a game of *Chutes and Ladders*? Of course, I could. Would it be nice if the kitchen was clean and the dishes were washed? Sure. What's more important, though, playing a game with my child or washing a dish?

One time, when I was frying a chicken for dinner, my oldest son rushed into the house and begged me to go outside with him. I turned off the burner, moved the skillet off the heat and went outside to see what was so important.

A heavy frost had covered the entire farm. Every tree looked as if it had been covered with white icing. I'd never seen anything so beautiful. My son and I walked through a tunnel of trees bowed almost to the ground from the weight of the frost on their limbs. The earth was silent; we were silent. It was a magical moment we shared.

I could have stayed in the kitchen and fried a chicken, but I didn't. I followed my son outside into a scene of beauty that never happened again. It was a once-in-a-lifetime memory. I'm so glad I didn't miss it.

When my young daughter asked me to go outside to look at the "melted butter" on the hill I went even though I wanted to finish watching a movie on television; there were only fifteen minutes left. I went outside and looked across the meadow. The hill must have had a thousand jonquils in bloom. When we got back to the house, we put jonquils in every vase, pitcher, glass and cup in the house. Every year after that, there were jonquils on the hill, but there were never as many as there were that spring. I don't remember the name of the movie I was watching that day, I don't know how it ended or what it was about, but I'll never forget collecting those armloads of jonquils with my daughter.

"Come quick, Mom!" one of the kids would yell, and I always stopped whatever I was doing and followed them outside to the woods, to the meadow, to the pond or to wherever they led me.

We saw wild geese flying past the full silver moon, honking to each other and landing on the pond with the reflection of the moon on the water. We watched kittens being born in the hayloft in the barn and witnessed the miracle of five new lives. We waded in snow, swished through piles of autumn leaves, danced in the pouring rain, listened to the thunder that was so loud it shook our hearts. On hot summer nights, we'd lie on a quilt on the grass for hours and watch the sky for shooting stars.

Years later, my son Peter said his favorite thing about his childhood was that no matter what I was doing, I'd always stop and give him one hundred percent of my attention, even if it was just to look at a shiny rock he'd found.

Did I make mistakes? Oh, yes, hundreds. Do I have regrets? Yes, I do, but one regret I don't have is that when my kids asked me to do something or to go outside and look at something or to play a game, I never considered it an interruption. I considered it an invitation. They were inviting me to share their life, their special moment, and it was an honor and always an unforgettable experience and a blessing.

Dirty dishes, laundry, sweeping, cooking can wait. These things will wait patiently for an hour or a day or for several days. But moments with my children were really just moments, gone in the blink of an eye. Sometimes you only get one chance to do something.

My children are grown now. They are fine, decent, funny, warm, loving, compassionate people. I'm proud of all four of them. They have never caused me shame or grief.

I watch my children with their own children now. When their sons and daughter come running up to them and say, "Come with me, Daddy. I want to show you something," they stop what they are doing and let their children lead them to adventures.

If I did anything right as a mother, that would be at the top of the list. When children ask you to spend time with them, it's not an interruption. It's an invitation to share miracles, adventures, blessings... and you only get one chance.

~April Knight

If It's Tuesday

Few things are more delightful than grandchildren fighting
over your lap.
~Doug Larson

From the kitchen I hear the crash and the baby's wail. "Oh my gosh!" I shout as I reach the scene in the living room. The bouncer is upended, baby and all, and her two-year-old brother stands beside it, wide-eyed, lips quivering. I pull the baby into my arms and check her body for welts and bruises. All clear. Hugs and kisses calm her, and I turn my attention to the culprit, who stretches his arms upward.

"Up," he cries. His eyes fill with tears. "Up."

I sweep him into my free arm. "It's all right, lovey," I say between kisses. "You have to be gentle with baby sister; you could hurt her."

It is Grandma day at my house, and I'm hoping my grandson's rambunctious activity is a result of Easter candy and not his recent second birthday.

I am not the kind of grandparent I intended to be. After raising five children, I planned to model this phase of life after my mother, who defined her grandmotherly intentions days after my first child was born. "I will not babysit. In fact, I'll be happy to hire a baby-sitter for you, but I will not baby-sit."

There was no doubt my mother loved the children, and they loved her, but all were content to sit across the table from one another sipping tea and eating oatmeal cookies for an hour twice a week. There was no diaper changing, lap sitting or neck nuzzling in my mother's house. Just short, polite visits and occasional dinners, always with me in attendance, the keys to the car in my pocket in case someone forgot the rules.

It worked for my mother, and I imagined it working for me. But when my son placed my first grandchild in my arms, I fell in love. Defenses melted, and the hardness in me turned to mush.

"Do I have to give him back?" I asked.

My waking hours following the birth of this baby were filled with a longing like one feels for a new love. Dropping by for baby hugs became part of my daily routine. It was a gift to hold this new little life close and breathe in his newness, to watch his face when he slept and his eyes wander around the room when he was awake. I couldn't get enough of him.

And so when it was time for my daughter-in-law to return to work, I found myself offering to baby-sit one day a week.

"Are you sure?"

I wasn't really, and I thought of telling them I'd changed my mind. *What are you thinking?* I asked myself. *This is your time. You've raised your children, cut back on work. You're free. You have time to write, read, do whatever you want. Don't you remember how old you are?*

"I'll give it a try," I told my son and his wife. "We'll see how it goes, whether it's too much."

That was the beginning of our Tuesdays together. They belonged to little Gordie and me. Everything else was put aside — appointments, phone calls, bills. I fed, diapered and cooed. I reveled in his smiles and tickled him into giggles. We played peek-a-boo and so-big and read *Goodnight Moon*. I searched his gums for budding teeth and watched as he took his first wobbly steps between the couch and coffee table, applauding himself when he reached his goal. We went to the beach and threw rocks in the water and went "so high" on the swings in the park. We stopped at the bakery and ate cookies before lunch. I heard his first words. And then words formed sentences.

The mother/disciplinarian in me from years ago no longer exists.

I stand by calmly as he empties the ice tray in my refrigerator or the bowls from a kitchen cabinet. I get down on my knees with him to wipe up the water he spills from the cooler. Cheerios on the floor, a broken dish are no problem. I don't scold. I am Grandma.

Now there is a little sister who joins us on Tuesdays. Caitlin is a chubby baby who spends her days eating, sleeping and smiling. She is the promise of more firsts.

So every Tuesday my son pulls his SUV into my driveway and unloads babies and bags of diapers, clothes and bottles. A little boy strolls up my walk, smiles and holds out his arms for me to pick him up. Behind him is his father carrying an infant seat overflowing with baby girl. Her eyes crinkle in recognition when she sees me.

"Any time you feel it's too much, just let us know," he says.

Not a chance.

~Alice Malloy

Ten Precious Minutes

At the end of the day, the most overwhelming key to a child's
success is the positive involvement of parents.
~Jane D. Hull

As a courtesy I grab my daughter Marissa's backpack and load it into the car before our ten-minute ride to school. The last time I checked she only had books and folders in the backpack. As I lift the backpack it feels as if it has been loaded with bricks. I feel for my daughter.

Then I do a double take as I notice that my little girl has grown into a young lady. She has much more style than I ever had or ever will have. Her hairstyles have become more sophisticated. She walks gracefully but with a purpose and asks if we have everything we need for the day. I tell her that her glasses, backpack and water bottle are all loaded in the car.

I open the garage door, fire up the engine of my Toyota Camry and back out of the driveway. Another day is beginning for both of us. It is about a ten-minute drive to school if there is not too much traffic. My daughter takes only a second to reach for the knob of the car radio. She changes channels quickly trying to find a song to her liking.

Soon Katy Perry and Snoop Dogg are telling me why California Girls are so wonderful. She loves the song and I secretly do too. I talk about the Beach Boys and how they sang about those California Girls too. I always tell her about the "old school" days when the music was the best. She doesn't care and someday down the road her kids won't care about her music either. Actually, they might care but they won't admit it openly.

The good thing is that we are talking. Music is a common bond between us. I love the fact that my daughter has inherited my love of music. Sometimes, she will fall in love with a song I like or a group I think is great and vice versa. This broadens each of our musical horizons and I must admit it also keeps me young, or at least young at heart.

The music also becomes a perfect conversation opener that often leads us into other discussions. How my daughter's friends are doing, what's going on during the day, how her classes are this week, etc. Because she is a teenager the answers are usually quick. Still we are conversing and I have gotten a brief summary of the upcoming day in her life. Out of the blue the DJ tells a funny story and we both relate to it and laugh. We hear some shocking celebrity gossip and we each gasp and look at each other.

When your child becomes a junior in high school the moments when you can bond become fewer and farther between. You learn to truly appreciate each moment you get. You also feel guilt for the times you have missed. Earlier in my daughter's life it was vital for me to get to work earlier and put in a long day. Thankfully, my wife, who has always been the ultimate mother, drove my daughter to school day after day without complaint. I am deeply appreciative.

From preschool until high school I missed out on a gift, the gift of time with my daughter. Knowing that I missed that gift has led to guilt and in some cases sadness as I understand that even ten minutes a day can have a positive impact on both her life and mine.

It is actually pretty easy to find those extra ten minutes a day to spend with your child. When I first began the task of taking my daughter to school, I grumbled and looked at it as something that I didn't want to do. It was similar to starting a new exercise program. I had to motivate myself to do it. I didn't think I could give up ten minutes a day. In the end, those ten minutes a day have become precious. Like ten minutes of exercise, they have helped my physical and mental well-being.

My daughter grabs her backpack as we arrive at the drop-off area of her school.

She lugs the pack onto her back and taps me lovingly on the knee and I tap her arm. It's a simple ritual we have. We tell each other to have a good day as Lady Gaga sings "Poker Face" in the background. I watch the young lady that I am so proud of walk into school. I pull away and quickly switch the music to a U2 song. Bono is reminding me that it's a "Beautiful Day." Thanks to those ten minutes I get to share with my daughter each morning, every day is a little more beautiful to me.

~David R. Warren

The Garage

Some of the most important conversations I've ever had occurred at my family's dinner table.
~Bob Ehrlich

As we sat and ate dinner in the garage, it occurred to me that we were not like most families. Surrounding this dinner table were baseball hats, war memorabilia and beer steins. We sat in a garage heated by an old wood-stove, and cooled by a sliding window above the countertop where my father sat in his favorite barstool. This was the kind of place that was warm, inviting and where every stray dog, cat and person could easily find a warm place to sit and a cold beer to drink.

Dinners here were special. They often, but not always, had a purpose. A big promotion, new job, new house or new friend would be reason enough to put out a big spread of cheese and crackers, coleslaw and meat of some kind on the handmade table. Tonight, we would gather to remind each other that we were family. Tonight, we would talk and laugh, all to avoid a more serious issue that was looming over us. As a family, we were facing Dad's cancer surgery, and as a family, we gathered in our meeting place to enjoy each other's company.

The garage was special. If walls could talk, I wondered what secrets they would share. They had definitely heard of hard times, worries and shortcomings. They had had their share of good news as well. All sorts of events were celebrated in the garage, and even a perfect summer day or magnificent snowstorm would be cause for celebration. On one night, an unexpected blizzard blew through town and we laughed, telling stories until the snow piled up so high outside we were all stranded at Mom and Dad's house. The woodstove popped, the window frosted up and we enjoyed the magic of family and the solace of the garage.

Part of its magic was that it did not discriminate. The garage had held us together during the most trying of times. Together, we sat in silence at the loss of those closest to us, and wonderment as to the reasons that must exist for sudden passing. We watched the Red Sox do the unthinkable, and then only days later we gathered to deal with a personal crisis. We watched in silence as our nation was attacked, and prayed even when praying was not what we were best at. What most people did individually, we did as a family, in the garage.

By looking at it, it was certainly nothing special. No fancy decorations adorned its walls and the furniture was either handmade or handed down. It was special, though. The garage was a safe place. It was a place to share secrets, problems and great stories. It was in the garage that I learned how to heal from a broken heart, how to ask for help, and how to listen with both ears. It was there that I learned the secret of life.

As we sat around, laughing and sharing stories of long ago moments, I caught my father's eye. I saw something I had never seen before. He was sitting back in his tall bar chair admiring his family. (My father's family extended well beyond blood relations. He welcomed friends and neighbors into his family and never let anyone forget how lucky he felt to have such wonderful people in his life.) As he sat quietly, listening to us jokingly discuss what it was like to grow up in a Polish, English and Irish household, his eyes glistened. It was then that I knew that he, too, had learned the secret of life.

The garage had given us a place to grow up, grow old and grow together. Although an outsider may think it odd that we ate in the garage, anyone who knew us would see something different. It was in that garage that we were most ourselves. We were family.

~Christine A. Brooks

Mommy, Can You Come Up?

Always kiss your children goodnight — even if they're already asleep.
~H. Jackson Brown, Jr.

From the time my son could talk, he had something to say. Every night after we put him to bed he'd call down the stairs, "Mommy, can you come up?" And every night I would answer the call and go back upstairs to hear what was on his mind. Sometimes he had something serious to discuss and other times, not so much.

We discussed everything from his belief, at five years old, that he'd have to move to Florida when he grew up, to his curiosity about what was here before dinosaurs. When he was in elementary school he'd tell me about things his friends were going through and ask me what advice I'd give them. At about eight years of age he wanted to know if he'd have to move away from home to go to college. When I told him he didn't have to but I was pretty sure he'd want to, he assured me that he wasn't going to leave home — ever!

At one point he changed his request from, "Mommy, can you come up?" to "Daddy, can you send Mommy up?" I'm not sure why this happened but the result was still the same; I went up. One night my husband turned to me and said, "You know why he doesn't ask me to come up? He knows I won't go." My response was simple. "When Aaron becomes a teenager he's going to have serious things to discuss. I want him to know he can always talk to me. No matter what time of day or what the subject may be, I want Aaron to know that he can trust me to take it seriously and take the time to talk to him. It's going to matter."

I'll admit there were nights when I really didn't want to go back up and talk about anything. On one of those nights I asked Aaron why we couldn't talk about these things earlier in the day. His answer? "Because I don't think about them then." Enough said! It was at night, when the day was done and he was relaxing, that the mysteries of life invaded his thoughts.

Aaron is now a teenager and there are many more things to think, and talk about. Teenagers these days deal with a lot of issues. From drugs to grades, from teen pregnancies to friends' parents divorcing, the list of possible real-life topics is endless. And then there are the not-so-serious issues teens deal with like acne. On any given day my son is dealing with these issues. On any given day he knows he can talk with me about any of these issues. He knows I'll take them seriously and take the time to listen because when he was little I always answered the call. And as I knew then, it really matters now.

~Diane Helbig

Dusting Off Memories

The happiest moments of my life have been the few which I have passed at home in the bosom of my family.
~Thomas Jefferson

As a young girl growing up in rural Alabama, I never understood why my mom spent so much time baking bread from scratch, and making my brother and me help her. One day every other week was dedicated to making bread. My brother and I were in charge of grinding the wheat into flour while Mom prepped the remaining ingredients. One of us would pour the wheat, a little at a time, into the hopper while the other turned the handle, and then we would trade positions as our small arms tired. The grinder was attached to a metal desk in the corner of the dining room, and occasionally the vise-like grip would loosen and we would have to stop and tighten it.

Eventually, Dad bought Mom a motorized grinder and our routine changed from pouring and grinding to grinding and keeping the flour dust from settling on everything in the kitchen and dining room. Despite our best efforts, the flour dust always went everywhere. So at the end of the day, while the bread was baking in the oven, we dusted the white off every coated surface.

While I went about my bread baking chores obediently, I chafed at the hours spent in the kitchen. I would wistfully look out the window as my horses grazed contentedly in the nearby pasture. I preferred to be outside with my horses. Looking back, I never appreciated my mom's idea of quality family time with my brother and me, at least when it came to time in the kitchen.

Years have gone by and I have become a mother myself. Home is now North Idaho. I handle kitchen chores with more grace as an adult, but I prefer to leave most of the cooking and baking to my husband. He's quite good at it, too.

It was on one such occasion that my husband, Christopher, was preparing dinner. I was at the kitchen table going through the day's mail when our two-year-old son, Cody, asked his Papa if he could help him cook. Christopher smiled and tried to explain that the stove was hot and it wasn't safe for him to be near it. Undeterred and resourceful, Cody grabbed a chair from the nearby table, and with all his effort began dragging the chair toward the nearest kitchen counter several feet away. While he struggled with the chair over the carpet, he made fast progress on the linoleum and soon had it placed in front of a counter centered between the refrigerator and the pantry. I sat there amused at his determination.

Cody climbed up on the chair and reached for a glass on the counter containing two dozen or so wine corks that Christopher had collected. With corks in hand, he pointed to the coffee pot on another counter. His Papa handed him the unplugged coffee pot. His final request was a wooden spoon. I put the mail down and watched as Cody carefully removed the glass pot from the brewer and placed the corks inside the pot. He stirred the corks with his wooden spoon for several minutes before returning them, and the pot, to the coffee maker.

"What are you doing?" I asked.

"Helping Papa cook," he replied with a big smile on his face. "I'm making cork soup!" It didn't matter that Christopher was behind him tending food in the oven. He was in the kitchen helping his Papa and that was all that mattered to him.

At that moment, something from within me stirred. I thought back to all those times as a kid when my own mom asked for help in baking bread, and I had grudgingly, but obediently, complied. Perhaps she was trying to create something more than just fresh baked bread. Maybe Mom was trying to instill a sense of togetherness through family time. Maybe she was trying to create a few lasting memories.

As I watched Cody take the corks in and out of the pot and stir them with all the dedication of a two-year-old, I realized that he had created a forever moment for me, a moment in time in which Christopher's willingness to let him "help" in the kitchen created a profound sense of family for our son. When the wine corks were sufficiently stirred to Cody's satisfaction, I got up from the table and offered him the small counter scale. Weighing the corks would let the moment linger even longer as I savored my newfound appreciation for the experiences my mom had given me years ago in her kitchen, a place where I was welcomed and belonged, flour dust and all.

~Jenny R. George

Multitasking a Marriage Too

It's what you learn after you know it all that counts.
~Attributed to President Harry S. Truman

I am a planner. With each stage in my life I thought I had it all planned out. I married my high school sweetheart, and after five years, during which time I earned my college degree, we felt we were ready for the next phase of our lives... parenting. We discussed the perfect time to have a baby and said things like "this baby is joining our lives, we are not joining his." How wrong we were!

We thought we had the perfect plan, my pregnancy was easy and I worked all the way up to my due date. There wasn't a doubt in my mind that I would have no problem delivering our baby and going right back to work, as we were going to stay a two-income family. Plus, I loved my job and I was positive I was the queen of multitasking and could do it all. I thought I had it all under control.

The delivery day arrived and my six-week maternity leave started and all I could think about was who could I possibly trust to love and take care of my baby as much as I did. I was fortunate enough to have my mom and grandmother to fill in on days when my husband was at work. With his job as a firefighter he was home every other day to be Mr. Mom.

My husband works twenty-four-hour shifts, so he would arrive home in the morning and I would hand him our baby at the door and head out for my one-hour commute. During his "Mr. Mom" days he handled everything: the feedings, napping, and household chores. When I would arrive home anywhere between six and seven at night he then would pass the baby to me at the door and head to the gym for some alone time. I understood his need to "get away" and he understood my need to bathe and bond with the baby. When he would return home we were both so exhausted from our day that we would have a quick bite to eat and fall asleep on the couch.

This routine went on for the first year of our son's life. We did not ask for help on the weekends or evenings as we felt my family was chipping in enough during the week. We didn't know of any babysitters. From the outside it all seemed perfect, but in reality we were living very separate lives centered on the baby.

What happened to the baby joining the life we already had? Now our lives consisted of taking care of the baby but we had forgotten that we were also a couple, not just parents. Without either of us realizing it we had become roommates, not companions. I am sure it was a gradual change but before we knew it everything had changed. We were too young to live as roommates and deserved more, but neither of us knew how to fix it… so, he moved out!

I worked so hard trying to prove I was a superwoman I forgot about the man I vowed to love and spend the rest of my life with. Now we were even more stressed, with double household bills and even more passing of the baby back and forth.

Asking for help may have been one of the hardest things we had to do, but we wanted our family intact. We started seeing a marriage counselor. We learned that being multitasking parents didn't mean we could stop being multitasking spouses. Date nights were important, babysitters were a necessity, and putting each other first was a must. With open minds, help from others, and a lot of love we were able to put it all back together for the better.

That was sixteen years ago, and while the road has not always been easy we learned to appreciate each other and value the stolen moments we have alone. We are best friends, lovers... and parents. When people compliment us on the success of our twenty-one-year marriage, I am the first to tell them that creating a wonderful family and life is easy if you always remember to take time to nurture each other.

Our son is now seventeen and has his own social life and will be going off to college in a little over a year. We still are very involved in his activities but once again we are rediscovering each other, spending Friday nights home alone, going on random date nights, and loving every minute of it. When I watch our son hold his own girlfriend's hand I know it is because he witnesses firsthand the love his parents have learned to share.

~D'ette Corona

Worth the Wait

When you look at your life, the greatest happinesses are family happinesses.
~Dr. Joyce Brothers

accepted Bruce's invitation to dinner at his house with a tiny bit of discomfort. This time, his children were going to be there, too. I'd met Megan, Brent and Kevin once before at a picnic. But my sister and her family were also there so I wasn't alone with them. This time it would be obvious Bruce and I were a couple. I was uncertain how the children might react to that idea.

The weather was unusually hot, even for July. Bruce wanted to keep it casual but thought we needed something to do so we wouldn't be sitting around staring at one another. He decided we could wash our cars. Playfully spraying one another with the hose kept us all cool and provided the diversion we needed. Everything seemed to be running smoothly and I was beginning to relax.

Bruce had planned bacon, lettuce and tomato sandwiches for dinner and Megan insisted on cooking the bacon. I was a little skeptical about letting a nine-year-old work with hot bacon grease, but Bruce said she'd be fine. Even so, I went inside to supervise.

The aroma of maple bacon already filled the room. Seizing the opportunity to avoid her father's censorship, Megan wasted no time commencing her own agenda. The questions came quickly. Did I have a husband? Kids? What kind of jobs had I had? Which one did I like best? Why? Where did I live? Did I like dogs? Had I ever owned any? I'd been in job interviews that were less comprehensive. I was amused and suggested I'd set the table while I answered her questions. Forgetting the kids had no idea I was familiar with the kitchen, I automatically went to the cabinet containing the plates. Four-year-old Kevin eyed me with suspicion.

"You don't have to steal those," he said.

Megan didn't notice my faux pas and began yelling at him for being rude. I was about to ask him for some clarification when she let out a yowl. Distracted by her annoyance with her brother she'd brushed the hot tongs against the bare skin of her thigh.

By the time Bruce and Brent came inside, I was finishing up the bacon and Megan was perched on a stool on the other side of the room cooling her burned leg.

"Nice job, Megan," cracked seven-year-old Brent, surveying the damage and shaking his head.

She'd barely paused my interview, so I knew the damage wasn't bad. Bruce took a cursory look and pronounced it "no big deal." Still, I wished it hadn't happened.

After dinner, the kids begged Bruce to pull out the projector so they could show me photos of "when they were little." I was curious, so I went along with the idea—until I understood which pictures they wanted me to see. They were combing through slide carousels in search of the photos that showed each of them being born! I had some friends who'd taken some pretty graphic photographs of their kids entering this world. I was definitely not prepared for that much information and began to squirm. Bruce and I exchanged stressed looks as he tried unsuccessfully to dissuade them. But they were so excited for me to see these particular photographs that I couldn't say no. I searched out a good spot to focus my eyes so I could look away without being obvious, but I didn't need to. Bruce quickly pulled most of the shots that included his ex-wife so he could focus on the individual photos of each child swaddled in pink or blue blankets. All three were convinced I'd taken in every detail and they were thrilled.

By the time we were married I had read every book our library had on stepfamilies. Most were about stepparents with full custody. Our situation was much different. Bruce's ex and her husband lived nearby so the kids popped in and out unpredictably. One moment we were newlyweds and the next we were a family of five. By our first anniversary I was struggling. I'd had no problem moving to the house Bruce had shared with his first wife. In fact, I rather liked the cozy little Dutch Colonial. And it was the best possible situation for the kids as they still had loads of friends in the neighborhood. What I wasn't prepared for was the growing feeling that I didn't belong.

Bruce put everything he had into helping me feel comfortable. He let me redecorate the kitchen with beautiful hickory cabinets and new counter tops. He even gutted and tiled the upstairs bathroom for me, installing a wonderful jetted tub. He never questioned my ability to handle the kids. In fact, he had more faith in me than I did. Still, I couldn't shake off the feeling of not being part of the family. Every time they visited, the kids brought their memories of family life the way it used to be. I began to feel like I was the stand-in for the real mother as I listened to a running dialog of "remember when" stories. Initially, I'd found them interesting, encouraging their talk. But eventually, I felt myself closing down as soon as they started. I tried to control my increasing sadness and jealousy. I didn't want to be that person and I felt angry with myself for letting it get to me, for being so immature. I knew they had a life before I arrived. The fact that they wanted to talk about it shouldn't have been any surprise.

I wondered whether this feeling was normal, whether it would go away. I knew of no one else with this kind of experience. So I kept searching for answers in books. I don't remember where I read it, but I finally found the one line that hit home: "You need time to develop your own history."

I can't say that everything was immediately fine. I'm not especially patient so I still went into a funk for a while when the kids had one of their "remember when" visits. But instead of giving in to my feelings, I began planning things for us to do together. We started traditions like make-your-own pizza nights and New Year's Eve hors d'oeuvres parties. We had winter floor picnics — roasting hot dogs in the fireplace and gorging on devilled eggs and potato salad as we lounged on my old quilt spread on the living room floor. I searched out tree farms with horse drawn wagons where we could cut our Christmas trees. And I initiated story times, reading aloud to the kids, often as we snuggled together during raging thunderstorms.

All of a sudden, I began to hear stories about the time we went to the apple orchard where we'd seen beautiful dappled gray ponies pulling a wooden cart or the exciting day we got to meet my sister's new parrot, and I realized it had happened. We finally had our own history. It took time and patience. I don't remember exactly when it began. But I can tell you it was worth the wait.

~Barbara Ann Burris

Busy

If you are too busy to laugh, you are too busy.
~Proverb

ll my life, I thought it was good to be busy. Idle hands are the devil's work. I was a busy kid, a busy teen, a busy student. I graduated on a Saturday from college and began my master's on Monday. After that summer of courses ended, I taught school while continuing my studies with night classes. The next summer break, I completed my advanced degree and launched my career. I taught high school, pursued an administrative certificate, joined clubs, and dated my boyfriend. I married, moved, acquired a new job and kept doing what I'd been doing, including taking groups of students to France on spring break. Then, at thirty, I had my first child and quit work. Life as I knew it came to a grinding halt.

I doted on that baby, and the one who came twenty-one months after him, and the one who came two years later, and the last one who came twenty-one months after the third. I stayed busy. All the while, I kept adding duties: sundry volunteer jobs, clubs, subbing, pets.

My father-in-law often advised that folks need to take it slow when raising kids. When I'd tout the educational benefits of some toy, he'd say, "Let the kids bang on pots and pans." When I'd sign up for some exercise class that would take me out of the house, he'd say, "Vacuum more." I'd furrow my forehead at the suggestion, and he'd add, "Grow a garden!"

"Next year, maybe," I'd say, not really planning on doing it.

"I like sweeping myself, and it's great exercise," he'd comment and pick up a broom and sweep out my garage. I thought he didn't want me to spend money on babysitters or classes. He encouraged more domestic work. I dismissed his advice and did as I pleased, which is what most thirty-something mommies would do. And then our folks got sick. My mom passed first. Then my father-in-law became gravely ill.

I remember the last time we saw him, wheelchair-bound, pale and aged. He called each of the boys to him. He gave a marble weight to one son, a brass eagle weight to another, and a signed baseball to the third boy. He hugged my little girl and rubbed her head. He delighted in watching them run around the lawn. In his last hours of his last days, he liked nothing more than to sit on the stoop and gaze at the kids romping around his front lawn. He'd been a busy man with a demanding career. He was a joiner. He had engaged in multiple civic duties and sundry clubs and Sunday school, but in the end, he sat serenely viewing his grandchildren doing nothing, just existing.

As I noted his fading eyes pore over them, I pondered the joy he gathered studying their movements and taking in their energy as they frolicked and rolled around on the grass. Something occurred to me. Maybe it's not good to be busy all the time. Maybe being a good mother doesn't mean you have to sign your kids up for every activity that comes down the pike. Maybe you yourself don't have to participate in every social function. It's good to plant a garden and watch the flowers grow without having to till it constantly.

One of the last things I said to my father-in-law that day, the last time I saw him alive, was this: "I'm going to become calmer. I'm going to become less busy."

He smiled weakly as he tilted his head up at me and said, "That's a good idea, Erika." And then he returned his gaze to the kids tussling under the magnolia tree. He smiled.

~Erika Hoffman

Chapter 3

Raising Great Kids

Be an Advocate for Acceptance

Mother-and-Son Moment

We know that we are beautiful.
~Langston Hughes

I can remember the look that he had on his face. So young, cute, innocent and a creation from me with God's help, of course — a true miracle indeed. A blessing that is worth more than anything. I'm talking about my son. I'm talking about raising this little guy as a single mother into a responsible black man.

One day my son caught me by surprise when he came to me and asked me a question. It was a Saturday morning, and I was busy typing away on my computer as I always do. I could hear the Saturday morning cartoons on in his room, which was right across from my bedroom. And here this little guy comes. Face still needs to be washed, eyes big and alive, with his black and gray Batman pajamas on, one pant leg higher than the other.

He says with his arms folded, "Mommy, why am I black?"

I could still hear myself clicking away at my keyboard, when what this little four-year-old boy had just asked me caught my complete attention. My eyebrows raised and I stopped what I was doing. I looked at him. And we were both looking at each other.

I sat straight up in my chair and said, "Baby, why do you ask me that?"

"Well, Mommy, my friend at day care said white is better than black. He said his daddy told him so. So I wanna know why God made me black?"

At this moment I could feel the anger slowly overcoming me. However, I stopped it in its tracks. I looked at my son, and I just shook my head as I took hold of his little hands.

"Baby, white is not better than black, and black is not better than white. We all are the same, just with different colors. Like your box of crayons, there are a lot of different colors but they are all in the same box. God wanted to make different colors of people. So he did. He didn't want to make everybody the same color because that would be boring. Don't listen to everything everybody says. Some people may not like others because they are a different color, but that's mean and that's not right. God loves us all. Nobody is better than anybody else. Even our hands, we all have different colors. This is a good thing, not a bad thing."

I stopped there, just to see what his reaction was.

He looked at me with his eyes still big, and he said, "Okay, Mommy, nobody's better than anybody else. God likes black people and God likes me. Okay, Mommy." He started to leave, then he came back. "So is that why Elmo is red, and the Cookie Monster is blue and Kermit the Frog is green?"

I smiled at him, "Yes, that is why." What could I say to that sort of reasoning?

Hours later that same day, I went into my son's room to see what he was doing. He was very quiet, which was not usual at all. What I found left me speechless, to say the least. My emotions were mixed between, should I get mad? or should I compliment him on getting the point?

My son had drawn different colored hands all over his wall — red, blue, green, brown, orange... I looked at the wall, keeping my emotions balanced, because I knew it had to be cleaned sooner or later. My son had never drawn on his wall before. Okay, on his dresser drawer, but not his wall.

As I stood there looking at these little small hands all over his bedroom, he tapped me on my side. From behind his back my son pulled out two pieces of paper. One was black construction paper with a lot of little white hands on it, and another sheet of paper was white with a lot of little black hands on it.

My son said, "Look, Mommy! Look what I drew. Look at my two papers. I wanna take them to my day care tomorrow and show my teacher and friend."

"That's good, baby, you do that. I like your two papers," I answered, leaving the wall out of it, still in shock and not yet sure how to handle it.

"I like them, too. I have to teach my friend and his daddy the truth."

I watched him as he went over to his little backpack and proudly stuffed the two papers inside.

I shook my head laughing to myself as I walked back into my bedroom thinking, *Kids are so smart. My baby is so smart. Why not, I'll let those hands sit on his wall, just a few days longer.*

I thought about what happened for the rest of the day. *Another job well done as a single black mother,* I thought.

~Tinisha Nicole Johnson

Purple Principles

Imagination continually frustrates tradition; that is its function.
~John Pfeiffer

"Mom?"

That nap hadn't lasted long, I sighed. I glanced from the newspaper as my four-year-old entered the room.

"What is it, Puss?"

"Can I have my toenails painted today?"

Asleep one minute and toenails the next; I blinked. What went on inside that head? I was constantly amazed by this little pinball-machine mind.

"Er, why do you want your toenails painted?"

"Because Ben and Ollie had red toenails yesterday, and it looked so good."

I considered that for a moment. Was he talking about the O'Neill twins? "Ben and Ollie are boys, right?"

A puzzled nod and a raised eyebrow told me I'd asked a dumb question. "Who painted the twins' toenails?"

"Their mom, of course."

"So," I inquired, casually, "do the boys have their toenails painted often?"

"Yes, and now I want you to do mine. I want red toes, too."

I stared at his pleased little face and shifted uncomfortably on the stool. I considered saying I'd run out of nail polish—much easier than explaining that boys don't usually wear nail polish. But I wasn't up for an endless round of the *why* questions it would evoke.

"Do you know something else, Mom?" He pulled off his socks and tweaked his toes at me. "Sometimes Ben and Ollie's mom even paints each toe a different color."

I looked at him cross-legged on the rug, eyes wide with admiration for someone else's mom, and instantly I reached a decision.

"Right, Paddy!" I swooped him off the floor. "Let's see what we've got in the bathroom."

"No red, only purple."

"I love purple," he whooped.

"Me, too," I whooped right back.

We painted our toenails in a sweet mother-and-son moment. I thought about Ben and Ollie's mom—with whom I vaguely remembered exchanging a hurried greeting or two as we flew in and out of the preschool Paddy attended four days a week since I'd returned to work. His grandparents kept him on Fridays.

I imagined her as a strong cookie-figure, regularly painting her sons' toenails, thumbing her nose at gender stereotypes and flying in the face of convention. I, too, could be that sort of mother; I decorated Paddy's toenails with flourish, vowing to tune in to all reports of Ben and Oliver O'Neill from now on.

But my newfound confidence took its first jolt about an hour later when my husband returned from work and Paddy gleefully told him how we'd spent our time.

"Well, that's great," I heard him say in a curious, strangled voice. He took the stairs in twos to reach me. "Why did you paint his nails?" he mouthed urgently, eyes wide in horror.

"Oh, relax, Pete. Ben and Oliver O'Neill have their toenails colored, too," I reassured. He seemed a little mollified but looked askance at the offending nails for the rest of the week.

And he wasn't the only one. Living on the other side of the world did not stop my Scottish mother from voicing her opinion in the toenail debate two days later.

"Gran wants to speak to you." Paddy relinquished the phone after thirty minutes, during which time the subject of toenails had evidently been discussed.

"What are you doing painting that boy's toes?" she asked. "It's terrible! You'll turn him into a girl."

My father-in-law apparently felt the same way. At the end of the week, I picked up Paddy from his Friday stay with Pete's parents.

"Grandad says I'm a sissle," Paddy informed me as we got into the car.

"A what?"

"A sissle. And I don't want to be a sissle, Mom." His voice was forlorn. "We'll have to take off my nail polish when we get home."

"Why?" I was baffled.

"Only a sissle wears nail polish," he said, sounding remarkably like his grandfather.

"Oh, you mean a *sissy*," I corrected him.

He nodded sadly.

"What do you think that word means?"

"It means you're a big *girl*."

"So, is Mommy a sissle... I mean a sissy, then?"

"No, Mommy," he almost smiled. "Only boys can be sissles. Grandad said."

Bloody Grandad.

"But what about Ben and Ollie?"

"Grandad says they're sissles, too."

In a fleeting moment, I saw him step back from his magical world of innocence and make-believe, of dress-ups and suspended reality, and I knew that something precious was about to be lost.

Not today, though. Not if I could help it. I resorted to guerrilla tactics.

"Well, that's a shame," I said carefully. "I liked your purple toenails and, you know, there's nothing wrong with being a sissle. Sometimes Grandad is one, too." Through my rearview mirror, I watched his eyes widen.

"When?" he asked, still unconvinced.

I thought about the photograph of my husband's father taken by me two years ago. He'd played the part of Juliet in his local theatrical production of "Romeo and Juliet — with a Twist." Posing for my camera had been the least he could do after I'd just sat through that painful debacle.

No nail polish, but plenty of purple tulle. Nice one, Grandad.

"Well, Paddy," I began, "I've got this photograph...."

Somehow, I was betting the purple toes would survive to fight another day.

~Maureen Johnson

Cats Are Cats

I think there's just one kind of folks. Folks.
~Harper Lee, To Kill a Mockingbird

aving been raised in Florida for half my life, I had been exposed to all races, colors and religions. When my family moved to Vermont, I barely noticed that most of the population was Caucasian like my family.

When my son, Shawn, was born in Vermont, it did not occur to me that he was being raised in an almost all white population since race had never been an issue with my family. So when I got a veterinarian technician job after college and we moved to central New York when he was three years old, I had not realized that he had never encountered a person who was not white.

When Shawn got home from pre-school his first day, he was very quiet. He seemed distressed but wouldn't tell me what was wrong at first. Finally he said very quietly that most of the kids at school were "funny." I asked him what he meant by funny and he told me, "They are brown and black, all different shades," and, "The teacher yelled at me when I tried to ask her about it." Then he started to cry.

I was flummoxed! How do you explain diversity to a three-year-old who has never encountered it before? I cuddled him in my arms and dried his tears while I thought for a moment.

Then I smiled and asked him to look around the room. Our seven cats lounged around, along the back of the couch, in a chair, curled in a corner. I asked him to look at the cats.

Cream-colored Diva with blue eyes and dark chocolate points accented by white boots, a gorgeous Snowshoe. Orange-striped Simon with dark amber eyes, a somber longhaired Turkish Van mix. Simon's short-haired sister, Brindle, a crazy tortoiseshell of black stripes over brown, tan and white patches, with multiple toes was our only poly-dactyl. Dapper tuxedo Sylvester in his black coat with white chest and paws. Fluffy Sassy, a Persian-cross with her snubbed nose and long brown-striped coat, a brown tiger. Black and white patches with a black mustache made Minx look like a clown. Solid blue-gray Ashley was an elegant girl.

I asked him to think about what he saw. After a few moments he said, "They are different colors." I could see the wheels turning in his mind as he thought about it. After a moment, he looked at me. "So people come in different colors too?" "Yes," I replied, "people come in different colors just like the cats, but we're all people just like they are all cats."

"Oh, okay." He gave me a perplexed look. "Why did my teacher get mad when I tried to ask her about it?"

"Well," I replied, "not everyone likes cats. There's no good reason for it and they usually don't like them because they don't know any better. Some people are like that about people who are different colors. It makes no sense but some people are like that. She probably thought you were having that problem and didn't realize you were just asking."

Shawn thought about that for a moment and then smiled at me. "I like cats," he said, "and people too. They're all pretty." He gave me a hug and then scooped up Brindle in his arms. A bright boy who likes everyone because of their differences, just like our cats.

~Tory S. Morgan

What Makes
Her Special

*True beauty is the flame of self-confidence that shines from the
inside out.*
~Barrie Davenport

When my twin daughters, Melody and Jessica, turned seven, I stopped by their school to drop off birthday cupcakes (for Jessica's first grade class) and doughnuts (for Melody's). Mrs. Connelly, the principal, spotted me and asked me into her office. She must have seen the look on my face — or perhaps she's merely accustomed to how people react to being called into the principal's office — and set me at ease, saying, "I need to brag about Melody."

"Did Melody tell you what happened last week?" she asked after we were seated.

"I don't think so." Both my daughters had told me a lot of things that had happened the previous week, but none of their stories featured anything principal-worthy.

The principal told me that one of her fourth graders, normally a sweet boy, had been acting up recently. In one incident, he sat next to Melody at lunch and asked her what happened to her face. Melody began to cry.

At this point in listening to the story, I began to cry too, which made the principal join in. Before I continue with the tearfest, let me give a little background.

I don't think it's merely maternal pride that makes me think that both Jessica and Melody are pretty. They are identical twins, but by developmental happenstance, Melody was born with a frontonasal dysplasia, or a facial cleft, similar to a cleft palate, but higher in her face and not affecting her palate. Jessica was born without the cleft. Melody has been seeing a craniofacial specialist since birth. The appointments were every three months at first, then slowly changed to yearly, and are now every two years.

She hasn't needed surgery, and there's nothing wrong with the function of her nose. It just doesn't have a defined tip. The cleft also causes her eyes to be wide set and has given her a widow's peak hairline. All of it combines, in my mind, to give Melody an adorable china doll look.

Melody's doctor warned us that, even if there was no functional issue with her nose, kids get mean about appearance around age seven. We could always opt for surgery if it was needed for Melody to have a healthy self-image. Honestly, I never gave surgery much thought. Melody is a well-adjusted kid.

It's not like Melody's unusual look has never come up before. When kids have asked why she has a "funny nose," I've responded by saying it's so that we could tell her apart from her sister. When I overheard a little girl telling Melody that her nose was "too small," I responded by focusing on its purpose. "Does it breathe?" Yes. "Does it smell?" Yes. "So is it too small to do its job?" No.

I've told Melody that she has the world's most kissable nose, and she permits me five kisses exactly at bedtime on her "kissy nose." A while ago, Jessica told someone that a good way to tell her apart from her twin was her pointy nose, in contrast to Melody's flat one. I considered taking her aside to have a serious discussion about thinking before we speak, but realized that she wasn't attaching a value judgment to one look over the other. She was just stating a fact.

Part of me worried, though, that having an identical twin would come to show Melody what she would have looked like without the cleft, and that she would resent Jessica. It's never come up, though. I hope it never does. It helps that, while my girls value their twin relationship, they also relish being individuals and having some differences from one another.

Let's return to the principal's office. As you may recall, we were crying.

The fourth grader had been mean, and Melody had cried in front of all her friends. It took a while for the older boy to admit that he'd acted wrongly and with intent to hurt. By the time he was ready to deliver a real apology, Melody was back in class. The principal called her out into the hallway, and the fourth grader apologized.

"It's okay," she told him. "You already said sorry, and I forgave you. People say that stuff to me all the time. It's fine."

Now it was the little boy's turn to cry. He was ashamed.

"It's not fine," the principal told her. "You're a beautiful girl, and it's not okay that people say mean things."

"But I forgive them," said my amazing, extraordinary child. "I love this school!" And she skipped back to class.

That night at dinner Jessica was distracted by her dessert, so I took the opportunity to talk to Melody about this whole thing. "I heard you were extremely forgiving at school. Mrs. Connelly was pretty proud of you."

Melody beamed.

"Do you want to tell me about it?"

She told me essentially the same story I'd heard in the office. I reiterated what her principal had said, that she didn't need to just accept people's cruel words.

"But Mommy, it's okay. They can say what they want. It's my job to forgive. I just don't get it. I don't understand why they would want to be mean about what makes me special. My kissy nose makes me special. What's wrong about that? I don't know why it's like this, but it makes me special."

There was nothing wrong with that, I told her. By a major act of self-control, I kept my tears at bay this time. Would she like to know why her nose was special? She did want to know, so I explained in very simple, objective terms the nature of her cleft. I also pointed out that it was responsible for her widow's peak, which she calls her "heart hair," since it helps give her a heart-shaped face.

"I love my heart hair!" she said. "That is part of what makes me special too."

She went on to tell me that her teacher had told her about being teased as a child for not speaking English well. Her sister's teacher told her about being teased for having a big nose. I added my own story about being teased for my eczema. I told her that I'd never realized I was pretty until I was eighteen.

She gasped. "But Mommy, you're beautiful."

"So are you, baby girl. I'm so glad you already know it."

"Me too. I've known ever since Nicole [her friend from infancy] told me I was beautiful when I was very small. That's why she's such a good friend," she said.

There was nothing more to say.

~Sadia Rodriguez

Different Paths

*While we try to teach our children all about life, our children
teach us what life is all about.*
~Angela Schwindt

"And where is your daughter going to college?"
the woman asks my friend Ellen. We are at a
fundraising luncheon, networking with the best
and the brightest. My friend's face tightens. Her
daughter has been struggling through her alcohol addictions in a treatment center and won't be going to college next year.

"She's going to work for a year," Ellen tells the woman.

Ellen and I move deeper into the crowd. "I hate it when that happens," she says. "I feel so embarrassed. I never know what to say."

We find our table. Kate is there, a woman I haven't seen for several years. Her son Mark and my daughter went to high school together. While our kids were easy friends, I always felt inadequate in conversations with Kate.

We greet each other and she instantly tells me what a success her older daughter is. "... Harvard Law School and now works for a big New York firm and has a darling little girl and a husband who's in environmental architecture. What about Jessica?"

My mouth feels dry. How can I tell Kate that my daughter dropped out of college, that she's bounced from job to unemployment to job? How can I explain to someone so put together and achievement-oriented that my daughter struggles with depression and cannot move ahead on a straight path? I have spent hours looking for the words to convey the brilliance and individuality of my daughter, brilliance not proven by any advanced degree or outstanding job success.

"She's still searching," I say.

My mouth is stretched into someone else's smile as I prepare for Kate to assault me with the litany of Mark's successes. But surprisingly, her face loses its starch.

"I am so relieved to hear you say that. Mark, well you know he started out at MIT, but he dropped out after a year and moved to Florida. He works as a janitor and he shows no signs of going back to school. At first, I couldn't believe it. We didn't raise him to be a janitor and well... but anyway, he seems happy so I guess that's all that really matters."

I take a breath and relax. A happy child is all we really want.

"Tell me more about Mark," I say, and Kate's smile returns.

Later that evening, I drop by my daughter's apartment for a quick visit. I am exhausted from the luncheon and from a long meeting. I spent the last hour of the meeting trying not to stare at the glossy photos of my client's children in various poses of glory — graduations, award acceptances, medal winning, weddings. While I was listening to him discuss the project, I was battling envy — these children were easy to talk about in a crowd. These photos proved he was a good and able parent.

Jessica answers the door, dressed in sweats and carrying a book. Her hair is uncombed, which means she probably didn't go to work today. "What are you reading?" I ask.

"Culture and advertising," she says beckoning me into her book-strewn living room. "It's really interesting the impact that both gender and advertising have on us."

She gestures to a stack of books, telling me the salient points of each and the status and professional qualifications of each author. She has read more in the last month than I have in the last year. She has learned as much about the subject as she might have at graduate school. She has done this on days when she was too depressed to face the outside world.

I pick up a couple of books and settle in the blue armchair that was in my living room when Jessica was growing up. She opens one of the books and dissects an ad. She tells me about the subtle but strong messages that impact us every day.

As I listen, I realize I am imprinted with some of those messages. I am wishing my daughter were easy to codify, easy to explain to people, easy for me to understand.

I think of all the stories I've heard, quietly, from parents who felt their children didn't turn out "right." Some of these children suffered with mental or physical health issues, struggled with learning disabilities, were trapped in addictions to drugs, alcohol, or food. Other children weren't able to excel in high school, to go college, get a good job, find a wonderful spouse, and live happily ever after. Still other progeny were rebels, adventurers, preferring to follow their own paths.

Yet as my daughter's face shines with her intellectual discoveries, I realize the gift she is giving me. She is pushing me out of my stereotypical thinking and into brave territory where I celebrate her for who she is. She is stretching me beyond my own narrow pre-conceived notions and inviting me into her world — a world of struggle, a world of hope, a world of creative excitement and possibility.

I put the books back on the chair when I leave. I hug my daughter goodbye. My daughter is making a difference in the world by talking about what she has learned with me. She is making a difference by showing me it's fine to struggle, to not conform, to explore who you are.

My mother has two children. One finished college in four years; the other ran off and got married after her sophomore year, and didn't get a degree until years afterwards. During those unschooled years, I learned enormous amounts about life and myself. During those years, I learned tolerance for those who don't follow the prescribed path. And what I didn't learn then, my daughter is thoughtfully teaching me right now.

~Deborah Shouse

She Already Knew

I would maintain that thanks are the highest form of thought;
and that gratitude is happiness doubled by wonder.
~G.K. Chesterton

I was fourteen. My girlfriend at the time was in southern Georgia while I was in Metro Atlanta, and we had only met online, never in person. We'd gotten into the habit of staying up late on the phone, even falling asleep sometimes, because my sisters or parents would constantly interrupt during the day. Nighttime was the only time we were sure to be unbothered.

I'd gotten comfortable in the routine: my dad would fall asleep on the couch, Mom would help him sleepwalk into their bedroom, my sisters and I would each go to bed, and my mom would turn in for the night after cleaning whatever dishes were left in the kitchen. I'd hear my mom's door shut and immediately text my girlfriend for her to call me.

This particular night, however, my mom was taking a very long time to go to bed. My girlfriend grew impatient, so I let her call but warned her that I would have to whisper until my mom went to bed.

What I didn't know was that my mom was in the living room, on the other side of my bedroom wall, reading a book with no intention of stopping any time soon. Eventually, I got too complacent and loud, and she heard me. My heart jumped out of my chest when she burst through the door, hissing at me to get off the phone and go to sleep. I quietly whispered what had happened to my girlfriend and hung up, burying under the covers so that I wouldn't have to face my mom's glare.

The next day, I was a wreck at school. I knew my mom wanted to talk to me about why I had been up so late, but we wouldn't have a chance to be properly alone until she drove me to orchestra that night. At school, I was constantly expressing my worries to my friends, all of whom already knew I was gay, asking them what I should say. I've always been a generally good kid; I wasn't used to getting in trouble, but there simply wasn't any credible excuse I could give to my mom to explain why I had been up so late without coming out to her.

Then I thought about what my mom's reaction would be if she did know it had been my girlfriend I was on the phone with instead of just a friend, like she'd thought. Her being my girlfriend was the only reason I would stay up with her on the phone, after all. I voiced the idea to my friends. Although they said that it was a brave decision to make on a whim, I had their support in whatever happened.

I wasn't particularly worried about my mom's reaction, necessarily. I'd been thinking about what would happen if I came out to her for a while; I didn't think that she would go so far as to kick me out or anything, but I had absolutely no idea what her opinions were on LGBT issues. I was sure she wouldn't hate me, but that didn't mean she would accept my sexuality.

Usually, I would sing along to the radio when riding in the car, especially when it was just my mom and me. However, that night, the ride to orchestra was spent with me in silence, constantly wondering when she would bring up the late-night phone call. When she dropped me off, she assured me that we would talk on the way back home.

Well, that didn't assure me at all. It only served to make me more nervous, so during rehearsal, I forced myself to get completely lost in the music we were playing so that I wouldn't have to think about what was to come. As soon as I started packing up my violin, though, all the nerves came back. I felt sick to my stomach, wondering what was going to happen once I told my mom that I was gay.

We were five minutes into the car ride when she asked me, "So, what made you think it was okay to be on the phone at two in the morning?"

This was it. This was my chance. I willed for my voice not to crack as I spoke, but it felt as if my heart was trying to claw its way up my throat. "Because she's my girlfriend," I replied.

There was only a half-second pause: "Okay, so why did you think it was okay to be on the phone at two in the morning?"

I was shell-shocked. Out of all of the reactions I'd imagined, I definitely hadn't thought that my mom would simply gloss over my Big Coming Out Moment.

That wasn't the case, however. After chastising me for staying up on the phone and promising me she'd take it away if she caught me again, my mom started asking me about my initial answer. She asked if I was gay, and then how I knew; I told her yes, and that I'd simply never wanted to be with a boy, but girls had always gotten my attention.

She was completely fine with it all. "If I'm being completely honest," she told me, "I kind of already knew." Apparently I'd had a fixation with girls since I was little, be it the pink Power Ranger or my fifth-grade student teacher. She promised that she didn't love me any less or any differently.

That was nearly six years ago. Since then, my mom has been my support system within the adults of my family. When I came out to my dad and he didn't react very well, she was right there to reassure me that everything would be fine. She asks how my girlfriend is doing when I'm dating someone, and she can always tell when we've broken up. She doesn't question my clothing choices and lets me be who I am.

A lot of people don't get so lucky when they come out to their parents. A lot of teenagers are kicked out onto the street simply because of who they love. My mom has been the most accepting, loving parent I could ever wish for. I knew I was lucky to have her before I came out, and that belief was confirmed once I'd told her the truth.

I know that she'll always be by my side, supporting me in who I am and what I do. She's the best mother I could ask for, and I will never be able to thank her enough for that.

~Ayanna Bryce

My Father's Approval

*You don't raise heroes, you raise sons. And if you treat them like
sons, they'll turn out to be heroes,
even if it's just in your own eyes.*
~Walter M. Schirra, Sr.

t was a cold night in late November. A perfect night for high
school football. The harvest moon drowned out the stars as it
hung high above the stadium lights. I was a senior and team
captain as a middle linebacker. We were a good football team
with a 12-1 record so far in the season. This particular game was the
semi-final round of the Alabama 5-A State Championship Playoffs.

We trekked from Eufaula to Mobile via Greyhound to meet our
cross-state nemesis. If we won this game we would play Etowah High
School in the State Championship game in December.

JaMarcus Russell, a mere freshman at the time, played quarterback for our opponent. Russell later played college football for LSU
and then became the first pick in the NFL draft in 2007, going to
the Oakland Raiders. Another kid by the name of Carnell Williams,
also known as "Cadillac" Williams, played running back for Etowah.
He later played for Auburn University, and then the Tampa Bay
Buccaneers. This was a tough team.

That November night the chilling air stung our noses and
burned our lungs as we ran during pre-game warm-ups. The stadium engulfed the one hundred or so faithful fans that followed us to

our battle. The opposing legion roared with ten thousand strong. My parents sat dead center on the fifty-yard line about halfway up in the section closest to the field.

Our team was the closest any Eufaula team had come to winning the State Championships in nearly twenty years. But first we had to cross this Goliath-sized hurdle in Mobile to move on to the finals in Birmingham. Playing in the championship game in Birmingham was something my dad did as a senior in high school. Hoping to make it that far was a dream of mine. I wanted to do something my dad had done, but better.

The game commenced and we burst out of the gates fighting. It was a fight to the finish with both teams leaving everything they had on the field. We scored first. 7-0. Then they reciprocated. 7-7. Then we pulled ahead with another touchdown. 14-7. They scored again but we blocked the extra point. 14-13. They took their first lead of the night with a little over seven minutes left in the fourth quarter. A failed two-point conversion made the score 14-19. With under a minute left in the game we fumbled. They ran the clock down and then took a safety with nineteen seconds left on the clock. 16-19. With three seconds left to score, we fought, bit, scratched, tore, grabbed, and ripped to break through the end zone one last time but time ran out.

I tackled a lot of guys but I also missed a lot of tackles. I made some good calls and made some bad ones. One play that haunts me was my chance to sack JaMarcus Russell. I closed in on him as we both neared the sideline. He cut left and I cut left. He shook right and I shook right. I was about to sack a future NFL quarterback but just before I placed my helmet on his shoulder pads I tripped. I fell and lunged for his legs and we both rolled out of bounds, however, not before the ball spiraled out of his hand and into the receiver's for the first down.

I was humiliated. I had my chance and blew it. I completely screwed up. The embarrassing part was that we rolled out of bounds into my team's sideline. I knew where my parents sat and hid my face from their seats. I could hear the disappointment in the sighs of the crowd. I couldn't bear the thought of what my dad was thinking.

The clock struck zero signaling that our chances of making it to the finals were over. We were numb. No tears, just disappointment. Not enough energy to cry. Time slowed to a crawl and the cheers of our opponent echoed in our helmets. I remained silent. My head throbbed. I didn't want to speak to anyone. No cheerleaders, no coaches, not my fellow linebacker whom I had played next to for six years, and especially not my dad. I feared how the conversation would go. I didn't want to hear, "Good game" because I knew it wasn't true. I didn't want to hear, "You'll get 'em next time" because there was not going to be a "next time." I didn't want to stomach, "You should've made this tackle or that tackle." I wasn't ready to face the reality of falling short in my father's footsteps.

With my helmet in one hand and my shoulder pads in the other, I walked alone across the field to the clubhouse. I looked up into the stands where my parents once sat. Empty. Every seat was empty. I guessed they'd decided to leave early. Could it have been my missed tackles? Was it the score that drove them away? Was it something worse, something as bad as shame? I didn't blame them; I was disappointed too.

It is funny how the air can be cold, your body hot and your emotions frozen as a familiar sound falls on your ringing ears. It was a whistle. A familiar whistle. Amidst thousands of cheers, a marching band, air horns, fireworks and sirens, I recognized that whistle. It came from the sideline. My head jerked and zeroed in on the source.

There he stood dressed in his game attire: red hat, red shirt with my number embroidered on his left breast pocket, khakis and a red tiger-pawed stadium cushion. It was my dad's whistle. Why did he come to the sideline? What would he say? What could be so important to call my attention away from my self-pity? What news couldn't wait until I got home? Why was it so important to remind me of the disappointment I had become?

Our eyes met; both red from heartache. I stared at him awaiting the verdict. He didn't say, "Good game," or "You should have done better." No expression fell on his face. Then he said something I'll never forget for the rest of my life. He extended his muscular arm, raised his thumb in a thumbs-up gesture, and said, "I love you, son."

He loves me? Even though I screwed up? Even though I blew it? Even though the weight of the game rested on my shoulders and I messed up? He loves me? That's exactly right. He loves me! All of those negative scenarios left my head. I didn't have a father whose love was contingent on my successes or failures. I had a father who loved me because I am his child and he is my dad. My dad approved of me because I am his son, not because I do or do not adorn a State Championship ring. So, thank you Dad. Thank you for showing me the perfect picture of my heavenly father's love.

~Bryan Gill

To Read When You're Alone

Home is where you are loved the most and act the worst.
~Marjorie Pay Hinckley

I was thirteen years old. My family had moved to Southern California from North Florida a year before. I hit adolescence with a vengeance. I was angry and rebellious, with little regard for anything my parents had to say, particularly if it had to do with me. Like so many teenagers, I struggled to escape from anything that didn't agree with my picture of the world. A "brilliant without need of guidance" kid, I rejected any overt offering of love. In fact, I got angry at the mention of the word love.

One night, after a particularly difficult day, I stormed into my room, shut the door and got into bed. As I lay down in the privacy of my bed, my hands slipped under my pillow. There was an envelope. I pulled it out and on the envelope it said, "To read when you're alone."

Since I was alone, no one would know whether I read it or not, so I opened it. It said "Mike, I know life is hard right now, I know you are frustrated and I know we don't do everything right. I also know that I love you completely and nothing you do or say will ever change that. I am here for you if you ever need to talk, and if you don't, that's okay. Just know that no matter where you go or what you do in your life, I will always love you and be proud that you are my son. I'm here for you and I love you — that will never change. Love, Mom.

That was the first of several "To read when you're alone" letters. They were never mentioned until I was an adult.

Today I travel the world helping people. I was in Sarasota, Florida, teaching a seminar when, at the end of the day, a lady came up to me and shared the difficulty she was having with her son. We walked out to the beach, and I told her of my mom's undying love and about the "To read when you're alone" letters. Several weeks later, I got a card that said she had written her first letter and left it for her son.

That night as I went to bed, I put my hands under my pillow and remembered the relief I felt every time I got a letter. In the midst of my turbulent teen years, the letters were the calm assurance that I could be loved in spite of me, not because of me. Just before I fell asleep I thanked God that my mom knew what I, an angry teenager, needed. Today when the seas of life get stormy, I know that just under my pillow there is that calm assurance that love — consistent, abiding, unconditional love — changes lives.

~Mike Staver

Too Many Children?

*Don't spend your precious time asking, "Why isn't the world a
better place?" It will only be time wasted. The question to ask is,
"How can I make it better?" To that there is an answer.*

~Leo Buscaglia

work for a very large company with many employees, most of
whom I do not know. As I was walking in one morning shortly
after Thanksgiving, I overheard two ladies talking about the
needy family that had been "adopted" for Christmas by her
husband's company. She was very upset over the family that had
been selected because they had "too many children" — they should
not have had that many if they couldn't take care of them.

My blood was boiling, but I bit my tongue.

She continued to relate that she and her husband decided not to
give anything this year because they didn't want to help a family that
"just didn't know when to stop." The second lady agreed.

I couldn't help myself. I turned around and, as calmly as I could,
I asked them what they really knew of this family. The lady who had
been doing most of the talking explained that there were seven kids,
the oldest of which was only ten. The parents were only thirty and
"obviously they started too young, instead of getting an education to
provide for their family." She knew their first names, their ages, favorite colors, and the items they needed and wanted for Christmas. The
list of wants/needs was pretty basic: hats, mittens, coats, a doll for little

Susie, a truck for Joe, etc. — nothing extravagant at all. The "problem" was just that they had "too many children."

At that point, I introduced myself, explaining that I was also in my early thirties and had "too many children." I had seven children, and my oldest was only eight.

The women decided my situation was different because I was working and providing for my children and that they were not being "adopted by strangers for Christmas."

I then told them that most of my kids also had their names on Christmas want lists and would very desperately love to be adopted for Christmas — permanently adopted by a "real" family. You see, six of my seven children are *foster* children.

They stammered, stuttered and apologized; they had never thought of that. I gave them a few other possible instances of how a family can end up with "too many children." It could be anything: death of the parents, blended families, grandparents raising grandchildren, and on and on. After hearing this, the ladies said that they wished they would have done something to contribute, but it was too late because the collection already had been completed and turned in.

I knew that they could see things differently now. I explained how I often got rude comments at the grocery store when I took my kids and used government vouchers (subsidies for food for low-income families and for kids in foster care). We heard cruel comments like, "You shouldn't have so many children if you can't afford to feed them." One day after hearing this, my oldest asked me, "Mom, can we afford all this food?" She was truly bothered by these comments (we routinely spend three hundred dollars a week on groceries, after the vouchers). I don't explain it to strangers in the store because it would only hurt the kids even more. They all have come to dislike the "F word" (as in, *foster*), which not only makes them different, but also gives them a feeling of being unwanted or unloved. But many of our family and friends are teaching others not to be so quick to assume and judge.

The ladies and I continued to talk for a while, and I showed them pictures of my seven kids. We talked about the number of children in foster care in the United States, as well as in overseas orphanages, waiting to be adopted. It's incredible that there are so many children in need. In some way, she was right: the "problem" is that there are just "too many children"; too many who need to be loved and cared for—even adopted, not just for Christmas but forever.

The following morning, when I arrived at my desk, there sat two bags of Christmas gifts for "my" kids. It's amazing how much people really do care when they really know.

~Kathy Gerst

A Mother's Love

There came a time when the risk to remain tight in the bud was more painful than the risk it took to blossom.
~Anaïs Nin

Think back to the early '90s, before Ellen "came out" and *Will & Grace* was not yet all over prime-time television. Before Matthew Shepard received national attention, and being gay got the public support it has today. Imagine a nineteen-year-old Mexican son coming out to his mother and seeing the heartbreak in her eyes. Picture her heart breaking into pieces so small they could fit through the eye of a sewing needle.

Living in Texas, growing up Catholic with a strong Mexican ancestry and influence, it was difficult coming to terms with my own homosexuality. I can remember many nights when I prayed the entire rosary and begged God to change me. As the years pushed on, I gradually accepted who I was and learned to love myself despite my machismo-rich heritage. However, that was only the first step.

All Latinos know how important family is, and I am not any different. Accepting my sexuality was a big move for me on my journey to self-discovery. Yet, the burning question was, would my family accept me as well? The thought of losing them and being disowned frightened me more than death.

In our culture, we are taught that family is everything. I could gladly meet any of life's challenges as long as I had my family by my side to face them head-on. Nonetheless, the time had come, and I needed to be honest with them.

Easing into the task, I came out to my younger brother first. Surprisingly, his reaction was good and more or less indifferent. He was of the mind-set that I was his brother, and my sexual orientation was not important. Feeling particularly confident about the experience, I decided to come out to my mother.

It was October 11, 1994, National Coming Out Day. She cried, yelled, screamed and ultimately blamed herself. It was a nightmare. By the end of the night, our eyes were red and puffy from all the crying, and our noses dripped with mucus. We were exhausted and retired to our respective rooms without saying good night. I never expected her to react the way she had, and I worried that our relationship was forever damaged.

That night I lay in bed and thought about a TV talk show that I had seen earlier that day. The focus of the show was National Coming Out Day, and the guests were a variety of non-Latinos coming out to their families. Their experiences on the show were much better than mine that night, and I could not comprehend why my mother had reacted so awfully. For the next few days, the house was covered with a blanket of awkwardness.

The next day I came out to my sister, and a month later I came out to my dad. I was able to delay telling my father as my parents divorced when I was in middle school. I could not bear another episode like the one I experienced with Mom. Nevertheless, their reaction to my news was much like my younger brother's, and I was very much surprised by my father's kind words. He said, "You're my son, and I'll always love you no matter what."

I wish I could write that my mother soon thereafter came to her senses and we promptly mended our relationship. The truth of the matter is, the road to her acceptance and understanding was a long one. In the months that followed, we had many emotional discussions, and she had several questions. She was determined to figure out what went wrong. Mom would encourage me to continue to pray, and I know that HIV and AIDS were huge concerns for her. A lot of people, especially at that time, believed that being gay was equivalent to an AIDS death sentence.

Today, eight years later and thanks to a lot of determination and persistence, my mother and I have a very healthy and open relationship. In a lot of ways, she is my best friend. Recently, we've watched movies with gay themes as she tries to gain a better understanding of my life. Her favorite is *The Broken Hearts Club*.

As far as my seemingly open-minded brother, sister and father and our relationship today, they have adopted the philosophy, "Don't ask, don't tell." We are all still close, and I now have a sister-in-law, a three-year-old niece and one-year-old nephew. But they turn a blind eye and deaf ear to those things they choose not to know. Unfortunately, that means there are parts of me missing from their lives. My mother and I had a rough start as 1994 came to an end, but today she is the only one in my family who knows me completely.

My Mexican-proud mom had survived an impoverished childhood on the north side of town, coupled with years of adolescence tormented by Texas-style bigotry and hatred for our race. And just when she probably thought she was in the clear, her first-born son professes he is gay. But falling back on our faith and cultural importance of family, that no longer matters to her. Come what may, we promise to be there for one another and to stand together.

People's reactions vary when I come out to them today, but as long as I have my mother supporting me, I am happy. What more could a son ask from his mother than her continued support and love? Nothing can compare to a mother's love, and being a mama's boy is a good thing. My mom has been the rock in my life, y no puedo imaginar mi vida sin ella.

¡Gracias a Dios por ti mamá, gracias por quererme sin límites!

~Johnny N. Ortez, Jr.

Raising Great Kids

Encourage Independence and Responsibility

A Mother's Faith

Fall seven times, stand up eight.
~Japanese Proverb

C hristmas with my brother, Ken, was always a magical time. He never got "too cool" to be excited over the holidays the way the rest of us did. Ken was born smack in the middle of my parents' twelve kids. He was born a month early in an era when pediatric intensive care units weren't what they are today. Halfway through the delivery, the doctors realized the umbilical cord was wrapped around Ken's throat cutting off the oxygen to his brain. By the time he was in the doctor's hands, it had been cut off long enough to leave him with cerebral palsy, mild retardation and profound deafness. But God is good and he more than compensated for Ken's disabilities by lavishing on him a sparkling personality, gusto for life, childlike faith and a magnetic smile that drew people to him.

Because my brother, Mark, was born less than a year after Ken, and my sister, Gail, had been born ten months before, babying Ken was not an option. He was part of the gang from day one, and although he didn't walk until he was twelve, he never had trouble keeping up with the rest of us, or the passel of neighborhood kids and cousins who hung around our house.

In the hospital, the doctors had advised my parents not to see Ken, to put him in a "special home" and forget they'd had him. They predicted he'd never walk or talk, never feed himself, and wouldn't live past his tenth birthday. Ken was seven by the time I was born and I'm glad the doctors never told him any of the above. The Ken I knew was lean and taut, feisty and impish and ate anything that didn't eat him first. He loved a party, loved being the center of attention and loved everything to do with Christmas.

One of my favorite Christmas memories was a year when our grandparents sent us a new swing set. From first glance, Ken was fascinated with the slide. He spent the holidays on the ground offering a blow-by-blow commentary as the rest of us slid down. He'd squeal with delight as we started down the slide, throw his head back and laugh when we landed with a splat at his feet, then chase us on all fours trying to grab us and tickle us before we could crawl back up the ladder again. (You did not want to get caught, because when Ken tickled you, he did not know his own strength.) He never tried to traverse the ladder himself. His scrawny, twisted legs just didn't work the way they needed to.

The day the rest of us started back to school, Mama knew what she had to do. She bundled Ken up, took him out to the backyard, pointed him toward the ladder and began to pray.

"Okay, Lord, Ken wants to go down the slide. I'm gonna need all the help I can get to let him try."

Years later, she told me how hard it was watching him climb and fall, climb and fall again and again. He tore both knees out of his pants, which he generally did most days anyway (his patches had patches), cut one elbow, bloodied his forehead and had one particularly bad tumble that left him rocking on the lawn crying and holding a knot on the back of his head while Mama forced herself not to run to his aid.

The neighbor to the back of us came to the fence and yelled at my mama, "What kind of woman are you? Get that baby off that ladder!" Mama told her as nicely as she could that, if it bothered her, she'd have to close her curtains and stop watching. Ken had decided he was going down the slide, and down the slide he would go, no matter how long it took him.

By the time the rest of us got home from school, Ken was black and blue and smiling from ear to ear. Not only could he get up and down the slide with lightning speed, but heaven help any kid who got in his way.

That swing set was a generous gift my grandparents gave us. I'm sure it set them back a bit. But the real gift came from my mom — my mom who loved my brother, Ken, enough to watch him struggle, to pray for the courage not to interfere, knowing how important it was for him to do things on his own.

That was almost fifty years ago. I wish I knew where those doctors are now. They were so ready to tell us all what my brother would never do. Obviously, they didn't know the God we knew. What would they say if they could see Ken now at age fifty-five, living independently and holding down a job? They didn't know back then that God had a much bigger plan for my brother and they didn't know the mama who loved him enough and trusted God enough to give him the best Christmas present he'd ever receive.

~Mimi Greenwood Knight

Music to My Ears

God is the answer. What is the question?
~Jay Robb

uring my pregnancy there had been no sign of anything wrong with the baby. I took my vitamins, ate lots of fruits and vegetables, and did my stretching exercises. I expected everything would go as smoothly as they had when my first son was born: an easy delivery and a "perfect" child.

In the delivery room, squeezing my husband's hand and hearing our baby's first cry, I was not prepared for what followed. The look on the nurse's face expressed her alarm as clearly as her words: "Mrs. Gardner, something's wrong here!" I looked in horror as she pulled back the blanket to show our son's face: one eye sealed shut; the other a milky mass; no bridge to his nose, and a face that looked crushed. Although I knew I should take him in my arms, I couldn't. I just couldn't. He was whisked away by the nurse as I was wheeled to the recovery room.

I lay on the hard hospital bed, the tightly pulled curtain shutting out the world. Still, I could hear other new mothers cooing to their babies. I heard one bemoan, "Not another boy!" and I was filled with jealous rage.

I thought of all the dreams I'd had for this child, of cuddling with him, of reading to him from brightly colored picture books, of his singing or painting or playing the piano like his older brother Jamaal — of his eyes, like Jamaal's, studying the keys.

Instead, my baby was blind and painful to look at.

Slowly, deliberately I walked to the phone and dialed my mom. My agony poured out between sobs: "It's a boy. His eyes won't open. His face is deformed. Mom, what am I going to do?"

"You will bring him home. You will bring him home and nurture him," she replied simply, firmly.

A nurse appeared at my side, led me to a rocker, and placed a small, blanketed bundle in my arms. Taking a deep breath, I looked down at my son. I had hoped he would look different — but he didn't. His forehead protruded. Under the sealed eyelid, an eyeball was missing, the other was spaced far from it. His bridgeless nose was bent to the side of his face. The doctors called it *hypertelorism*. I didn't know what to call it.

As we rocked, my mom's words echoed in my ears. I began to talk to him. "Hello, Jermaine," I said. "That's your name. I am your mommy, and I love you. I'm sorry I waited so long to come to you and to hold you. Please forgive me. You have a big brother and a wonderful father who also love you. I promise to work hard to make your life the best it can be. Your grandpa has a lovely voice, and can play the piano and sing. I can give you music." *Yes,* I thought, *that I can do. That I will do!*

Over the next few months, my husband and I poured our energies into filling up the darkness in Jermaine's life. One of us carried him in his Snugli or backpack at all times, constantly talking or singing to him. We inundated him with music — mostly classical, some Lionel Richie, some Stevie Wonder. His four-year-old brother was already taking piano lessons, and whenever he practiced, I sat next to him on the piano bench with his little brother on my lap. After a while, I began strapping Jermaine into his high chair next to Jamaal when Jamaal practiced.

However, I seldom took Jermaine out of the house because I couldn't stand anyone staring at my baby. Since blind infants cannot mimic a smile they cannot see, they often do not smile. It hurt that I got no smiles from Jermaine.

Every day my younger sister, Keetie, called, reminding me that God had a plan for each of us.

One day, Jamaal was practicing the piano, playing "Lightly Row" again and again, his little brother secure in his high chair next to him. Jamaal had just finished practicing and had come downstairs where my husband and I were sitting, when we heard a familiar *plink plunk-plunk, plink plunk-plunk* floating down the stairs. I looked at my husband, and he looked at me. It couldn't be Jamaal. He was jumping up and down on our bed. We stared at each other for a second, then tore upstairs!

At the piano, head thrown back, a first-ever smile splitting his face, Jermaine was playing "Lightly Row"! The right keys, the right rhythm, the right everything!

In response to my husband's immediate and astonished, amazing-news phone calls, the house filled with family and friends within an hour. I sat Jermaine at the piano in his high chair, as we all stood around expectantly.

Nothing.

I hummed "Lightly Row" and played a few notes. Jermaine sat silent, his hands motionless.

"It was just a fluke," my husband said.

"No," I replied unabashed. "It couldn't have been." I was certain our eight-and-a-half-month-old son had perfectly replicated a tune.

Two weeks later, he did it again, this time playing another piece his older brother had practiced. I ran to the piano and listened as the notes became firmer and the tune melded into its correct form.

From then on, there was no stopping Jermaine. He demanded to be at the piano from morning until bedtime. I often fed him at the piano, wiping strained applesauce off the keys. At first, he only played Jamaal's practice songs… and then he played Lionel Richie's "Hello" after hearing it on the tape recorder. At eighteen months, he played the left-hand part of Beethoven's "Moonlight Sonata" while my sister played the right-hand part. When he gave his first concert, I crawled under the piano to work the foot pedals his little legs could not possibly reach.

By the time he was out of diapers, I was desperate to find him a good piano teacher. I sought out a teacher at the Maryland School for the Blind and called, explaining that Jermaine was already playing the piano.

"How old is he?" the teacher asked.

"Two and a half," I replied.

"A child that age is too young to start piano lessons," he said disapprovingly, just as strains of "Moonlight Sonata" filtered in from the other room.

"By the way, Mrs. Gardner, who is that playing in the background?"

"That's the two-and-a-half-year-old."

"Bring him in!" the teacher replied promptly.

Soon, invitations for Jermaine to perform poured in. He appeared on national television. He played at the White House for two first ladies. Stevie Wonder invited him to play with him at his studio in California. A pair of Texas philanthropists who saw Jermaine on TV flew him to Dallas for a special surgery to rebuild his face.

As I reflect on his accomplishments, I think of my sister Keetie's words when I had despaired: "God has a plan for all of us," she'd said, and "God has a plan for your son." Indeed, I believe He did.

~Jacqui Kess-Gardner

Editor's note: Jermaine Gardner grew up to be a well-known concert pianist and recording artist.

The Slide

There are two ways of exerting one's strength: one is pushing down, the other is pulling up.
~Booker T. Washington

I have worked with people with disabilities since I was in college. Honestly, though, I have always said, "This really isn't where I belong." I did not study special education in college. I was a psychology major. When I pursued my master's degree, I chose early-childhood education hoping to open a parenting center in my community to teach expectant parents the wonders of newborns and very young children.

Yet, time after time, I kept finding jobs and opportunities in the field of developmental delays and disabilities. My husband and I were blessed with two little girls when I was working as the director of an early-intervention program for children from birth to age three with developmental delays and disabilities. My young daughters were raised around a kitchen table where stories were shared about the triumphs, challenges, joys, and struggles of parenting children with disabilities. They heard many of my "soapboxes" about stereotyping people with disabilities. They cried or laughed at wonderful stories from those infants and toddlers and their families who opened their lives to me.

Each year, our program had an end-of-the-year graduation for those children who would be moving on to the next stage of their lives.

For some, that would be community programs; for others, they would begin the special-education process. It was a big to-do at a local park with many families in attendance. All of the staff's families attended, too. There were balloons, fried chicken, graduation certificates, lots of pictures, and certainly many hugs and a few tears. The graduation picnic was just getting started when my youngest daughter, Gracie, age four, asked if she could go down the slide. This was one of those "cool slides" with about ten steps and a steep incline. The slide was all metal and slippery.

Since my husband had a work commitment that night and was unable to join us at the picnic, I greeted families as they joined us and kept one eye on the slide as I watched my two little ones head off. The picnic paraded on with the charm of a small town. Parents laughed and reminisced. Children ate ice cream and chased lightning bugs. Gracie could hardly take time to come down from that slide to eat.

Pretty soon, a little girl who had been in my program several years earlier made her way to the slide. She, too, wanted a turn on the "cool slide." Lena, who was seven, had Down syndrome. Due to complications from heart surgery, she had incomplete paralysis from the chest down. She wore a body brace and "bear-walked" on her hands and feet. Lena had been the very first baby I had seen as an early interventionist. Lena's mother was now a member of the staff at the early-intervention program. Quickly, I went to find Lena's mother to see how she wanted to "handle" this. It took me a few minutes to locate Lena's mother in the crowd. When I explained the situation, both of us went running back toward the slide.

As we made our approach, we both stopped, frozen in our tracks. Lena was pulling herself up the first few steps of the slide ladder. Gracie was behind her, lifting one of Lena's feet onto a step. She then moved to the other side, lifted the other foot, and gently pushed her bottom. Lena then used her arms, which were very strong, to pull herself to the next rung. Gracie then began the process again, lifting one foot and then the other, with a little bottom nudge. When Lena made it to the top, she smiled triumphantly, laid down on her belly, didn't even blink, and *whoosh!* Down she came! In a flash, Gracie was on her belly right behind her, squealing and laughing all the way down! At the bottom, the girls giggled and carried on, and slowly made their way back to the ladder. It was time to do it all again! Lena and Gracie played on the slide until the last flicker of evening light gave way to the early glow of the August moon.

As we drove home that evening, I thought I would try to talk to Gracie about how proud I was of her. I also thought that perhaps all those talks around the table had made some impact, and maybe, just maybe, I had played a role in this remarkable child's ability to relate to a child with a disability. And so I said, "I guess you see that Lena is really much more like you than different from you."

Gracie was very quiet in her car seat. Finally, she said, "Oh, you mean, how her eyes are squinky." For the life of me, I could not understand how we could be talking about Lena's eyes when Gracie had just spent the last two hours lifting Lena's legs and helping Lena get up a slide because she could not move the same way as Gracie.

Ever the early interventionist, however, and never one to pass up a "teachable moment," I decided that Gracie must be talking about Lena's facial features related to having Down syndrome. I began a monologue about facial features that people with Down syndrome may have. When I finished and asked Gracie if she understood, she simply sighed and said, "Lena's eyes are squinky because she smiles so big when she laughs!"

At that moment, humbled by the wisdom of this little child, I knew that God was teaching me many lessons through Gracie and Lena. When we truly look at the person, we see beyond all disabilities. Lena's smile captured Gracie's heart, and a friendship blossomed. And for that moment, on that August evening, all that mattered was how many times you could ride on that cool slide!

~Corinne Hill

Coach Dad

Whether you think you can or think you can't — you are right.
~Henry Ford

Thanks to my dad, I learned to intercept life's fumbles and turn them into winning plays. Decades later, I still use his guidance when I overcome obstacles with my optimistic outlook.

"It's how you respond that counts," he coached. "Have a positive attitude. Do your best. Enjoy life. Do your part. Be resourceful. Believe in yourself. Believe in others."

Dad lost his youthful dream to coach football when he couldn't afford college. Yet he didn't let disappointment bench him from a productive life. He held varied jobs until the end of the 1930s. Then he founded and ran Parks Sand and Gravel Company until he retired.

By the time of my birth in 1951, my parents had been married twenty years and my sister had celebrated her thirteenth birthday. We lived in Emporia, Kansas, where my dad had earned respect as a hardworking businessman who mentored others.

Dad boosted floundering souls and freed the daring spirit in those around him. He set reasonable expectations. He offered support and feedback. He created opportunities to build strengths and demonstrate competencies. I heard stories about his kindness from those who stopped to say, "Wes, thanks for believing in me and for giving me a chance."

Dad had become a coach after all: a coach about life, a model of strength, courage, and integrity.

As his daughter who had hearing and voice impairments, I benefited from the same "believe in yourself" approach. Coach Dad taught me that we become stronger when we face our setbacks. We shape our strengths and sharpen our compassion. From his viewpoint, the disabilities and challenges I braved became scrimmages to train my coping muscles to manage the ups and downs of life.

I had the typical childhood tasks to master along with tough medical issues to tackle. My ear malformations and hearing loss in both ears required several surgeries. Lifesaving throat surgery at age twelve damaged my vocal cords and nerves and muscles to my face and tongue. I had countless sessions of speech therapy due to my hearing loss, and later for problems I had using my tongue and voice.

My parents encouraged me. They made a terrific team with my dad's inventiveness and my mother's faith that all things worked out in one way or another. Growing up under their "I can" philosophies, I gained the strategies I needed to face my challenges.

Dad focused on finding solutions, not whining. He didn't let fear, failure, or worry immobilize him and rob him of innovative ways to solve problems. He expected no less from me when I grappled with frustrations during my younger years.

Sometimes I didn't hear crucial information at school. When I tired, my face drooped. My weak voice gave out. I disrupted class with incessant coughing spells. I ate at a slow pace to avoid choking. Sometimes I got weary from studying hard to make up for missed information. Even though I practiced relentlessly to improve my speech and my voice, I often felt my progress was too slow.

With his head cocked to the side, Coach Dad listened. Then he'd ask, "Did you do your best?"

"Yes," I'd say. "I tried."

"Well then, that's all you can ask of yourself."

He'd pause then continue, "What did you learn?"

To him everything — good or bad — provided a learning opportunity. A chance for self-improvement. A clue to solve a problem. A way to help others.

Coach Dad didn't cut me any slack. He held me accountable for making positive contributions. When the church high school youth group elected me president, I didn't want the leadership role. I thought it would tax me with my hearing loss and voice limitations.

"I can't do it!"

Coach Dad listened. "Sounds like others have faith in you."

"That doesn't matter!"

"I wonder — what would it take to make it work?" He nudged me to list ideas. Then he stepped back to allow me to take charge.

I learned resourcefulness by using my strengths to find solutions. I observed, listened attentively, carefully chose my words, and facilitated ways to help all feel included. I taught others to keep background noise to a minimum, to talk one at a time, and to look at me when they spoke.

Coach Dad followed up. "How did it go this time?"

"Great, Dad!"

"What did you learn?"

"I can do it!"

He smiled. Point made.

During an eventful year, Coach Dad stood by me as I graduated with my master's degree in social work, moved to Iowa to start my career, and subsequently survived a medical emergency and two grueling surgeries. When I recovered and returned to my job, he knew his coaching had paid off. I bounced back despite the serious setbacks that had blocked my path. Most importantly, I had conveyed confidence in my ability to tackle tough times.

Before the end of that year more turmoil arrived when Coach Dad was diagnosed with pancreatic cancer. He knew he couldn't control the existence of the cancer, but he could control his response. As he faced life's last game with dignity and grace, the core truth of his coaching became clear: He had taught me and many others the skills we needed to direct our own lives.

I was twenty-four when Coach Dad died. That was over thirty years ago. Every day since, I've been grateful for his legacy of values and lessons about resilience.

He taught me to believe in the irrepressible quality of the human spirit. He empowered me to learn from both the joys and challenges of life. He coached me to use my strengths to respond in positive ways to life's fumbles. He instilled in me the kindness of sharing my hard-earned wisdom.

Today Coach Dad cheers from the grandstand of my heart. I continue to call upon his wisdom to tackle whatever life throws at me, an inspiring tribute to his lifelong influence and the relevance of his lessons.

~Ronda Armstrong

Polka Dots and Stripes

It's always the badly dressed people who are the most interesting.
~Jean Paul Gaultier

'm at my wit's end," my daughter complained. "Maddie insists on wearing that old pink tutu over her clothes everywhere we go. It's embarrassing! And why are you smiling?"

Yes, I was smiling as I thought back to a time twenty-eight years before when it was this very daughter of mine who was "embarrassing."

Life with two daughters had been happy and normal for several years... until my younger started kindergarten and wanted to choose what to wear to school each day.

Oh the struggles we had! Like clockwork... every morning. She wanted to wear polka dot shirts with striped pants, or plaids with teddy bears. The colors didn't even come close to matching. Of course, I insisted she choose from the clothes I picked, which resulted in tears and drama. She would leave for school wearing perfectly matched clothes and unfortunately, a frown on her face. I'm sure I wore a frown too.

Although I hated to send her to school feeling unhappy I did anyway. Why? I was concerned about what others would think, or say, about her appearance. Would her teachers think I was colorblind? Or even worse, that I did not get up and get her ready for school? Or that I just didn't care?

Unhappy school mornings were becoming the new "normal" around our house and I didn't like it. Fortunately, a change did come about, thanks to the wisdom of a kindergarten teacher.

During a conference with my daughter's teacher I learned that her morning disposition was interfering with her learning. She would seem sad and unable to focus at times. Tearfully I told the teacher of our daily power struggles over what she should wear to school.

Her teacher told me that as long as my daughter was dressed appropriately for the weather I should let her decide what to wear and stop worrying about what others would think. "Let her go to school happy and ready to learn. Parents have to choose their battles."

I took this teacher's words to heart and began letting my daughter wear whatever she wanted. (Although I often cringed when she came out of her room with her polka dots, stripes and smiley face on.) Her teacher saw immediate improvements in her grades and interest in learning. My husband and I were enjoying our stress-free mornings. Such a simple change, yet it made all the difference.

Why was I smiling? As I watched my little granddaughter spin around the room dressed in a T-shirt, jeans, and pink tutu I noticed that she too had her smiley face on.

"Let me tell you what a wise teacher once told me, " I said.

~Carol Emmons Hartsoe

Privilege Coupons

Successful enterprises are usually led by a proven chief
executive who is a competent benevolent dictator.
~Richard Pratt

t's frustrating to be a child. Adults are always telling them what to do, and kids crave some control over their lives. As the 19th century writer Josh Billings said, "To bring up a child in the way he should go, travel that way yourself once in a while." In other words, imagine what it feels like to have no say over your life, even for little decisions as to whether you get to stay up an hour past your usual bedtime. After years of skirmishes with my kids over the little things, I realized there had to be a better way for us to coexist with me in charge but with the kids feeling like it was not a total dictatorship. So I decided to make it a benevolent dictatorship.

I had always found that my kids behaved better if I gave them some control over the things that didn't even matter to me, such as how they styled their hair or what clothes they wore. My daughter could wear her brother's pants to school with her pink shirts, and my son could wear a red cape to nursery school for an entire semester if that made him happy. My theory was that if I let them make decisions about the unimportant things they wouldn't feel the need to rebel about the things that mattered, such as doing their best in school or avoiding self-destructive behavior.

One Christmas, when they were preteens, I surprised the kids with homemade coupon books. I took their most requested privileges, made coupons for them, and stapled them into a little booklet that included:

1 coupon for "Shopping spree at the mall"
2 coupons for "A day with Mom doing anything you want"
2 coupons for "Have a party for whatever reason you want"
4 coupons for "Pick a game to play with Mom"
4 coupons for "Double your allowance this week"
4 coupons for "Triple your allowance this week"
4 coupons for "Get candy while shopping with Mom"
5 coupons for "Order pizza whenever you want"
12 coupons for "One can of soda whenever you want"
12 coupons for "Stay up one hour past bedtime"
12 coupons for "Watch one hour of TV on a school night"
12 coupons for "Watch one hour of TV on a camp night"

In the early years, I included coupons like "Have Mom read a book to you" and in the later years I included things like "Get a ride for you and your friends to the movies."

The kids loved their booklets. They presented me with a coupon whenever they wanted to exercise one of their privileges. They had power, we had peace, and we could spend more time enjoying each other instead of negotiating. They learned how to budget their TV time; they chose when it was really important to stay up late; and they learned to view candy and soda as occasional treats over which they had control. After all, they had to make those coupons last an entire year until the next Christmas.

I continued to give them their privilege coupons through their middle school years. I think it was one more contribution to making them the responsible adults they are today. They still talk about those coupons and how much they liked them, and I won't be surprised if my grandchildren end up getting coupons from their parents too!

~Amy Newmark

A Deed a Day

Happiness is a by-product of an effort to make someone else happy.
~Gretta Brooker Palmer

I cast a warning glare and mouthed the words "Just a minute!" as my daughter tugged my hand. I was stirring chili with the other hand and balancing the phone between my shoulder and chin. The clothes dryer buzzer sounded as my husband walked in with our other daughter. The dog was scratching at the door, and we had about twenty minutes to eat before we had to take the girls to their next activity. My husband seemed a bit annoyed that dinner was not already on the table. The girls started arguing about who had to let the poor dog back into the house.

That night, I had a heavy heart thinking about how mindless my family's routines had become. We were becoming taskmasters who performed each day's activities as if we were on an assembly line. We had become absorbed in our own activities and not very considerate towards those around us. We needed to do something to bring back some meaning into our lives. It needed to be something that would refocus our own agendas and energize us toward the common good.

I purchased a journal, labeled it "Our Deed Diary" and held a family meeting. I told my husband and our daughters that I wanted us all to think about doing a kindness for others every day. It could be for each other or for people outside our home. The purpose was to reduce the focus on ourselves and brighten someone else's day in the process.

We talked about what a good deed would mean for this "project." We decided that a good deed was doing something nice for someone else that they were not expecting. It could be as simple as making a card for your teacher or going out of your way to give someone a compliment for something he or she did. We decided to record our deeds every day and discuss them over dinner. The girls seemed excited at the prospect of this new "game" we were playing. My husband rolled his eyes. I said a little prayer.

When I first conceived of this project, I thought that one deed a day was too easy. Let me tell you; it is harder than it seems. We all, of course, do things for others on a regular basis; but this had to be something above and beyond what we already do. Sending birthday cards to people that we already send cards to every year would not count. This had to be an unexpected effort on our parts.

We had a rough start. We were supposed to talk about our good deeds and write them in our Deed Diary at dinner every day. On some days, someone would forget to do a good deed, while on other days, we would forget to write our good deeds in the diary. After a few weeks though, I found myself waking up in the morning trying to decide what good deed I could do for someone that day. My daughters began to rush to me after school to tell me a good deed they had done for someone that day.

We have been doing good deeds for nearly a year now. I am happy to say that it is making a difference in our lives. Instead of always wondering what the day will bring for us, we think about what we can do for someone else. At dinner, we have an instant conversation starter, as we all share our stories.

I have expanded the deed experiment to my first grade classroom. I started out by having every student write a letter to someone in the school to thank him or her for something he or she does for us. It was most touching to observe the janitor, nurse, librarian, and other school staff hang our notes on their walls while beaming because they felt appreciated.

In my classroom, every student does not have to do a good deed every day, but our class, as a whole, tries to show at least three kindnesses to others each day. We record them and I am most boastful about how thoughtful the students are towards others. When a student spills his or her crayons, you wouldn't believe how many kids scurry over to try to help and clean them up! Just as with my family, keeping and sharing a Deed Diary changed our whole outlook on life.

Who would have thought that trying to do a simple kindness a day would be so rewarding? I feel my daughters and first grade students better understand the old saying that "it is better to give than to receive." They have felt that indescribable feeling of inner joy that you can only experience by giving to someone else from your heart. The best thing is that you feel so great about doing something for someone else, you don't even look for or expect anything in return. So, when someone does reciprocate, it is an enormous and positive bonus. When someone does something nice for me, I now think of it as, "What a great idea! I'll have to do that for someone too!"

~Shannon Anderson

Always Show Up

Commitment means staying loyal to what you said you were
going to do, long after the mood you said it in has left you.
~Author Unknown

rolled over in bed to look at the clock. I needed to get up if I was going to be on time for work. I'd pulled what the resort called a double shift the day before — 5:30 a.m. until 9 p.m., until everything was washed, wiped down, swept up and stored away for the next morning's crew at the summer vacation resort where I served as an event waitress.

I worked there during their two big months — June and July — and we'd served over 400 people the day before. The soles of my feet felt sore and puffy and my back was stiff, but I was due back for a single shift and I needed to get up. I put my head back down on the pillow and considered my options, and produced the most obvious one a self-centered, pampered sixteen-year-old girl was likely to choose.

I would simply call in sick. I would apologize for not making it to work today, but I figured they'd be fine without my services just this one day.

My mother walked into my room.

"You have to work today, don't you, Bec? You better be getting up or you're going to be late." She stood there watching me, not showing any sign of leaving me to my state of exhaustion from all my hard work the prior day.

"I don't think I'll go in today. I'm too tired," I said. "I'm going to call in sick."

I felt a slight tinge of guilt, maybe even a bit of premonition because as soon as the words were out of my mouth, the expression on her face changed, and it wasn't in my favor.

"What do you mean you're calling in?" she demanded, her eyes hard and glaring. And I knew this whole scene was far from over. It's funny how even a sixteen-year-old does know deep down she's botched this one.

She didn't miss a beat. "When you accepted that job, you were telling those people you wanted that job," she said. "You were telling them you would show up and work for them when they asked you to. You were telling them you would respect their giving you that position and that they could count on you."

My mother didn't yell at me to make her point, nor did she swear or threaten me with some bogus form of punishment should I not hoist myself out of that bed. She should have been a lawyer because she used the best weapon there is: shame mixed in with a healthy dose of blunt honesty.

But she wasn't done with me yet, this woman who produced three homemade meals a day for her family of six, and who did all of the laundry and ironing, made the beds, baked and canned, cleaned the house and washed the windows; this woman who walked wherever she needed to go in our small town because she didn't drive a car. The same woman who went to business school to become a legal secretary, but instead fell in love, got married and ended up with four children to feed, clean up after and raise, but who never got to call in sick when she was tired.

"You know, Bec," she continued, "there are so many times I wish all I had to do was get up, splash a little cold water on my face and head into class or to a job." Her wistful expression drove her point to the center of the bulls-eye, and I saw her in a different light, and I knew I had no right to call in sick simply because I was a little on the tired side that morning.

My mother considered a job outside the home something to be

appreciated, even if it was just a summer waitressing job.

"Now, get yourself out of bed and into work."

I did, and I survived.

She taught me many things through the years, either by example, or by silence at the right time, or through our late-night girl chats over hot cups of tea that we shared so many, many late evenings when I'd come home to visit as a married woman with children of my own.

The scene presented itself full circle years later. There I was, a mother of two preteen daughters and your typical working wife and mom. We'd finished dinner and I was cleaning up in the kitchen when I commented to the family that I wished I could take tomorrow off from work because I was feeling extra tired that particular evening.

As if on cue from Providence, my younger daughter offered what I'm sure seemed the most logical response to such a request.

"Why don't you just call in sick tomorrow then, Mom?"

And I had to wonder if my mother was just around the corner, listening to see how I would respond to that one.

I think she would have approved.

"I can't do that, honey," I told her. "When you tell someone you're going to work for them, you need to show up, even if you're a little tired."

To this day, both of my daughters remember and honor that tenet my mother drilled into my head so long ago.

~R'becca Groff

Teamwork

Act as if what you do makes a difference. It does.
~William James

I n early spring of my daughter's ninth year, her life's passion was to play soccer. She had been active and successful in softball, karate, ballet, and basketball in the past, so it was with enthusiasm that I took her to sign up for the recreational soccer league in town. However, when we arrived, we found out there were not enough coaches to start a new team and there was no room on any existing teams.

Since there were a couple of other girls awaiting a new team, the league director suggested that I coach. My daughter's confidence in my abilities outweighed my concern that I had never played the sport before, or even watched a game. I immediately ran to the library and got every book I could about the game and about coaching soccer. I had coached other teams before in the sports that I myself had played, so how hard could this be?

The coaches of the other teams were instructed to donate one of their players to our team so that we would have a full roster. Well, as you may have guessed, I did not get their star players; but I did have a group of ten girls who were excited about playing.

I wrote up drills and charts and team building activities and went to the first practice with only mild trepidation. The first activity was simply to familiarize the girls with the size of the field, so we all gently jogged the length of the field. It was then that I realized that I had some girls who could not jog the length of the field without taking a break.

During the next drill I positioned myself at different spots on the field with a stack of numbered cards. The girls were to walk with a soccer ball and gently kick it and then immediately look up and shout out the number of the card that I held up. I wanted the girls to get comfortable with looking down at the ball and then quickly looking up, as they would have to do that during a game. I quickly found out that I had a team of mixed capabilities, with some girls tripping over the ball and their feet, and others zigzagging down the field at great speeds.

I knew that what mattered most was for each girl to achieve her personal best and for the team to support each girl's efforts to do so. So we put all of the equipment away and sat on the field and talked. The rules for our "talk time" were to listen to each person and not make fun of what anyone said. I encouraged the girls to be honest, silly, and revealing by providing them a safe atmosphere to express their feelings. At the first "TT" (how we referred to talk time), each girl had to tell us her name, what school she went to, how many siblings she had, her favorite desserts, what she liked about soccer, and what she hoped to be able to do by the end of the season. It was a great way for the girls to start seeing each other as friends who wanted to work together.

We continued to practice twice a week, and we were really improving, except for one girl, Melissa, who was struggling with being overweight, uncoordinated, and discouraged. She would often hang her head and fight back tears. So, during the next TT, I had the girls go around the circle and tell each player something positive about her progress.

We lost our first game and the second, so during the next TT we sat and talked about what mattered most, with a focus on having fun, learning teamwork, and making friends. Those aspects were just as important as winning… even more important. It was exciting to win our third game and our fourth, but when we lost our fifth and sixth games, the girls needed a morale booster. So the theme of the next TT was "believe in yourself and work towards your goals." During this session I asked several parents to tell stories about their own personal experiences centered on that theme. The end result was we were building not only a team, but a family as well.

We ended up winning half our games and having a terrific time in the process. Since my daughter was recruited by a travel soccer team, I did not coach soccer the next season.

After my daughter started middle school, I stopped by the grocery store one day to pick up a few things for dinner and heard someone shout "Coach Judi." I turned and recognized that the woman behind the bakery counter was Melissa's mother. She came around the counter with her arms open wide and a huge smile on her face. We embraced and I asked how Melissa was doing, and she said that Melissa had made the middle school soccer team.

She told me an inspiring story. When Melissa went to the try-outs, the coach suggested that she might have better luck with another activity. (Melissa was still overweight.) But Melissa looked the coach right in the eye and said that she wanted a chance. Needless to say, the coach was taken aback but allowed Melissa to try out. When she was selected to be on the team, the coach asked her what motivated her to try out even when he initially discouraged her. She said, "When I first starting playing soccer, I could not even run the length of the field, let alone kick a ball and run. But my coach told me at the time that if I believed in myself and worked hard, I could achieve my goals. I figured if this person who barely knew me believed in me, then I needed to believe in myself as well."

Melissa's mom and I openly wept as she told me this story. After another big embrace, she said that she wanted to give me a gift. She went behind the counter of the bakery and returned with a pie. She said, "You always let the girls know that sometimes life would give them lemons, but you also taught them how to turn them into lemonade."

My throat was so filled with emotion that I could barely speak, but I smiled and choked out my reply, "Lemon meringue; my favorite."

~Judith Fitzsimmons

Too Bad You Lost
Your Jacket

*"I must do something" always solves more problems than
"Something must be done."*
~Author Unknown

When my children were little we went to Disney World every fall. My friends thought I was crazy, but the kids loved it and I think I enjoyed it even more than they did. Except for one thing. Souvenirs. The kids would drive me nuts asking for souvenirs, to the point that in the stores I would try to block my daughter's view of the stuffed animals and my son's view of the superhero items.

Then I discovered Disney Dollars! The next time we went to Disney World, I gave each child fifty Disney Dollars to spend on souvenirs. They started evaluating every possible purchase as if they worked for Consumer Reports, and we returned home with half their Disney Dollars unspent.

That gave me an idea a few years later when I was at my wit's end over my son's remarkable ability to lose his clothes. Our school had a dress code and it could get expensive. I'll never forget when my twelve-year-old son Mike went off to the first day of school in a brand-new navy blue blazer and came home wearing a bedraggled old one that barely fit him. The $100 blazer that I had bought just a little too big for him, so that it would last the entire school year, was gone. He said his friend Gideon needed a larger jacket so they swapped.

That was the last straw in a series of clothing disappearances. I decided it was time to change the dynamic in our household. I sat the kids down and laid out their annual clothing budget. Their father and I would give them half their budget in the fall and half in the spring. My daughter opted for a debit card that I refilled every six months; my son opted for a savings account.

It was heavenly. I drove them to the stores, we shopped together, and we each paid for our own purchases. If my son lost something, it was not my problem, and he learned a lesson about caring for his possessions. There were no arguments over clothing, no pleading for more, and no frustration on either side. We actually had fun shopping.

The advice columnist Abigail Van Buren summed it up perfectly when she said, "If you want children to keep their feet on the ground, put some responsibility on their shoulders." I gave my children the responsibility for what they wore on their shoulders, literally! My son became much more careful, although he did lose his blazer one more time, the night before an important ninth-grade event. With my new attitude, I just thought it was funny when he had to wear a pastel plaid jacket from the lost and found.

~Amy Newmark

The Pie Chart of Me

*At times our own light goes out and is rekindled by a spark from
another person. Each of us has cause to think with deep gratitude
of those who have lighted the flame within us.*
~Albert Schweitzer

The infamously rigorous International Baccalaureate program was always the most popular topic of discussion for everyone, from seasoned alumni to anxious Pre-IBers. Stories of sleepless nights sustained by cans of iced coffee and mental breakdowns at 1 a.m. were passed around like urban legends.

Those of us entering grade eleven didn't have time to be fazed. But the panic first started setting in when we received our physics lab on the third day of school.

"This is harder than anything you've done," our teacher chuckled — almost snidely — as he passed around the instruction sheets. "No one will get above ninety." My confidence was shaken as I looked at the page of tauntingly unfamiliar symbols.

With a heavy heart, I managed to make it through the rest of the school day. When I finally dragged myself home, my father only added insult to injury. Pointing out my lack of progress in the SATs, my dad reiterated for the millionth time that I would not be able to get into a prestigious American university without good SAT results.

The last straw was the e-mail from the Red Cross. As the vice president of my school's Red Cross chapter, getting rejected from the Regional Red Cross Youth Council was a possibility that never crossed my mind. It simply couldn't happen. Not only was the Red Cross my passion and inspiration, but it was also what I relied on to set me apart from all the other college applicants with ninety-five percent averages.

My future had seemed so bright and certain, yet in reality it was so fragile. Any small blockage could force me to veer off the narrow path to success. I felt like a rubber band — it can only take so much stretching before it snaps. After that e-mail from the Red Cross, I snapped.

I ran out of my room and the first person I saw was my mother, the woman who left behind her family, her friends, and her life in China to emigrate to a foreign country just so I could receive a better education and have a brighter future. The woman who gave up her highly esteemed job in Beijing and could only find a job as a part-time office assistant in Toronto. My mother had spent her life bringing me to the most advantageous starting point, and yet I did not have enough stamina to reach the finish line.

When my mom finally noticed me, I was already a sobbing mess. "What's wrong, baby?" she asked, her face a mixture of alarm and worry.

My answer was "everything," and so that's what I told her about. My mother let me blabber on and on.

After I was done, she stared at me with so much emotion in her eyes. Her brows were furrowed as she bit her lip. I recognized the expression on her face. It meant she had too much to say and didn't know how to get her message across, which rarely happened. The only other time I clearly remember seeing that look directed at me was when I was six and took a bouncy ball home from kindergarten. It was years later that I learned that, at that time, she thought she was a failure as a parent because I didn't understand the fundamental principles of integrity and honesty.

"This pie chart here," my mother began hesitantly after a long silence, tracing a circle into the felt table cover with her forefinger, "represents your time."

At this point, I was thoroughly confused. Rarely has my mother chosen to use mathematics to prove a point; it just wasn't her forte. It was me, rather, who had such a dominant left-brain that I saw the world around me in numbers and statistics.

"Eighty percent is school work," my mom carefully darkened the majority of her impromptu pie chart.

"Ten percent is the SAT and ten percent is extracurricular activities."

It made sense. I mentally recorded everything my mom was saying.

"But most importantly, at one hundred percent," my mother's voice was starting to shake and she was tracing the circle so furiously that it was starting to look like a shapeless blob, "is your mental health."

I stared at her, a little dumbfounded, because that just didn't make sense. She looked back at me with the same look as when six-year-old me asked why it was wrong to take home the kindergarten's bouncy ball. It was a look that said "Trust me" in the most affectionate way possible.

"Nothing is more important than your health, Aileen. Why do we want you to go to a good university? Because you are more likely to have a good, well-paying career. Why do we want you to get a good job? Because you'll be less stressed if you're financially stable. This, right here, this is not healthy. This is not happy. If you feel so burdened by every little mistake and mishap along the way, then this isn't worth it. If you're happier working flipping burgers, so be it. There's absolutely nothing more important than your physical and mental wellbeing."

Maybe, to another girl in another family, such a lecture was the norm, but not to me. My parents did not immigrate halfway across the globe so I could be healthy. Yet I couldn't help the immense relief I felt in my chest. A rubber band doesn't have to keep stretching. A rubber band that wraps around your hair during the day and is allowed to rest on your nightstand at night won't ever snap.

That night, my mother and I stayed up all night chatting about my plans for the future, yet there was no impending sense of doom. The incessant fear of failure no longer seemed so terrifying.

To an outsider, perhaps nothing changed. I was still the girl who arrived at school at 7:30 a.m. to study before tests and stayed behind until 5 p.m. to get as much extra help as I could. Yet to me, everything changed. When I received a less-than-satisfactory result, there was no calm façade that crumpled as soon as I was safely hidden in a bathroom stall; there was only me carefully analyzing my mistakes so I could improve in the future.

I'm still reaching for the moon, but I'm no longer afraid. For I know that if I miss, I will land right in my mother's arms.

~Aileen Liang

My Bubbie's Bulkalah

Learning is a treasure that will follow its owner everywhere.
~Chinese Proverb

When I was nine or ten, my father would sometimes drop me off at my grandmother's house on Saturday morning when he went to work. Time spent with my bubbie meant one thing: baking. Mostly, though, she would bake while I would sit at the kitchen table and watch. Later, I'd get to sample the delicacies.

My grandmother had the heart, soul and hands of a baker. She could take everyday ingredients and somehow spin them into heavenly treats. Whenever I picture her, I see her with flour up to her elbows, rolling dough to make yet another kind of dessert.

My mother and sister liked my grandmother's roly poly, a rolled dough filled with raisins, Turkish delight, and nuts. Not me. I loved her cheese bulkalah, bite-sized pastries filled with an egg, cheese, sugar and raisin mixture, dusted with cinnamon.

I remember the first time I helped. She placed all her ingredients for the dough into a large bowl, plunged her hands into the bowl, and mixed everything together. "You see what I am doing?" she asked, bits of wet dough clinging to her fingers. "Sometimes it is good to get your hands dirty. You must be able to feel the dough. It is not enough to think; you must feel."

"Here, touch it," she said, once she had the right consistency. "That is what dough should feel like."

I patted the dough lightly, trying to imprint the texture on my mind.

Then, she tipped the dough out of the bowl and rolled it out on her counter until it formed a big sheet about half an inch thick, which she then cut into small squares. Once the dough was ready, it was time to make the filling and put everything together. Greasing several old, banged-up muffin pans, she placed a square of dough in each cup, forming a pocket with the corners sticking up.

"So, Harriet," she said, "do you think you can spoon out the mixture?"

Proud that I would finally be helping, I took a large spoon and dipped it into the bowl. I spooned a huge mound of cheese onto the dough.

"Not too much," she said. "Just a hint. Cheese is very expensive. Flour, on the other hand, is not. So, we hide the jewel in the middle, like a surprise when you bite into it."

I laughed at the thought of a jewel hidden in my favourite dessert. I removed half of the filling from the first pocket and put it in the next one. Then one by one, I carefully filled each dough pocket with a little filling, making sure to divide the raisins evenly among them.

My grandmother nodded her approval.

Once I had spooned on just the right amount, she took over. She pinched the four corners of each square together and then sprinkled cinnamon on top. After pinching the last one, she placed the muffin trays in the oven.

Over the next fifteen minutes, her kitchen filled with the heady aroma of cheese bulkalah.

"Is it ready yet?" I asked, five minutes after they'd started baking.

"Of course not, I just put them in. If I took them out now, they would not taste good. You must learn to be patient. Remember, good things take time."

I sighed and waited a few more minutes before repeating my question.

"Not yet," she said. "Soon. Soon. What did I tell you?"

"Good things take time," I repeated, not realizing I was learning much more than baking.

When she finally took the bulkalah out of the oven, their tops were lightly browned. Without thinking, I reached out for one and burned my finger on the hot pan. I screamed, more in surprise than in pain. My grandmother grabbed my hand and dragged me over to the sink where she ran cold water over my finger. "See what happens when you don't think?"

Disappointment overwhelmed me and tears flooded my eyes.

My bubbie turned off the water and looked at me. "It is only a little burn. Nothing to cry about."

I gulped. "That's not why I'm crying."

"So, what's wrong?"

"You'll think I'm stupid and not let me bake with you again."

My grandmother walked me over to the kitchen table and sat me down. Then she showed me her wrist, which had a long pink scar on it. "You see this? I burned myself three years ago. And I am not a little girl just learning to use a stove. It happens. You learn. That is life." She rubbed the scar. "And sometimes you have to learn more than once."

She went to the fridge and got me a large glass of milk. "Drink. The bulkalah will be cool enough to eat in about fifteen minutes. Since you were such a good helper, I will send you home with some. But," she paused, "you must share with your family, because the best part of cooking is sharing with others."

I nodded. "But you know, bubbie, they like your roly poly. I'm the one who really, really likes your bulkalah."

A hint of a grin played on her lips. "I know how much you like them, but you still have to share. However, that doesn't mean you can't eat a few extra before you go home."

Laughing, I sat at the table with my bubbie, eagerly awaiting my treats. Even now, a lifetime later, I remember the sweetness that filled my mouth when I took my first bite of the still-warm bulkalah. And I realized that if you're like my bubbie, you bake love into everything you make.

~Harriet Cooper

Chapter 5

Raising Great Kids

Be Kind to Strangers

Night Watch

Not he who has much is rich, but he who gives much.
~Erich Fromm

"Your son is here," the nurse said to the old man. She had to repeat the words several times before the man's eyes opened. He was heavily sedated and only partially conscious after a massive heart attack he had suffered the night before. He could see the dim outline of a young man in a Marine Corps uniform, standing alongside his bed.

The old man reached out his hand. The Marine wrapped his toughened fingers around the old man's limp hand and squeezed gently. The nurse brought a chair, and the tired serviceman sat down at the bedside.

All through the night, the young Marine sat in the poorly lighted ward, holding the old man's hand and offering words of encouragement. The dying man said nothing, but kept a feeble grip on the young man's hand. Oblivious to the noise of the oxygen tank, the moans of the other patients, and the bustle of the night staff coming in and out of the ward, the Marine remained at the old man's side.

Every now and then, when she stopped by to check on her patients, the nurse heard the young Marine whisper a few comforting words to the old man. Several times in the course of that long night, she returned and suggested that the Marine leave to rest for a while.

But every time, the young man refused.

Near dawn the old man died. The Marine placed the old man's lifeless hand on the bed and left to find the nurse. While the nurse took the old man away and attended to the necessary duties, the young man waited. When the nurse returned, she began to offer words of sympathy, but the Marine interrupted her.

"Who was that man?" he asked.

Startled, the nurse replied, "He was your father."

"No, he wasn't," the young man said. "I've never seen him before in my life."

"Then why didn't you say something when I took you to him?"

"I knew there had been a mistake by the people who sent me home on an emergency furlough. What happened was, there were two of us with the same name, from the same town and we had similar serial numbers. They sent me by mistake," the young man explained. "But I also knew he needed his son, and his son wasn't there. I could tell he was too sick to know whether I was his son or not. When I realized how much he needed to have someone there, I just decided to stay."

~Roy Popkin

The Thank You Note

Kindness, like a boomerang, always returns.
~Author Unknown

Many times we do something positive or say something kind, but we don't see the impact it has on other people. We may practice these "random acts of kindness," but we never know what happens next. One time, I was lucky enough to find out.

I was returning from a business trip to northwest Wisconsin when I stopped to refuel and get a snack at one of those travel plaza/gas station combos on the expressway. It was late, I was tired, it was starting to rain, and all I wanted to do was get home, but home was still more than two hours away. I was feeling slightly crabby, and my back hurt from all the driving.

I went inside to buy some veggie chips and a sparkling water. The checker smiled at me, and we chatted for a moment. I don't remember exactly what she said, but I do remember the kindness she showed me. Our brief interaction brightened my spirits, and when I got back in my car, I had a smile on my face. My car and my stomach were both refueled, but more importantly, I was refreshed. Her small act of kindness kept me going on the last leg of my journey home.

The next week, I was cleaning my purse, and I came across the receipt. The receipt reminded me of the clerk's warmth, and it had the address of the store. On impulse, I decided to write a quick thank you note to her manager. I normally don't write thank you notes—in fact, except for my wedding, I've never written many notes of thanksgiving or gratitude—but I've learned to heed such promptings.

Initially, I felt a little awkward, embarrassed even, to be writing a thank you note to a gas station manager, but I set aside my "feelings" to listen to my gut. I told the woman's manager exactly what I've just shared with you—that his employee's kind words and caring attitude stood out to me, brightening my trip home. It took all of five minutes to write the note and affix a stamp to the envelope. I dropped the missive in the mail, and that was that.

That is, until a week later, when I received a thank you note for my thank you note. That clerk—Robin is her name—wrote me back. As a result of my note, she received a commendation from her manager, a company award pin, and then, to top it off, a merit raise. I was stunned, and the note brought tears to my eyes. Robin's kindness inspired me to return her positivity, and there it was—a small, mini chain reaction of goodness.

In these challenging times, it's especially important to spread joy and gladness whenever and wherever we can. Whether it's a note or a kind word or even just a smile, a little gratitude goes a long way. More people complain than give thanks, and I've heard it said that it takes ten kind words to overcome a single harsh one. It sometimes takes a conscious effort on our part to say more positive words than negative ones, and to do more positive things than negative ones, but the ripple effect of that goodness is powerful.

Mother Teresa advised us to "do small things with great love." Oftentimes, when we do such small things, we don't get to see the effects of our kind words or deeds, but every so often, we're blessed to discover the positive outcome. If there's one thing I've learned from writing that short note it's to give in to the impulse of kindness when it strikes.

You never know what good may come of it or where it might lead you.

~Jeanette Hurt

Bus Stop Blessing

A bus is a vehicle that runs twice as fast when you are after it as when you are in it.
~Author Unknown

She ran for the bus with all of the strength and determination of an Olympic sprinter, but the bus pulled away from the curb without her — the driver not seeing her or just not caring. She collapsed on the bus bench in a heap of failure, disbelief and sobs.

I could have just kept on driving. It was the first day of my vacation and I was off to wander the local mall, and, besides, it wasn't my problem, I didn't know her. Another bus would be along soon. But there was just something about her. There was an intensity in her need that I could not ignore so I stopped my car and went up to her.

I sat down on the bench next to her and gently mentioned that another bus would be along in half an hour or so. I introduced myself and asked, "What's your name?"

"My name is Sarah. I'm sorry to make such of a scene but I need to get to the hospital to be with my sick baby," she responded through lessening sobs.

Sarah explained to me that she was a struggling single mother and her one-year-old son was in the hospital. She had gone home late the night before to get some sleep and when she started back to the hospital in the morning, her car battery was dead. I could tell from Sarah's face that she was exhausted and that she felt overwhelmed.

"What's wrong with your son?" I gently prodded.

"My baby has pneumonia and he has been very sick," Sarah replied. "I don't want him to be alone and afraid, I need to get back to him."

My heart melted and my plans for the day took a detour. "Please," I said, "let me give you a ride to the hospital." Seeing a little hesitation in her eyes, I continued, "Please, it would be my pleasure." Sarah's face softened and I saw the first hint of a smile as she nodded her head yes, and we began walking toward my car.

On the drive to the hospital I learned that Sarah's boyfriend had left her when he found out that she was pregnant and that she did not have any other family in the area. She has been struggling to work and raise her baby in a loving home. Though rough at times, things were going fairly well until little Daniel got sick. Daniel's illness set Sarah back financially and emotionally.

As I listened to Sarah's story I decided to do everything I could to help her out. I dropped her off at the hospital, gave her my phone number and asked her to call me when she got home. I assured her that my brother would come over and help her with her car battery. Though reluctant, Sarah took my number and promised to call me.

I shared the day's event with my Bible study group that night and asked the group to pray for Sarah and Daniel. The group did much more than that. One person had baby clothes left over she wanted to donate, another friend wanted to donate food and we even took up a collection of money to help Sarah out.

Sarah was very grateful and humbled by the help my group was able to give to her during the illness and recovery of her son. My brother went to help Sarah that night with her car battery and, not only did he get that battery to "spark" once again, sparks began flying between my brother and Sarah as well and now Sarah is my sister-in-law!

You never know what blessings God has waiting for you if you just take the time to stop and try to meet someone's need. Sarah and Daniel are a precious addition to our family, and that would never have happened if Sarah had not missed her bus on that fateful day.

~LaVerne Otis

Playing Santa

The most vivid memories of Christmases past are usually not of gifts given or received, but of the spirit of love, the special warmth of Christmas worship, the cherished little habits of home.
~Lois Rand

very Monday night, nearly 100 students from around the world come to our free school for English as a Second Language. For seven years we've taught, befriended, and helped men and women of all ages from Bosnia, Kurdistan, Mexico, China, Vietnam, Korea, Africa, Russia, South America, Iran, Pakistan, and more.

The people have many differences in languages, customs, food, and clothing. They are excited, shy, and sometimes afraid. They are always grateful, and we are always left rejoicing in the help we can give them. We also have many similarities that blur our differences: mainly, we love our children.

Three weeks before Christmas, one of our students from Iraq approached my husband and surprised him by asking for help in creating a Christmas celebration for his children. We were surprised that a Muslim family would request this. We were curious why he would want this, but his children went to public school and were feeling left out of this exciting holiday.

The father was on disability from a job injury and the family had little. We put out the word to the other volunteers who taught, drove buses, and helped in child care for the English classes every week.

Six days before Christmas, we went to the family's apartment, loaded with a gift for each of the four children, fruit, a basket of olive oil and spices, homemade cookies, beans, and rice.

We were greeted with smiles and led to the sparsely decorated living room. While we talked with the children, their parents put together a tray of sodas and sweet bread.

We talked about how they were doing with practicing their English, how they were adjusting to America, and we joked with the children, whose eyes strayed to the wrapped packages nearby. When I couldn't stand it any longer, I asked their parents if the children could open their gifts.

Everyone helped the eighteen-month-old daughter, who was almost completely blind. Familiar with the child's problems, one of our volunteers had purchased a push button toy full of sound and bright lights. We laughed as this little girl, who had smiled very little when we came in, now laughed, and clapped her hands as she pressed the buttons of the toy with her hands, feet, and mouth.

The two-year-old daughter hurriedly unwrapped her gift, a see-through backpack full of blocks. Soon miniature buildings filled the living room. The twelve-year-old son gasped when he opened his package containing two small remote-controlled cars inside. And the fourteen-year-old daughter, her English near perfect, couldn't wait for me to cut open the plastic that held her new cassette player and headphones. Soon, like any teenager, she was nodding her head to the rhythm of her favorite music.

Their mother smiled and made us promise to come back soon for dinner. We felt like the three kings bearing gifts; my husband, daughter, and I couldn't imagine a nicer feeling. We made a new connection with this family that Christmas week.

Yes, there are many differences between us and our students. We speak different languages, eat different foods, celebrate different holidays, and see the world just a little bit differently.

But the reality is that when Muslims and Christians become simply parents, we are very similar.

~Kathryn Lay

An Angel in Chains

It's not so much the journey that's important; as is the way that
we treat those we encounter and those around us, along the way.
~Jeremy Aldana

t was only a few weeks before Christmas when Becky, our four-and-one-half-year-old daughter, cheeks flushed with excitement, climbed over the fence of the corral where I was bottle-feeding an orphan calf, and squealed, "Mama! Mama! You have to come see! Angels wear chains!"

I was about to ask, "Becky, what on earth do you mean?" when my heart plunged to the pit of my stomach.

Outside the wooden gate amid the cactus and mesquite towered a stranger, his skin gleaming like oiled mahogany in the blistering Arizona sun. Nearly eight feet tall in giant-sized motorcycle boots, he wore a red sweatband that failed to control the black braids leaping wildly from his head, and in the early morning December breeze he seemed to sway like a genie uncorked from desert sand.

Heavily muscled arms stained with purple tattoos burst from a leather vest. A deep scar crimped his left cheek and a small silver dagger swung from one ear. But it was the chains on his boots, chains on his belt and chains cascading down his massive chest that made me wonder, Why does Becky think he's an angel?

Then I spied the Harley-Davidson beside the water pump at the end of our long dirt road. On the far side of the barbed-wire fence a gang of wind-whipped, grease-streaked, smoke-shrouded motorcyclists milled around, "HELL'S ANGELS" glinting across the shoulders of more than one black jacket.

This was 1974. I'd read about the Hell's Angels — terror-riddled tales of large groups of men who adhered to no boundaries of human decency, infamous for murder, rape, theft, guns and drugs. My husband was at a bull sale in Casa Grande. The children and I were alone. Why was this group here on our ranch a hundred miles from Tucson?

"His name's Rip because his muscles ripple," Becky piped as she ducked beneath the fence and took the stranger by the hand. "His motorcycle broke." She tugged him toward me, and although he seemed bigger with each step, I noticed he looked down at my little girl as though seeking reassurance.

Finally, he bowed his head and his uneasy, hooded eyes met mine. "Rip Balou, missus. I know it's gettin' late, but two of my buddies took off for the city to get me a new clutch. They won't get back till morning and I wondered if we could camp near the gate for the night? We won't bother you none... and... all we need is water."

Dared I say no? It was a chance I had to take, yet something beyond Rip Balou's frightening appearance — and The Hell's Angel's reputation — made it seem safe to say, "Sure." I glanced at the group by the gate. "But please," I said, "don't smoke. Fire danger is at a peak right now."

"Don't you worry yourself none about no fire," Rip said. The thought seemed to have humbled him a bit. "Those warning signs are posted all the way from New Mexico." He thanked me before walking back toward his friends.

"But Mama, what about supper?" Becky asked. "They don't have any food."

"How many are there?"

"Eleven... no, nine. Zack and Ty went to Tucson... and Rip makes ten." She answered so quickly.

Zack?... Ty?... Rip? I wondered how long she'd been down by the gate. Long enough to count — to know their names — and to make a friend! Such a natural thing for a child to do, especially one without playmates. I vowed to keep a closer eye on her, but at that moment, my thoughts were on food. I fed everyone else who stopped by — ranchers, cowboys and Mexican mehados hoping for work. What harm could possibly come from feeding a band of… Angels?

Later, back at the house, ten men sat at the picnic table under the cottonwood tree drinking iced tea from Styrofoam cups while Becky held them spellbound with a Barbie-doll fashion show. As they wolfed down tacos and beans, I asked questions. "Where are you going?" "Los Angeles," they chorused. They had been on the road for two years, ever since they had met at the Harley-Davidson rally in Sturgis, South Dakota. Before that time, some had come from major cities across the country. Chicago. New Orleans. Boston. New York. "What about home and family?" I asked. Few responded, but Rip, the obvious leader, muttered "Baltimore, 2,647 miles away."

The following morning, Rip's huge frame darkened the kitchen doorway. He didn't look happy. "Zack's back. They had to order the clutch from Phoenix," he said. "It'll take a couple a days. Could we stay? We could rake… clean stalls… do somethin' to help out?"

"Okay. I guess you can't get very far without a clutch." I thought I was being funny. He didn't.

"And missus. There's twelve of us now." I knew he was referring to meals.

Soon, more hands than I would ever need, or find again, unloaded a double semi-trailer load of hay, repaired fences, and rode back and forth to Tucson to buy food that I hadn't even asked for. I noticed they laughed and talked a lot among themselves. Why not? I thought. No responsibilities. No family ties.

Strangely, it was big Rip Balou who not only worked the hardest but continued to be drawn to Becky — and she to him. She let him help bottle-feed the orphan calf and collect eggs in a basket from the chicken coop where the ceiling was so low he couldn't stand up straight. Then, when she placed a day-old chick in his enormous hands, his mouth opened like a child who had just touched Santa.

Three meals a day at the picnic table left time to share more than her Barbie doll. Although not yet in school, Becky could read, and I watched a remarkable friendship tighten between her and the giant man as they hovered over a book together. Was it possible that a little girl could make a difference in his life? Rip's tough, big-shot countenance seemed to soften, and the face of a boy emerged; I saw a whole life flash by in his eyes as Becky ran a tiny finger beneath magic words that introduced an Angel to Beauty and the Beast. Rip watched. He listened. I wondered… could he read?

What did it matter? It was Becky's crayons and coloring books that caused those haunted eyes to brighten. "Red and blue are my favorite colors," she told him, "but we can share. Can't we?"

It wasn't long before the crayons in his pie-sized hands created magic of their own. Rip banished another Angel to Tucson to "buy more." During the two days that followed, he taught Becky how to coax pastels from primary colors and fill empty skies with sunrises, sunsets and rainbows. Gradually, every page in the coloring books became a Rip Balou masterpiece.

"I don't like ugly, dark colors," Rip told Becky. "Anyone can color like that." Then over and over again, he covered her small white hand with his huge dark one, and said, "Honey, the most important thing to remember is that you gotta stay inside the lines."

It was on the third day that Becky popped the question. "Do you have a mommy and a daddy?" Rip didn't answer. Instead, he flexed his muscles so the ship on one arm seemed to roll in a storm and the dragon on the other coiled to strike. But he'd shown her these wonders before. And now there was something else on her mind. She asked again.

Reluctantly, Rip unhooked a leather pouch from the chain around his waist and pulled out a photograph of a gray-haired woman with glasses. Her hand rested gently on the shoulder of a little girl. "That's my mama," he said, "… and that's Jasmine… my baby. She'd be just about your age now."

"I wish she could come play with me," Becky said.

Rip stared at the picture for a long time. "Mama's raisin' her," he said, "but she's got the glaucoma. She can't see so good no more."

Becky fixed her eyes on Rip and, in the infinite wisdom of a child, she asked, "If your mama can't see so good, who's going to teach Jasmine to stay inside the lines?"

Rip shook his head. "I… don't know." He answered softly, but I could hear the pain in his voice, his heart and his soul.

Late Thursday evening, the gang members who had gone in quest of the new clutch finally returned. Rip must have worked throughout the night to get his bike running for they were all ready to leave at daybreak. Although the barnyard and corrals had been raked and the men were filling their canteens with cool water I sensed unrest among them. "No breakfast, Ma'am," one Angel said. "We gotta hit the road." He glared at Rip. Had there been an argument? A disagreement?

Careful not to scare the horses and chickens, motors purred softly as one by one the Hell's Angels cruised over to say "good-bye" and "thanks." Rip Balou was last.

"Thank you, missus," he murmured, "… for a lot of things."

"And thank you for being such a wonderful playmate and teacher." I wanted to say more, ask him why he had chosen such a life, but suddenly his eyes were brimming with tears over which he had little control.

"I don't see Becky," he said, glancing over at the picnic table. "I… I need to tell her somethin'… remind her of somethin' real important…"

"She's down by the gate." I hugged him quickly, straightened the chains around his neck and found myself wishing I could do the same to the chains that had stolen his life. I pointed to a very little girl sitting alone on top of the fence. By now Becky was waving and shouting goodbye above the roar of impatient engines as one by one the Angels turned west on Frontier Road—west to Los Angeles—leaving the peaceful desert of moments ago drowned in swirling dust. "You better hurry, Rip," I urged. "They're going to leave you behind."

He smiled at me then—for the first time a big smile—before coasting down to Becky on the high ground between ruts worn by tires. I watched him set the kickstand before he dismounted and walked over to the little girl he'd grown to love. He lifted her off the fence and set her down on the leather seat. Then, crouching beside her so they could speak face-to-face, Beauty and the Beast talked… about sunrises?… sunsets?… rainbows? Who knows?

What I do know is that the good-bye hug he gave Becky brought tears to my eyes. Then the last angel swung a long leg over his gleaming Harley, revved up the engine and turned east on Frontier Road — east, to Baltimore — "2,647 miles away — in time for Christmas," where a little girl waited for a lesson on the importance of "staying inside the lines," and a daddy to show her how.

~Penny Porter

Emergencies of the Heart

We can do no great things, only small things with great love.
~Mother Teresa

Accompanying a friend to the emergency room at our local hospital, I dreaded the hours of waiting I knew that I most likely faced. I had heard horror stories of people spending all day—eight or nine hours, maybe longer—just waiting. Still, my friend needed me to take her, so I went.

I settled myself into an uncomfortable chair and started flipping through the outdated magazines that were donated by the local churches. At one time, I would have sat there, oblivious to everyone around me. This time, for some reason, I looked restlessly around me, unable to focus on reading.

There was a young mother with three small children. One was a little girl of about seven with a dreadful rash on her legs. She got into everything, even though her harried mother tried to keep track of her. The two younger children, a toddler and an infant, cried continuously, the decibel level increasing with each passing minute.

A young woman, sitting next to them, leaned over and said something to the exhausted mother. Smiling gratefully, the mother nodded, and the young woman gently reached into the carrier and snuggled the baby into her arms. When she offered a bottle, the baby began to nurse hungrily.

The mother captured the toddler as he climbed over a chair in an attempt to reach the window. His screams were those of frustration from not being able to achieve his goal. The mother stood holding him, rocking side to side, as she pointed toward the window. The rain cascaded, tapping against the glass. The mother began to tap, tap, tap her hand on the toddler's back in time to the rain as she crooned softly. It wasn't long before his head began to bob and finally nestled between his mother's chin and shoulder. Wearily she sat down, gently resting her head on his as he slept.

By this time, the seven-year-old girl was engaged in a conversation with an elderly man who had a bloody bandage around his leg. She was entranced by the story of how he had fallen out of a tree while trying to rescue his cat, describing how the fire department had to come to his assistance. I smiled at this corny old story.

A hospital representative came out. "We are ready for you now," she said to the young mother. "Let me help you take the children back."

I was surprised when the young woman who had quieted the baby stayed behind.

"Aren't you allowed to go back with your friend?" I asked. If that was the rule, I understood, but was incredulous nonetheless.

"Oh, I don't know her," she responded. "I could see she just needed help with those children. I'm here because I'm pregnant and I may be losing my baby."

Her eyes misted and her lips trembled. Before I could respond she also was called to go back.

Taking a deep breath, I prayed that she and her baby would be all right.

Blinking, I looked around the small waiting room and realized that the only ones who remained were the elderly man who had entertained the little girl, a young man whom I had not noticed before, and me. I looked over at the elderly man and he smiled invitingly.

"You did a great job entertaining that little girl with your harrowing story," I laughed.

"Well, it always works on the little ones," he said sheepishly. "I do like kids, even though I don't have any of my own."

"How did you really hurt your leg?" I asked.

"Well, when Daniel here came over to get my dog," he responded, nodding his head toward the younger man, "I lost my footing and fell down an embankment. When Daniel tried to help, he fell right on top of me."

Just then, the hospital aide came into the waiting area and wheeled the old man back to see the doctor.

Looking at Daniel, I asked, "Can you finish the story?"

"Sure," he obliged. "Mr. C had his dog for about fifteen years. It just died of old age, I guess. But he loved that dog and he couldn't stand the thought of burying him and leaving. You see, he and Mrs. C. are retiring and will be moving. He didn't have the heart to leave his best friend behind."

Daniel's eyes met mine. "So I was picking him up to have him cremated. That's what I do you see. I cremate people's pets."

At this point in the story, the hospital aide called Daniel's name.

"Darn the efficiency of this hospital," I muttered.

Alone now, I was left with my thoughts. I sat peacefully reflecting on my afternoon in the emergency room, of the many bittersweet stories here. Yet my spirit was uplifted and joyous because of them. I thought of the selflessness of the young woman who had put aside her own grief and fear over her unborn child to help a distressed mother care for her children, the elderly man who helped calm a little girl with his tall tales, while he sat bleeding and in pain, and the young man who, with such sensitivity, provided comfort to someone who had lost a beloved pet.

What happened that afternoon would inspire me for some time to come. I had waited, yes, but my time had not been wasted. At a time when there is so much focus on the dark side of life, my time in that emergency room was an unexpected blessing.

~Linda B. Breeden

Drawn to
the Warmth

*Compassion is not religious business, it is human business, it is
not luxury, it is essential for our own peace and mental stability,
it is essential for human survival.*
~Dalai Lama

Factoring in the wind chill, I knew the temperature was
below zero. The bitter cold cut through my Californian sen-
sibilities, as well as my enthusiasm as a tourist, so I ducked
through the nearest door for warmth… and found myself in
Washington, D.C.'s Union Station.

I settled onto one of the public benches with a steaming cup of
coffee — waiting for feeling to return to my fingers and toes — and
relaxed to engage in some serious people-watching.

Several tables of diners spilled out into the great hall from the
upscale American Restaurant, and heavenly aromas tempted me to
consider an early dinner. I observed a man seated nearby and, from
the longing in his eyes, realized that he, too, noticed the tantalizing
food. His gaunt body, wind-chapped hands and tattered clothes nearly
shouted, "Homeless, homeless!"

How long has it been since he's eaten? I wondered.

Half expecting him to approach me for a handout, I almost welcomed such a plea. He never did. The longer I took in the scene, the

crueler his plight seemed. My head and heart waged a silent war, the one telling me to mind my own business, the other urging a trip to the food court on his behalf.

While my internal debate raged on, a well-dressed young couple approached him. "Excuse me, sir," the husband began. "My wife and I just finished eating, and our appetites weren't as big as we thought. We hate to waste good food. Can you help us out and put this to use?" He extended a large Styrofoam container.

"God bless you both. Merry Christmas," came the grateful reply.

Pleased, yet dismayed by my own lack of action, I continued to watch. The man scrutinized his newfound bounty, rearranged the soup crackers, inspected the club sandwich and stirred the salad dressing—obviously prolonging this miracle meal. Then, with a slow deliberateness, he lifted the soup lid and, cupping his hands around the steaming warm bowl, inhaled. At last, he unwrapped the plastic spoon, filled it to overflowing, lifted it toward his mouth and—with a suddenness that stunned me—stopped short.

I turned my head to follow his narrow-eyed gaze.

Entering the hall and shuffling in our direction was a new arrival. Hatless and gloveless, the elderly man was clad in lightweight pants, a threadbare jacket and open shoes. His hands were raw, and his face had a bluish tint. I wasn't alone in gasping aloud at this sad sight, but my needy neighbor was the only one doing anything about it.

Setting aside his meal, he leaped up and guided the elderly man to an adjacent seat. He took his icy hands and rubbed them briskly in his own. With a final tenderness, he draped his worn jacket over the older man's shoulders.

"Pop, my name's Jack," he said, "and one of God's angels brought me this meal. I just finished eating and hate to waste good food. Can you help me out?"

He placed the still-warm bowl of soup in the stranger's hands without waiting for an answer. But he got one.

"Sure, son, but only if you go halfway with me on that sandwich. It's too much for a man my age."

It wasn't easy making my way to the food court with tears blurring my vision, but I soon returned with large containers of coffee and a big assortment of pastries. "Excuse me, gentlemen, but…"

I left Union Station that day feeling warmer than I had ever thought possible.

~Marion Smith

Fathers, Sons and the Angel in the Stadium

I see great things in baseball. It's our game — the American game.

~Walt Whitman

remember when I got the call that American Eagle Outfitters would be flying my ten-year-old son to New York for their fall campaign. Immediately, I was excited. Actually, I was over the moon about it, but then I stopped in my tracks. My son, Dalton, is a triplet and we have a daughter as well who was seven. Dalton would miss the whole week of school, but the bigger question was: Who would take him?

I was the obvious choice, but my husband is not the best at juggling things at home. Still, the one time he'd taken a child on a trip to a chess tournament, he missed the flight and had to be rerouted at five the next morning. It had been a total disaster. So, imagine, now my son was about to go to New York with his father for six days. I freaked. New York, to me, is scary, and the trip would involve more airports and planes with his dad.

"You have to hold on to him for dear life everywhere you go," I ordered. We live in Boca Raton, Florida and everything here is usually pretty quiet. New York is tough, or so I thought.

But to my delight, my husband was amazing. He took my son

places I would have never dared to go. He took him to Madison Square Park, on a ferry to see the Statue of Liberty, to the New York Stock Exchange, photographed him in front of Trump Tower, Chinatown for dinner, everywhere. He was also taken to many locations around New York for his photo shoot and they had a blast. My husband even had him on the subways!

A few nights into his trip, he wanted to take him to a Mets game — Michael and Dalton — just father and son. They walked around the arena looking for tickets from anyone who had any to sell. They came across a guy who had two over-priced tickets, but my husband did not have enough cash, and so the person selling them said, "Hey, you can leave your son with me while you go find an ATM."

"Uh, no thanks," my husband said. "I'll take him and we'll be right back."

Well, as the two of them continued to walk around the stadium to get some more money, an elderly man tapped my son on the shoulder and kindly asked, "Are you two looking for tickets to the game?" To which, my husband snapped around and said, "Yes, sir, we definitely are." With that, the man — who was with his wife — said, "Great, you can be our guests."

The gentleman informed my husband that he had two extra tickets for their friends that couldn't make it. He then said, "Here you go."

My husband said, "Wow, that's awesome. Thank you. How much are they?"

The man softly said, "Nothing. They're on me. Go get your seats and we'll see you inside."

Michael took Dalton to get a Mets sweatshirt and a hot dog.

"This is sooo cool," my son said. "And the other guy wanted so much money. I like New York!"

The two of them went to find their seats and meet their new friends. They walked into the stands, lower and lower and lower until they ended up three rows back from the first base line. Not a soul was sitting in front of them to block the view! It could not have gotten any better.

A short while later, the gentleman and his wife came and sat down next to them.

"I got to tell you," my husband said, "this is really kind of you. It's not every day that people do this kind of thing. My wife would never believe me."

My son was ecstatic. Not only was he doing a national campaign for an amazing clothing company, but he was three rows back at a Mets game for free! The four of them sat together, talked a bit and watched. About a half an hour into the game the concession guy came around selling beers, at which time my husband said, "No, no, I got it. It's a thank you."

The concession guy insisted that since there are cameras, he must ID everyone, and he meant, "Everyone." The gentleman took out his ID and handed it over, but when he went to put it back inside his wallet, something caught my husband's eye. It was a badge of some sort. My husband dared to ask his wife.

"Um, I noticed a badge in his wallet. Is he in some official department? Is he a police officer?"

The woman quietly whispered, "No, he's not a police officer. He is retired from the New York City Fire Department. He was a captain."

My husband then dared again. "Did 9/11 have an impact on him directly? Was he involved in any way at that time?"

The woman replied, "No, he was retired then, but his son is also in the FDNY and he never came home. He died that day."

My husband was speechless. Then the woman said something that made my husband's heart go heavy. After such a wonderful day, a beautiful sky, a perfect evening game, she said, "He used to come to these games with his son. Now, when our friends can't make it, he waits outside the arena looking for another father and son to share our seats with."

When my husband came home and told me this story, he was right; I could hardly believe it. Those short few moments of conversation spoke volumes. My son had shared — with two total strangers — an appreciation for the relationship of a father and son that will last a lifetime.

This is a huge "thank you" from me, the mom of that cute little boy and amazing father and husband. I hope that gentleman knows what he did for us that day.

~Marni Chris Tice

Reconnect

Three things in human life are important. The first is to be kind.
The second is to be kind. And the third is to be kind.
~Henry James

Joey paced back and forth at the top of the slide waiting for me to clear the puddle from the gravely dirt at the bottom, my last task on his takeoff checklist. I'd spent the past ten minutes ridding the slide of its seventeen dew droplets, barely visible to the human eye, by using a dirty paper towel I had found in the trash receptacle. After twenty minutes, and the completion of five tasks, Joey tentatively sat down and slowly slid his way down to the bottom. He then proceeded back up the stairs to slide down again, exactly the way he had climbed up and slid down the time before... my much-needed break had come.

I sat down on the bench and took pride in my ability to resolve his issues once again. As my eyes took a brief recess from watching him, I noticed a flock of mothers looking at me. Disgust, irritation and disbelief were a few of the emotions I saw in their faces.

"I've heard of spoiled but come on — dry off the slide?"

No one understood and I didn't want to explain what Joey's issues were. I wanted to yell out, "I am not spoiling him! I am just making his environment one he can tolerate for twenty minutes to slide down a slide a few times... to do everyday things your children do and you don't have to think about!" At times, I secretly wished Joey had Down syndrome or some other "visible" disorder that people would recognize immediately, thus feeling instant empathy towards me. Rather, Joey, like many autistic children, was an adorable little boy with blond hair and big brown eyes.

I leaned back, brushed the gravel off my jeans and their comments off my mind and closed my eyes, taking comfort in my isolation. I didn't want to spend time with people who gave us dirty looks or didn't take the time to understand.

Then one day I was on the playground taking my break as Joey slid down the slide and one of the mommies approached me. She sat down next to me on the bench and handed me a paper bag. I opened it to find some dishtowels and a small bar of chocolate. Confused, I asked what it was for.

"I always kept a bag in my car when my oldest son was about your son's age," she said. "I got tired of going through the trash to find something to wipe down the slide. The chocolate bar was my reward after I helped my son get down the slide comfortably."

Through tears of disbelief I thanked her and she hugged me. I had been so alone for so long, I could barely contain myself. I began to sob. "We wanted to help; we just didn't understand," said the other mothers as they handed me tissues.

Many people make negative or derogatory comments about things they don't understand or can't explain. I've learned to look beyond those comments and take the time to "understand" them so they in turn can understand me. Since then, I have handed out a lot of paper bags, some filled with dishtowels, some filled with extra baby clothes for a new mother, or a spa candle and bath bubbles for someone appearing overwhelmed.

I have grown to realize that, though our children may lead us down different paths, we as parents all have the same wishes and instincts and that is what unites us. It's worth trying to reconnect with someone you feel has hurt you. Make a point to have coffee with your neighbor or a family member that you have disassociated yourself from. Maybe they just couldn't understand what you were going through. There's a paper bag with your name on it waiting for you.

~Anne Moore Burnett

New York City's Greatest Underground Secret

Don't judge a book by its cover.
~Proverb

was four months pregnant, violently ill, and wished I was at home in bed. Unfortunately, I was at work in New York City. My home in Long Island was forty-five minutes away by train. I thought I had morning sickness. The company nurse set me straight.

"You have a forty-eight-hour virus. Go home and get some rest," she said.

I trudged downstairs and grabbed a cab to Penn Station where I could catch a train home. It was lunchtime and Penn Station was mobbed. Crowds of commuters and shoppers dashed to trains and subways. I shuffled out of their way and leaned up against the wall. My legs felt like rubber. Before I knew it, my knees buckled and I sank to the floor.

There I was, dressed in my sharpest pantsuit and long winter coat sitting on the floor of a train station. Some commuters stepped around me. Others tripped over my legs. Almost everybody looked at me in disgust. I couldn't blame them. I was a mess. I'm sure they were thinking that alcohol and drugs had done me in. I closed my eyes. Maybe I'd wake up and be home in bed.

I felt a tug at my sleeve and looked up. A toothless bag lady hovered over me. She had a ratty wool cap pulled over her hair. She smelled like a mixture of dirty clothes and rotten food. Not a good smell for someone who's pregnant. First I cringed; then I gagged.

"You don't look so good," she said.

I could have said the same thing about her. She waved over a fellow homeless lady and together they lifted me to my feet.

"You got to get out of the way," said the lead bag lady. "People stepping on you."

The two ladies stood on each side of me. One grabbed my handbag, the other my briefcase. I was too sick to panic. We staggered out of the lobby and headed down a flight of stairs. They led me through a maze of passageways. What had I gotten myself into?

Finally we stumbled into a dimly lit tunnel. A shopping cart filled with their worldly possessions sat to the side. For them, this was home, below Penn Station. The two escorted me to a wobbly wooden stool.

"Don't worry, you're safe here, honey," said the second bag lady.

Her kind smile showed me several missing and chipped teeth. She certainly wasn't worried about her appearance. Surprisingly, she seemed more concerned about how I felt.

The head bag lady disappeared for a moment. She returned with three cups of tea. I'm not much of a tea drinker, but this was by far the most delicious tea I had ever tasted.

"You lookin' better. Where you live?" she asked.

"Long Island," I said.

"We'll get you back to the trains, no problem. But first, you rest."

We chatted about the weather and family, as subways and trains overhead rattled the walls and ceiling. For a moment I felt like I was experiencing an Alice in Wonderland tea party moment with some major differences. While Alice fell down a rabbit hole into a fantasy world populated by outlandish creatures and conversations,

I plunged into an underground tunnel populated by two unbelievably caring people.

After tea, my two saviors led me back to the Long Island Railroad concourse. They checked the departure boards, walked me to my train and waved goodbye. I hadn't felt this good all day.

After resting for two days, I headed back to work. It was rush hour and the subway was jammed. As I waited for my train to arrive, I stood back on the platform away from the crowd of commuters. I wasn't alone for long.

"How you feeling?" asked my bag lady friend. She wore the same ratty wool cap.

I smiled. I couldn't believe she found me down here in the subway.

"A little tired, but much better. Thanks again for your help."

"No problem. Today, you need a seat on the subway," she said. "No standing for you." She displayed a mischievous grin.

Subway commuters traditionally jockey for the best spot on the platform, which is where the train doors open. Once the doors open, the subway riders push and shove their way into the train and grab a seat, even while exiting commuters try to leave the train.

As my homeless friend approached the coveted spot on the platform, the commuters backed away. (It's an unwritten rule that commuters always keep their distance from bag ladies.) It was like the parting of the seas. She stood alone. She waved for me to join her. Heads turned as I walked over to her. My new friend put her arm around me. I forced myself to stifle a laugh.

"You gonna get a good seat this morning," she said with a wink.

I didn't doubt her for a moment. The train riders were furious. They had lost their coveted position... and there wasn't anything they could do about it. The train arrived; I scooted on board and grabbed a seat. My nomadic friend quickly stepped back from the tracks and angry riders swarmed the train.

The train doors closed and I waved goodbye to my wool-capped helper. I never saw her again. But for those special couple of days, we shared some laughs, some smiles and some tea. And I realized how lucky I was to receive the gift of kindness from two extraordinary strangers. Sometimes good fortune comes to us when we need it the most and least expect it.

~Maureen C. Bruschi

Queen of Hearts

*They might not need me; but they might. I'll let my head be
just in sight; a smile as small as mine might be precisely their
necessity.*
~Emily Dickinson

After the great American poet, Emily Dickinson, died,
her home in Amherst, Massachusetts was sold to my
grandparents, Hervey and Ethel Parke. There in the
heart of New England, they raised their five children.
My father was born in the home, which is now owned by Amherst
College and is open to the public as the Emily Dickinson Museum.

The house at 280 Main Street was officially called a mansion, we
were informed, because it had four chimneys, not because the property included formal gardens and a grass tennis court. It also offered a
wonderful cupola high above the roof where children could peek out
and spy on the entire town. Doors and stairs creaked with mystery.
Walls were said to harbor old poems stuffed behind the plaster by the
famous former resident. Grand, sprawling, full of nooks and crannies,
it became the perfect playground for sixteen lively grandchildren.

We called our grandparents Nai Nai and Yeh Yeh, the Chinese
terms for revered grandmother and grandfather, not because we had a
wonton noodle in our heritage, but because my aunt and uncle served
as missionaries in China in the early 1940s, and they were the first
of the clan to supply grandchildren. Once their children used these

terms of endearment, the pattern was established and the rest of us adopted the same honorifics.

Nai Nai, by the time I arrived on the scene, was already an older woman. During the day, her snow-white hair was pulled back in a neat bun, but at night I remember sitting on the black leather chaise at the end of her bed and watching her brush out the long strands. To me she looked like the woodcut illustration of the first wife of Mr. Rochester in my child's copy of the Brontë novel, Jane Eyre. "Like the woman who was raving mad?" she laughed when I told her so.

My grandmother delighted in having fresh flowers from the garden appear in vases all about the house. She would walk in the gardens and point to the ones she wanted us to cut and indicate where they might look best. "Those would look nice on the mantel in the library. The others can go in the parlor."

Her heart always wanted the house to look its best because from time to time, random visitors knocked at the door and asked to see the place where Emily once wrote her poems. Without fail, Nai Nai would welcome these complete strangers and offer them a tour. Before they left, she would invite them to enjoy a hot cup of tea and read some of their favorite poems aloud. She knew the lines herself by heart. Her head would nod as she listened to her guest recite, "I'm Nobody! Who are you? Are you — Nobody — Too? Then there's a pair of us!"

Early in the evening, like a shepherd rounding up his flock, she would announce bedtime and shoo all of us grandchildren up the oval staircase to the Austin Room, the Emily Room or the Lavinia Room. As we grew older, we were still sent upstairs by 8:00, the hour she herself retired to her bed. Even as teens, we obediently continued to follow her lead, only to sneak downstairs half an hour later for a raucous round of games in the library.

Parlor games were an important part of our life in Amherst. Most of us learned to manipulate the cards in a playing deck well before we learned to read. We began with simple games of matching hearts, diamonds, spades and clubs. Then we spread the cards out on the floor and played Memory. Later we worked up to games with more and more complicated rules — Canasta, Cribbage, Canfield. Each game had its own rules, and no Parke ever relaxed the rules just because the opponent was a child. My cousins and brothers and I all knew Nai Nai's favorite phrases. If she was losing, she'd quote the dime novels she grew up with: "I'll get you yet, Nod Nixon, he cried, as he shook his fist in the villain's eye!" Or she would promise ominously, "The worm will turn!"

Nai Nai had no fears about her grandchildren becoming card sharks. Her theory was that learning to play cards was character-building. Card games taught a person to win and lose graciously. No one ever wins all the time, so the loser might as well learn to be pleasant even when he is "skunked" and then congratulate the other player. Just as importantly, when you were lucky enough to win, you were not to flaunt that victory at the expense of your cousin's humiliation. Nai Nai's personal attitude was that she never lost: Either she got the highest score or she won bragging rights about having "such smart grandchildren."

If our hearts are as warm and welcoming as my grandmother's, then we too will all be winners.

~Emily Parke Chase

Chapter 6

Raising Great Kids

Stay Positive

The Tent

We tend to forget that happiness doesn't come as a result of getting something we don't have, but rather of recognizing and appreciating what we do have.
~Friedrich Koenig

Water hit me in the face and trickled down my shirt. "We've been attacked by munchkins!" I hollered at my husband as I ran after our five-year-old son and three-year-old daughter. We were a family armed with water guns and giggles, and somehow the kids always got their best shots on me. My mom's eyes crinkled with delight as she watched us play while cradling our infant son.

"Lindy," she said, "you and Tom are more like older siblings to your kids than parents." This was an observation, not a criticism and Tom and I received her words like a badge of honor. We didn't take life as seriously as we probably should have. Our marriage was easy and our children a delight. We let the kids stomp in rain puddles and stay up too late. We felt we had been given this amazing gift of three little personalities and we were privileged to know these beings before anyone else. It was like we were harboring three beautiful secrets that we would introduce to the world one day.

When Tom and I married we knew we wanted to have kids and experience America. We had our own design business and could set up shop anywhere, so we did. We lived in some of the best tourist spots in the country. We lived in Atlanta, Georgia through its gorgeous spring months. We enjoyed Colorado's delightful year-round climate. For a time we lived in a two-story farmhouse, rich in character, on a pumpkin farm in Illinois and helped with several harvests. In the Northwest we chose to live in a little fishing village in the shadow of Mount Rainier. Later we moved to Montana where we were literally surrounded by mountains and taught our kids how to ski. The houses in which we resided varied widely. One was expansive with all the amenities, while another was a little duplex in desperate need of repair. Each one enriched our lives differently, but none as much as when we lived in the tent.

"The tent." Whenever I say those words my husband smiles knowingly. That was the one place in which we did not choose to reside. Tom and I had been living in the most impressive house we had ever rented. It was a two-story in Washington State with picture windows all the way up to the vaulted ceiling. We had bedrooms enough for everyone plus a writing room and a room for me to do my illustration work. The windows looked out on a lush, green meadow bordered by tall pines. We were often surprised by deer that were curious enough to peek into our family room window. We would have stayed there forever if it hadn't been so wonderful.

Now, we like wonderful. We like amenities and everything that this house had to offer, but so did the realtors, and because they liked it so much they were able to sell it right out from under us.

Although this complicated our lives and added to our expenses with deposits and moving costs, we were not worried. We had one really good design client. This company not only kept our bills paid, but also took the majority of our design time. They had us create newsletters, brochures and advertising pieces. We hadn't needed to pursue other clients, so we didn't. That, however, turned out to be a mistake.

The same week that we got the call that we had thirty days to move out of our house, we also got the call from our one and only client. He told us he had hired in-house designers and would no longer need our services.

Difficult circumstances, but not insurmountable. We planned to get in the car and hunt for a new place and new clients. That is when the final blow came. Literally! Our car's engine blew up and we were done. We were thirty-four years old, had three kids and found ourselves without a car, without a job and without a home.

As we had always done before, Tom and I put our heads together and brainstormed survival plans. We borrowed a beater pick-up truck from his brother-in-law and when the deadline came for us to be out of the house, we moved most of our belongings into a storage unit. We had still not found a place to rent so we took our tent and our sleeping bags and a few changes of clothes to a state park and set up camp. The kids were delighted! We had been on many adventures with them and this was just one more, but not for me.

The tent was meant to be a weeklong stopgap measure, but new work and another house were not forthcoming. The reality of being without a home was setting in and I began to feel fear and frustration. We weren't camping, we were surviving, and as the days rolled on with no income, our checking account dwindled. The prospect of having the required deposit and first month's rent to get into a new place was fast diminishing.

My husband began each day by driving to his office in town to buy a newspaper and searching for housing and jobs. Daily I shook out sleeping bags and amused the kids with nature walks and berry picking. My job was to keep them happy while I hid my own fear of the future. As long as the weather stayed warm we could continue this way, but early fall frosts were not far off. The days of no work and no house turned into weeks of anxiety.

One night when the three children were asleep in their bags, Tom and I talked quietly about our worries. I was feeling the full burden of our homeless and jobless situation and could not stop the tears from rolling down my face. Tom rubbed my shoulders and leaned in close. "We are the most blessed of people, you know," he said softly. I looked at him incredulously.

"What do you mean?" I sobbed. "We have nothing!"

Then he gently replied, "Honey, we have everything that matters right here. We have the kids, we have a roof over our heads, and we have each other."

It seemed so simple — too simple — but I knew he was right. I told him, "If anyone heard you say that they would think you had lost your mind!" We began to chuckle and then we began to laugh! We laughed and hugged until our tears of desperation turned into tears of tenderness.

We lived thirty-three days without a home that year. Miraculously, the landlord of a duplex trusted us to move in without having a dime of deposit to give her. Since that summer we have moved less often, and made contingency plans for unexpected hardships, but we have never forgotten our days in the tent. That was where my husband and I became grown-ups in our hope, in our faith and in our love. We make a point to vacation in the tent every summer just for pleasure. It is there that we remember we have everything that matters.

~Lindy Schneider

Chicken Soup for the Soul.

Lessons in Line

The indispensable first step to getting the things you want out of life is this: decide what you want.
~Ben Stein

Recently I was standing in line at the state university bookstore. I find myself there periodically for game gear and various sundry items I can't find elsewhere to cheer on the college team.

This day the line at the checkout counter was several people deep and into the aisle. I was in the middle of it. Ms. Perky Cashier had her fingers dancing across the keys of the cash register faster than my eyes could follow. They seemed to have a Caribbean beat as she punched in merchandise codes and prices for each customer. She was clever, witty and fast. She had the situation under control. She didn't need a second cashier. Although the people in line didn't talk much to each other, they smiled and seemed pleasant about the short wait till their turn.

Still several customers back, I was close enough to hear the conversation when a young man moved up to the counter with his dad. Ms. Perky Cashier took his purchases from his hands and set them on the counter. "You hardly seem old enough to attend the university," she said smiling. She had excellent customer service down to a science.

The young man was pleased she'd noticed. "Well actually I'm

Stay Positive | 211

not old enough," he said. "I'm only a kid. But my dad here said that maybe I needed an incentive, you know, a carrot." He pointed to the quiet older man on his right elbow. "You see," the kid went on, "I am just in high school so I have two years left before graduation. I really want to go here after I graduate. My dad says I will have to work really hard to get in." Unlike his father, the kid had no clue as to the fight he faced.

The young man had tripped over the word "incentive" and it was clear he was not a high-performing student. This was not the class president, high school valedictorian, or some political or business go-getter. This was a regular kid who had been passed over a lot because he didn't sparkle. He gave the impression, though, that he was hard working and sincere.

Ms. Perky Cashier's fingers danced again across the keys as she typed in the codes and prices for his really nice T-shirt and a hoodie in the university colors. She hit the subtotal and the register added the tax for her.

"Is there anything else you need?" she asked as her fingers stopped. She made eye contact with both the father and son while noticing the customer line had lengthened considerably. "Well," said the father shyly as he slowly raised his hand from his side. "It's not so long until I will be needing this, so I will just get it right now." He laid a university car-window decal across the sweatshirt Ms. Perky Cashier had folded on the counter. The kid smiled so wide it seemed his face would crack. He must not have seen his father pick up the rear-window sticker while they were shopping for gear.

The people in line turned away, their eyes moist. Even if this kid didn't get into college he would always know his father believed in him.

Ms. Perky Cashier was also taken back by the tenderness of the moment. Her fingers moved slowly across the keys as she added in the additional purchase and called out the amount due. The cash register yawned open. She regained her composure and put the items in a plastic bag with the university logo on it. The dad handed her exact change that she put into the open mouth of the register and shut it.

Taking the handles of the plastic bag, she again made eye contact with the kid. "Well, young man," she said. "We will be seeing you soon then." She spoke as if she expected to see him later in the week to buy books for this semester's classes. The kid thanked her and moved towards the door with his father behind him.

"May I help you?" she said to the next customer. But no one moved up to the register. The line of people was staring after the father and son, sensing the price of their own goods had just included a free parenting lesson.

~Pamela Gilsenan

This Is How We Practice Not Quitting

Perseverance is the hard work you do after you get tired of doing the hard work you already did.
~Newt Gingrich

'll never forget the day my then fifty-something professional sports executive dad became a marathon runner. After he finished his first race, the Disney Marathon in January of 1995, I watched him walk through our front door limping, battered, and bruised. He looked like he had been in hand-to-hand combat and was dragging home from the war. I remember wondering what in the world was fun about that. But a few years later when I watched him cross the finish line at the 1997 Chicago Marathon, I caught the bug. Whatever it was that made him want to do this, the satisfaction I saw on his face told me I wanted it too. So I started training for my first marathon. To date, I've run in nine of these epic events, seven of them right alongside my dad.

The first time we did the Boston Marathon together, I had trained hard for months, and Dad and I were both pumped. The first half of the race flew by, and I was on fire. I had energy like a madwoman, but Dad was struggling... so I did my best to keep him going. Kind of like Frodo and Sam, you know? Though the plan had been to stay together, Dad kept saying, "Go! Get a better time if you can... go ahead!" I debated it, but decided to stay with him. After mile thirteen, we stopped for a bathroom break — and that's when I cramped up really bad. Dad came to life after that, so for the second half of the race, he had to "carry" me! Miles thirteen through twenty-six were brutal, and sometime during mile twenty-one, as we were making our trek up the aptly-named "Heartbreak Hill," in agony and almost in tears, I looked up at Dad and cried, "Why in the *world* are we doing this?"

"People ask me that all the time," Dad said, "but you know why I do marathons? Because this is how I practice not quitting."

Wow! What a *great* perspective. Needless to say, it gave me a jolt of energy and we finished the race with smiles on our faces, hand-in-hand as we crossed the finish line.

I have reminded myself of that statement many times since that day and it has "carried" me through many situations. I still don't know what's *fun* about marathons, but I know the immense sense of satisfaction I feel after running one. It's a great "I did it!" moment. One more time, I forced my body to keep going long past the moment it wanted to quit.

Rich DeVos, cofounder of Amway and a family friend, likes to say that perseverance is stubbornness with a purpose. I think that is a terrific quote, and it reminds me that if you quit once, it makes it easier to quit the next time. After you start quitting, it's hard to put the brakes on.

I hear people say all the time, "Oh, I could *never* do a marathon!" And you know what my response is? "Sure you could! Most of it is in your mind." People look at me like I'm crazy, but trust me, marathons are as much a mental challenge as they are physical. Basically, from the moment you start, your body wants to stop. But then your powerful mind kicks in and says, "You started this thing... you're *gonna* finish it!" There really is nothing like that feeling — the rush — of knowing you've just beaten those twenty-six miles.

I don't have the kind of dad who will sit on the porch and drink beer with you. My dad is the one challenging *you* to keep up with *him* in a marathon. How cool is that? Because of his "not quitting" attitude, he's inspired me to take up the challenge too.

Today, whether it's running a marathon with Dad or finding my way in the country music world, I know I may not be the best, but I *can* guarantee you this: I will work the hardest, I will persevere the longest, and I will strive for lasting quality in my field, no matter what. Thanks, Dad, for one of the most powerful lessons I have ever taken away from you.

~Karyn Williams

The Crucial String

Courage doesn't always roar. Sometimes it's the little voice at the
end of the day that says I'll try again tomorrow.
~Mary Anne Radmacher

y husband and I had grown increasingly uneasy about our second child, Mickey. Though a warm, engaging baby, he showed no interest in playing Peekaboo, How Big Is the Baby, or waving bye-bye. At monthly visits the pediatrician assured us all was well. But by eighteen months, Mickey had only three words, and that's why we finally found ourselves sitting in a cubicle at a major teaching hospital. A team of unsmiling experts spent two hours poking, prodding, and measuring our son, asking him to draw a straight line, stack cubes, put pegs in boards. I leaned forward to catch the doctor's words more fully, hoping to hear how adorable, how promising, my child was.

Instead, she said, "Don't expect higher education for your son."

It felt as if we were looking down an endless, dark tunnel. Our radiant little boy had just been diagnosed with an autism spectrum disorder. How could she make such a prediction about a child not yet two? There was no doubt, she said, that he was "special." A puzzling word. For if he was special, did that make our other, older son Jonathan ordinary?

Just as you go through predictable stages of grief and recovery when someone you love dies, so too, learning to scale back your expectations and dreams for your child is an equally painful process. We began the endless rounds: speech therapy, occupational therapy, sensory integration therapy, physical therapy, vision therapy, auditory integration therapy, behavioral therapy, play therapy, dietary and biomedical interventions. At first my mood was only as good as the last therapy session had gone. I felt isolated as friends and relatives rushed to dismiss my fears. "Einstein didn't talk till he was four. Give him time and he'll snap out of it. Boys talk later. Don't compare your children."

In the next year and a half, Mickey learned to recognize letters and numbers, and he showed a keen interest in reading signs and license plates. I was waiting for a "Miracle Worker" moment, a breakthrough where he would suddenly begin speaking in paragraphs. Naively, I still assumed that with enough intervention he'd be fine by the time he reached kindergarten. One night at bedtime, he offered a first full sentence: "Mommy, snuggle me," and my eyes filled with tears.

Disability seeps into all the cracks, the corners, of one's life. It becomes the emotional center of the family. Sometimes I felt as if other, "normal" families were feasting in a great restaurant, while the four of us were standing outside, noses pressed to the glass. Birthday parties for other children were sometimes unbearable, as my child, so clearly different, was unable to bowl, do gymnastics, or participate in any other activity. People often stared at him. Equally painful were Mickey's birthday celebrations; I couldn't help remembering just how much his older brother Jonathan had been able to do at a comparable age.

I was adrift in a foreign country, without a guidebook, and I didn't know anyone else who lived there. Those first few years with Mickey were like living with someone from another culture, and it was our job to teach him the ways of our world. Slowly, we learned the language, as I dogged my son's therapists with questions and requests for more information and articles, reading voraciously, going to workshops and conferences, acquiring a new vocabulary.

You adapt. Mickey was impulsive, and would often dart away in public or dash out of the house; we put a special lock on the front door. He frequently dumped every book and toy from his shelves; we stripped his room to a minimum of play materials. Loud noises — even the whir of elevators — disturbed him so much he would cover his ears and hum; we avoided crowds and learned to take the stairs.

And yet, for all that he could not yet do, there was so much about him that was intact. He was unfailingly sweet, carrying his collection of Puzzle Place dolls everywhere, hugging and kissing them, feeding them pretend food. He would line them up under the bed covers, whispering, "Shh, take a nap." Given the depth of his issues, his warmth and his sheer vibrancy seemed extraordinary.

The summer before kindergarten, Mickey lost his first tooth. We hadn't even known it was loose, because he still lacked the words to tell us. It was a bittersweet milestone. I remembered vividly the flush of excitement when his brother Jonathan had lost his first tooth. Though Mickey seemed pleased to show off the gap in his teeth, and we cheered for him, there was no elaborate celebration this time. The tooth fairy was too abstract for him.

The age of five was also the magic cut-off point I'd always imagined when all would be well. But the first day of kindergarten, I stood in a huddle with the other mothers and watched through the window of the special ed classroom as Mickey lay on the floor and said repeatedly, "I go home." In the next year, though, he learned to follow classroom rules, and began to read. That year, when he told us his first knock-knock joke, we celebrated.

As the years have passed, I have learned to wear emotional blinders. I stay tightly focused on Mickey, celebrating every change I see. I try to tune out what other, neurotypical kids his age are doing, because the gap is still too painful. Mostly, I try not to compare him with his brother Jonathan, an excellent student who is athletic, funny and well liked. Their trajectories are so different. It was hardest when Mickey was a toddler; if I did not remember every one of Jonathan's developmental milestones, there they all were, lovingly chronicled — by me — in his baby book. Comparing the boys is sometimes tempting, but dangerous. I must have separate, realistic expectations for each.

Most support comes, not surprisingly, from other parents of children with special needs. When I finally connected with them after those first hard years, it felt as if I could take a deep breath after holding it too long. Today we talk eagerly, like war veterans sharing their foxhole experiences. And though each of our tours of duty is different, we all long for our discharge orders.

I am often asked how I do it. I give the same answer each time. I wasn't given a choice. I just do it, one foot after the other. I have to be his advocate, because as wonderful as the therapists and teachers are, they go home every night. We are his ultimate teachers, the ones who are in it for the long haul. There's nothing particularly noble about it. We do it because it has to be done.

Acceptance doesn't mean giving up, and it isn't a constant state. Grief and anger still rear up unexpectedly. I still get tired of the relentless effort, the struggle for normalcy, the endless round of therapies and school meetings and fights with the insurance companies. This process of healing is a destination without an arrival. There is no cure, no magic bullet. Joy and grief are joined in lockstep.

Ultimately, what buoys our family is hope. When I look at this child, I do not see "autism." I see my child: an animated, endearing, and handsome fifteen-year-old with a mischievous sense of humor, who despite the early dire predictions, has learned to speak and read and do math. Parenting this trusting, gentle boy has deepened me immeasurably. But would I trade in my hard earned equanimity and expertise if someone could magically make his autism go away tomorrow?

In a heartbeat.

A few years ago, I heard a story that changed the way I framed my feelings about having a child with a disability. Itzhak Perlman was giving a concert. He made his way on crutches to the stage, seated himself, and took up his violin. He began to play, when suddenly a string snapped. Perlman looked around, seeming to measure the length of the stage, how far he would have to go on crutches to fetch a new string, and then seemed to decide that he would do without it.

He lifted his violin and began to play, and even without that string, this man with a physical disability not only played; he played beautifully.

This is what it is like to have a disabled child. It feels as if you've lost a crucial string. And then, painstakingly, you must learn to play the instrument you've been given. Softly, differently, not playing the music you'd intended, but making music nonetheless.

~Liane Kupferberg Carter

A Turkey of a Thanksgiving

Enjoy the little things, for one day you may look back and realize
they were the big things.
~Robert Brault

I grew up with the crazy notion that cancer is 100% survivable. My mother's first bout with cancer came only a few weeks before my fifth birthday. She was diagnosed with thyroid cancer, and the surgery meant my mother missed my first day of kindergarten. My cousin Charlotte was the one who put me on the bus that morning. I don't really remember the day. My cousin's picture of me standing in my blue dress in front of the house is the only proof I have that my mother wasn't present. And the scar along the crease in my mother's neck is the only proof she'd had a tumor.

Mom survived the thyroid cancer, but as the years passed, the doctors kept finding skin cancer on her face and back. She'd have minor surgery to remove the malignant moles, and life would go on. Cancer didn't seem like such a dirty word to me. Just a nuisance that left my mother with another scar.

And then came my freshman year of college. I was home one weekend when my mother sat on the edge of my bed to tell me she had breast cancer. In hindsight, I should have been terrified, but my fear was tampered by Mom's track record for kicking cancer to the curb. Mom had survived thyroid cancer once and skin cancer more times than I could count. Surely, breast cancer would be just another bump in the road.

The impact of my mom's diagnosis didn't hit me until my dad called my four brothers and me together to discuss Thanksgiving. "Your mother's surgery is just a few days before Thanksgiving. She won't be able to lift anything heavy for a while."

I scratched my head. Why was he telling us this? And why would a mastectomy make it hard for her to lift things? Oh, yes, I was that blissfully ignorant. It wasn't until years later when a tumor was removed from my own breast that I understood how much even a small incision could impact arm movement.

"So..." Dad continued, "there won't be a Thanksgiving dinner this year."

"Wait. What?" My jaw hit the floor. Mom had cancer — again — and Thanksgiving was cancelled?

"What are we going to do instead?" my oldest brother asked.

Dad shrugged. "We'll go out to eat."

I had visions of the family in *A Christmas Story* eating Christmas dinner at a Chinese restaurant. My family would be doing the same for Thanksgiving? Inconceivable!

Apparently, my four brothers felt the same way. I don't remember which of them came up with the idea first, but one of them said, "We'll do it. The five of us kids will make Thanksgiving dinner."

Did I mention I was the only girl in this family with four boys? And none of us had any real cooking experience at this point?

It didn't matter. We quickly jumped on the bandwagon.

"Yeah. We'll each make a part of the meal."

"Mom can just sit in a corner of the kitchen and direct us."

"And tell us where she keeps things. Anyone know where the big roasting pan is?"

"Mom won't have to lift a thing."

"We'll do it all."

I saw the concern in my father's eyes. Could four young men and an eighteen-year-old girl make Thanksgiving dinner on their own?

My two oldest brothers were just starting their careers in computer-related fields. My third oldest brother was in his first year of medical school, and my younger brother was a sophomore in high school. Although I'd done a bit of baking, none of us really knew anything about cooking, much less a Thanksgiving feast for seven.

But we were determined we'd have a traditional Thanksgiving dinner with all the fixings. Being techy nerds, my oldest brothers decided to make a Gantt chart for the meal. For the less nerdy, a Gantt chart is a type of bar graph that illustrates the development of a project. The project is broken into smaller elements, and the start and end times of each element are displayed on the chart.

Thus, the Thanksgiving feast was broken into parts and tasks were divvied up. I would make the pumpkin pie. Mike would make the apple pie. Dave was in charge of cranberry sauce and bread. Steve would make twice-baked potatoes. The youngest, Tom, would make the stuffing, and with Dad's help, get it and the bird into the oven.

Then each of the cooks was assigned a time to work in the kitchen. It was absolutely imperative that each cook finish his or her task on time, so the next cook could step in. Mom was deemed Executive Chef, but her tasks were purely supervisory.

Working backwards, with an expected dinnertime of 5:00 p.m., my brothers filled in the Gantt chart.

On Thanksgiving morning, I made two piecrusts. I filled one of these with pumpkin pie filling and got it in the oven. The other I left for my brother's apple pie. He began work on his as soon as I'd finished the piecrusts. After clearing off my end of the kitchen table, Tom stepped in to prepare the stuffing.

By the time my pumpkin pie came out of the oven, Mike's apple pie was ready to go in. By the time his pie came out, the turkey was ready to go in. And so the day continued, each of us taking our turn in the kitchen.

At four o'clock, we set the dining room table with Mom's good china, wine glasses, water goblets, and silverware. At 4:30, the turkey came out of the oven. It was the most beautiful golden brown bird I've ever seen. At five o'clock on the dot, exactly the time prescribed on the Gantt chart, all the food was displayed on the table, and the candles were lit. It could have been a scene from a Norman Rockwell painting. We took pictures so we'd never forget.

We sat down to that Thanksgiving table thankful for so many things. Mom's surgery had gone well. She'd still have chemotherapy and radiation treatment, but she'd survive. Yes, we were also thankful that we'd saved Thanksgiving dinner, but that was part of Mom's doing, too. She had taught us not to fear trying new things. She had instilled in us the importance of family. She had raised us to work together to solve our problems.

Over twenty years have passed since that Thanksgiving. Mom has battled breast cancer two more times. She's had numerous more incidents of skin cancer. She is the very definition of a cancer survivor.

And to honor our mother, my brothers and I still aid in the making of Thanksgiving dinner. Sometimes Mom makes the green bean casserole and helps with the turkey if her health is good. My brothers and I stick with our traditional roles. What had once seemed like it would be a turkey of a holiday has become our standard for the perfect Thanksgiving dinner.

~A.J. Cattapan

Finish It for Me

My mother made a brilliant impression upon my childhood life.
She shone for me like the evening star.
~Winston Churchill

M y husband Jim and I fell in love while we were both in college. We married the same fall he started law school, and I buckled down to finish my under-graduate studies.

A year later, I was determined to find a job with my liberal arts degree, but in a college town the best paying jobs went to graduate students who taught beginning courses while pursuing advanced degrees. I enrolled as a master's degree student in French literature. My teaching stipend covered our basic living expenses.

Fast-forward two years. Jim had finished law school and was studying for the bar exam. He had a job waiting for him and soon we would move to a nearby city to start our post-college life.

I had completed all my graduate course work and was plodding through the final stages of my thesis, translating and analyzing an obscure medieval French literary work.

That's when it happened. The French use the elegant word *ennui*, which covers a multitude of ills: boredom, fatigue, depression, or just plain feeling "stuck." I could go no further with my thesis. Every day felt like moving through mud. I didn't want to share my dismal state with Jim; he was totally consumed with bar exam preparations.

I knew my friends would dismiss it as a bad case of almost-ready-to-graduate-itis.

I was daydreaming about walking into my thesis advisor's office and saying "I quit" when the phone rang.

"Hello?"

"Hi, sweetie, how are things going?"

My mom? How did she know? But then she always seemed to know when I was down, even though she lived half a country away and we didn't talk that often. My anguish tumbled out.

"I don't think I can finish my thesis, Mom. I just can't find the motivation. I doubt if the degree will ever do me any good. I'm ready to settle down and start a family."

Mom paused. "If you don't want to finish your degree for yourself, finish it for me."

Her words went straight to my heart. Mom had been a child of the Great Depression. Even though she was a talented pianist, she had turned down a scholarship to Juilliard to get a full-time job and contribute to the family finances.

She never made it to college. Neither did my dad. They had both told me on numerous occasions how proud of me they were. At that moment I realized how selfish I would be if I didn't go ahead and finish.

"Okay, Mom," I sighed. "I'll do it for you."

I successfully completed my master's degree and went on to teach college French and start a family. A few years later, after both kids were in school, I decided to make a career change and found myself back in school for three years to obtain a law degree. Mom was delighted, of course. I sailed along on my own motivation until it was time to study for the bar exam.

The bar exam, I knew from Jim's experience, was a grueling two days of essay questions with complex legal scenarios. Without passing the bar exam, one cannot be licensed to practice law. It's the "golden ticket" to being a lawyer, regardless of how many law courses you take.

Studying for the bar exam took up most of the summer. A small group of us met each day and grilled each other, sometimes late into the evening, drinking cup after cup of coffee to stay awake.

As the bar exam date loomed nearer, I felt more and more panicky. "I'll never be able to remember all this stuff," I thought. "I don't know why I ever thought I could be a lawyer. I'll never find a job at my age, anyway. Why put myself through this misery?"

My anxious mind dredged up every negative message it could think of. I was on the verge of quitting when Mom's words came floating into my consciousness: "finish it for me." Those words were my lifeline. I summoned a picture of my mother as a young woman, looking straight at me with her deep brown eyes. She nodded her head as she smiled, and I felt her heart reaching out to mine.

All my anxiety drained away. Two days later, I marched into the examination room with 200 other candidates and began to write. Whenever I faltered, whenever the old negative feelings threatened to take over, I heard Mom whisper "Finish it for me." Her words magically melted all the fears.

Six weeks later the letter came, informing me that I had passed the bar exam and requesting my presence the following week at the State Supreme Court to be sworn in as a practicing lawyer. Only then did I call Mom and let her know how her words had once again sustained me.

Although Mom's no longer physically with me, her heartening words — "finish it for me" — continue to inspire me to press on, to accomplish that next goal, whether it's writing an essay, planning a workshop, or dreaming up a special dessert. Thanks to Mom, I'm up to the challenge!

~Maril Crabtree

Always a Winner

He didn't tell me how to live; he lived, and let me watch him do it.
~Clarence Budington Kelland

The doctor's grim diagnosis sent a collective shudder through the family. It looked as if Dad had cancer. The X-ray showed a large mass inside his brain.

Prognosis: Bad, really bad. Treatment needed to begin immediately. According to the doctor, my father was in for the fight of his life.

Literally.

But if anyone expected Dad to launch into histrionics or some display of denial, they were soon proven wrong. After taking a deep breath, my father lifted his head, looked the doctor straight in the eyes and said, "Could be cancer, huh? Well, either way, I'm a winner."

The physician's office filled with silence.

No doubt, Dad must have felt a dozen bulging eyes fixed on him as his family sat, incredulous at his reaction to the horrible news.

Either way, I'm a winner?

What kind of response was that? The doctor said this was probably cancer — brain cancer!

Although stunned, we should've anticipated Dad's stoic response. After all, hadn't he always faced the unknown with this calm, yet fierce resolve? Not once in forty-odd years had I heard him ask "why me" or rail against God, blaming the Almighty for any setbacks or tragedies. Instead, he tackled life's cruel disappointments in a quiet, dignified manner. The severity of the situation didn't matter. Whether it was financial problems, conflicts at work, even a health crisis, Dad wrestled the issue calmly, always shielding his children from the awful truth.

Only then, as I looked back, did I realize how strong my father was—and how others leaned on him for support.

No doubt he found his strength at an early age. My father was born to an immigrant family. His dad hailed from Portugal and eventually Brazil while his mother came from Mexico. From his earliest days, he had to help his parents—usually as a translator.

The road wasn't easy for Dad. Eventually, he started to work after school to contribute to the lean family income. As a result, he didn't have many playmates or close friends. When his father died, Dad became the sole provider for his family. As a teenager, he attended school while working a stream of thankless jobs in the evenings and on weekends—a balancing act he continued until he graduated.

After a short stint in the army, Dad landed a good position with California's largest grocery chain where he eventually met my mother. His relentless strength was evident throughout his married life, raising children while still assisting his mother and various family members over the rough spots. During these years, he helped my mother take care of her parents as well.

As usual, there was no complaining, no wallowing in self-pity. Dad simply accepted the many challenges thrown at him and soldiered on. In fact, I never heard Dad complain about his childhood, which he always described as a happy, normal one.

His biggest test of strength came as an adult when my mother battled cancer, eventually succumbing to the disease. After Mom's death, Dad found himself alone for the first time in thirty-odd years. They had made such a strong team in life that my siblings and I were worried about Dad's ability to carry on without his spouse. Surely he wouldn't be able to make it on his own. The grief, we assumed, would take its toll on him.

The first few months proved to be his worst period as he lost weight and seemed a bit withdrawn. During my visits, I noticed the refrigerator and cupboards were not as fully stocked as they once were. Nor was the house as clean as I remembered it. He watched a lot of TV and seldom ventured beyond the living room.

It was obvious: Dad was depressed; life had finally beaten him.

Or so we thought.

Dad's recovery began a few months later as he returned to work and started to socialize again. He attended all the family functions and even met some new friends who helped him over the sadness of losing a spouse. Before we knew it, he had cleaned the house from top to bottom and even replaced some old furniture and appliances.

The message was clear: Dad had rebounded and was ready to move on. Somehow, he had found that quiet, unshakeable resolve and had risen from his grief stronger than before.

Ironically enough, I hadn't realized the magnitude of Dad's fighting spirit — or how much he had inspired me — until that pivotal day in the doctor's office. Only then did I understand the breadth of his philosophy that nothing in life was a safe bet, that struggles and setbacks will always follow us. In the end, we simply must know how to deal with them — and to fight with all the strength we possess. His life was an example that although there would be agonizing moments of quiet questioning, that we must accept whatever God throws at us and learn how to be thankful.

It was true. Either way, we're all winners.

My debt of gratitude for all the lessons my father taught me may never be fully realized in my lifetime. However, I have come to understand the priceless gift he has given me — the strength and will to survive, and maybe, just maybe, serve as a rock for others to lean on.

Thanks, Dad, for teaching me how to be a winner.

~Al Serradell

Two Little Words with a Big Impact

Too many people miss the silver lining because they're expecting gold.

~Maurice Setter

have always considered myself a positive thinker, an upbeat person and an optimist. I try to find the best in every situation. I've recently become aware of how two little words in my vocabulary have had a tremendous impact on people. I didn't even realize it.

I've been listening to myself lately, and I don't like the way I sound. As a veteran teacher, I know that praise can be a huge motivational tool. I realize the importance of developing a child's self-esteem. I generously sprinkle uplifting comments around my classroom like I am fertilizing flowers. Each new school year brings a garden variety of students, and they all blossom with praise and encouragement. I know how to thank my grown kids, my grandkids and my husband for a job well done. I toss compliments to the unsuspecting if it appears someone needs a lift. I also yo-yo my positive comments right back when I use the word that makes my preschoolers giggle — BUT.

When one of my students attempted to print her name, I oohed and ahhed. "Wow! That is a great A, and your letter, D is nice and tall, but your letter, E should be short; can you erase it and try to make it shorter?" I asked. She wasn't crushed by my comment. She tried to live up to my expectation. I thought I was helping, preparing her for kindergarten, showing her the difference in size between upper case and lower case letters. I don't believe that my comment would have any long term affect on her self-worth. I imagine though, if I'd substituted the word BUT with the word AND, she'd have been proud of her accomplishment instead of questioning the "right way" to print her name. I wish I had said, "I like your nice tall letters, AND I like how hard you are trying to make your letter E."

My recently divorced daughter called to tell me about a house she was interested in. I listened to her. I applauded her for moving forward with her life, and I said, "Honey, I am glad that you've found something you like, but..." There, I did it again! "Don't you think, with the gas prices, you might want to buy closer to your work?" As she told me all about the prospective house, I could hear the excitement and joy in her voice. The moment I spoke the word, BUT, it was as if I pricked a balloon with a needle. I could hear her slowly deflate. I sure wish I'd used the word AND. "Honey, I'm glad you found a house in your price range, AND I'm happy for you." She knows I freely express my opinions, and I know she's used to my mouth. I suspect that if I had leashed my tongue, her emotions wouldn't have flip-flopped, and we'd have both hung up feeling better.

Recently I visited my son and his six-year-old little boy and six-month-old daughter. I scooped up my grandchildren and bragged. He babysits while my daughter-in-law works weekends. I told him he was a great father; I praised him for his devotion to his family. He beamed as though he was a little boy, and then I flubbed. "You should be commended for spending your whole day taking your little boy to his sports events, but don't you think he might be worn out and ready for a bath?" There I was with my bad word again! My son's smile slid away, and he said, "He'll be fine. I'll get him to bed soon." I planted an ounce of doubt, when I should have been planting the seeds of confidence. I wish I'd said, "You're a good father, AND I admire your ability to recognize the children's individual needs."

My granddaughter showed up at my door dressed like a princess on her way to the prom. I told her how beautiful she looked. I told her I was proud of the young lady she has become, and I said, "Sweetheart, I want you to have a great time, but please don't drink tonight." I know she doesn't engage in risky behavior; she's responsible and sensible and trustworthy. She looked as though I'd snatched her crown. "Nana!" The tone of her voice indicated how I'd made her feel. How I wish I'd said, "I want you to have a great time, AND I trust you."

My dear husband helps around the house; he did the dishes, emptied the dishwasher, and folded the laundry. I was thrilled he had lightened my work load. I thanked him. I told him how wonderful he is, and I used that naughty word again. "BUT, why did you leave crumbs all over the counter?" Why? Why? Why didn't I say, "Thank you, AND I appreciate all you do around the house."

I've been doing some self-reflecting. I've given up on losing those twenty pounds. I've decided a walk around the neighborhood is a good substitute for vigorous exercise. I've watched dust bunnies cuddle under the sofa. I've prayed in the dark instead of at church more often than not. In other words, all those New Year's resolutions are now null and void. I lose a pound; I eat a chocolate; I gain a pound. The bar on my treadmill makes a nice rack for hanging laundry. I've attended church for grandchildren's christenings, and I pass the sanctuary on my way to the church office. I vacuum on weekends. I figure if the dust bunnies don't mind snuggling for another day, I don't care either.

My house isn't spotless, my thighs are heavy, my soul, like my face could use some uplifting, but I have decided that I simply cannot keep all those resolutions I made on January 1st. I'm ready for some spring cleaning. I'm tossing those old resolutions out and I am making one, just one, which I intend to keep. I am going to refrain from using the B word. I think I can do it, and I am going to give it my best. I know it will have a positive effect on others. BUT if I mess up, I will try again, and again, and again to remove that naughty little word from my vocabulary. I resolve to replace it with the word AND. This is a resolution I intend to keep!

~Linda O'Connell

Pinstripe Dreams

Keep true to the dreams of thy youth.
~Johann Friedrich von Schiller

sk a classroom of eight-year-olds what they want to be when they grow up and you'll hear they plan to become astronauts, professional athletes and scientists. Nothing is impossible to a child.

Ask the same question to a high school junior or senior and you'll get a much more practical response. Seems that getting older prompts us to reel in our dreams, trading them in for more realistic pursuits.

My oldest, however, a high school junior, is very specific about his career path. He intends to wear a pinstripe suit to work. No, he's not planning a career in business or law. He will complete his pinstripe ensemble with a pair of baseball cleats. He plans to play shortstop for the New York Yankees. He told me so when he was ten years old.

Therein lies my dilemma. At age sixteen, he's still a dreamer. Just like his mother.

At ten, it was okay to nurture those dreams with inspiration like, "You can be anything you want to be as long as you believe in yourself." At age twelve, you applaud all-star achievements and keep the scrapbook up to date. But somewhere around fourteen or fifteen, most kids begin to cut themselves from the team. They realize their limitations. Reality sets in. Sometimes, their parents even help them to this conclusion.

I started to question my eternal optimism and support for my son's dreams after I ran into a former Little League mom. She said that her son wasn't going to play baseball anymore. This was a kid I loved to watch. Not because he was the best on the team, but because he played like he loved the game. When I asked her why he was giving it up, she said she encouraged him not to play anymore. A loving and protective mother, she wanted him to pursue something that would enable him to enjoy more success.

When should a mom help redirect dreams, if at all? What if your child holds on to dreams well past the expected age? Do you protect him, as my friend was doing, or encourage him to go for it?

I knew early on that I enjoyed writing, and dreamed of bestsellers and book tours. I imagined myself signing stacks of books and being interviewed on talk shows. I knew the odds were against me. Everyone has a book idea. Few ever make it into print. And, the bestseller list? I'll probably win the lottery first.

But my parents always encouraged me. They were, and continue to be, my biggest fans. Their years of support gave me the courage to put myself in the vulnerable position of being rejected as an author. And I was, over and over again.

But guess what? One of my books did get published and the publisher sent me on a coast-to-coast book tour. They put me up in fine hotels and provided a driver and an author escort to each TV studio and radio station. The best part: writing my book led to an appearance on NBC's *Today* show. There I was, being interviewed by Katie Couric in Studio 1-A in Rockefeller Center. I was living my dream.

The bestseller thing is still probably out of the question. I mean, realistically, the odds are against me. But it sure is fun pursuing the dream.

Shortly after giving birth to my future Major Leaguer, I came across a powerful quote. It read: "Successful is the man whose mother is his greatest fan." I promised then to make that my motto. I think I'll stick with it. Like my parents stuck with me. Next time my son looks to me for encouragement, I'll steal a line from Thoreau: "Go confidently in the direction of your dreams. Live the life you've imagined."

I hope my son makes the big leagues. If he falls short, well, so be it. It'll have been a great ride. If he makes it, I will revel in the missed opportunity to buy him a tie to go with those pinstripes.

~Kimberly A. Porrazzo

Editor's note: The author wrote this essay more than a decade ago. Her son never played baseball in college, but he was hired by the San Francisco Giants in 2010 as a video scout. That year, his first year working in baseball, the Giants won the World Series and he received the ultimate prize in baseball: a World Series ring!

Thanks for Letting Me Fail

Few things are more satisfying than seeing your children have teenagers of their own.
~Doug Larson

Whether you've got kids or not, everyone has watched another parent and thought, "Okay, I wouldn't do it that way." It all seems easy until you actually have to do it yourself. For me, the hardest thing about being a father is watching my kids fail without interfering.

This is a tough one. I thought I'd just give them the space, watch them struggle, watch them cry and get frustrated, then I'd give them some magical tip and they'd succeed. Ta-daaaa! No problem. I didn't realize that my heart would break for them while I watched. I didn't realize that I wouldn't always have the magical tip. I didn't realize that sometimes they wouldn't even want it; that they actually might want to do it wrong.

Now that I'm experiencing this, I've been thinking back to when I was a kid. I would tell my dad about my hair-brained ideas, and he would just smile and say, "Hmmm, sounds interesting. Let me know how it turns out." If I was really struggling with something, he would ask me a bunch of questions, and usually I would come up with my own answer.

How did he resist the urge to talk me out of stuff, to help me before I failed? It must have been painful to watch, because I tried a lot of stuff, and I failed at a lot of it. And yet, Dad was always there for me, the ultimate coach and supporter. He never tried to talk me out of things, or coach me in the right direction unless I asked. He gave me the room to screw up on my own. Maybe one of the best things he did for me as a father was to have the strength to stand by and watch me fail—to let me figure it out on my own.

It has occurred to me that this was a huge factor in the fact that, for the most part, I don't fear failure. Don't get me wrong, I don't like failure, but the risk of it never stops me from doing anything. I have had a life rich with travel, adventure, and widely varying experiences and friendships, most of which can be attributed to going out and trying things that somebody should have told me would fail. It was a gift my dad gave me—the confidence to screw up on my own, to attempt anything and see what happens.

I want to give that same gift to my kids. When they're coloring outside the lines, putting tape on crooked, or trying to jam the Barbie shoe on the wrong foot. Kids are in a perpetual state of learning, so that means they're screwing up constantly.

Today at cross-country ski training, Cassidy, my seven-year-old, was falling repeatedly trying to get up a hill. I kept taking a step forward, closer, closer... thinking, "Okay I'll help her... no I better not. Okay, now I'll help her... no, let her do it!" Then, finally, she figured out a way to crawl up, and it looked silly and she giggled loudly as she did it, full of excitement that she had conquered that hill. It wasn't good skiing form, but mission accomplished, and my lip still hurts from biting it.

I have a lot of work to do on watching the failures with a smile. Maybe I'll come up with some plan, some way to deal with it. Maybe someone I know already has some good ideas. Maybe I'll bounce them off my dad.

He'll probably say, "Hmmm, sounds interesting. Let me know how it turns out."

~Tim Brewster

Little Things Do
Make a Difference

Start by doing what's necessary, then what's possible, and
suddenly you are doing the impossible.
~Saint Francis

t tore at my daughter Laurie's heartstrings to hear the sobs of my granddaughter. This was the third time in a week there had been bullying problems at the elementary school my granddaughter attended.

Creative juices flowing, Laurie realized she had the perfect answer. It would take a lot of planning and even more time on her part, but Laurie became a woman on a mission.

After gaining the approval of the school principal, Laurie developed a program that would help the students focus on positive actions and words. She was about to inspire and motivate hundreds of children, and she realized a lot was at stake. *It has to work,* she thought. *It just has to!*

Laurie explained to the school staff that the students were to be encouraged to file reports on one another for their kind gestures, no matter how small the deed. "The interesting thing about it all," said Laurie, "is that it truly was the little things that they all began noticing." She picked up two reports at random and read them. "When I was by myself, Jeffry sat on the swing with me." "I slipped and cut myself on the ice, and Sara sat with me." Similar reports handed in by the school children eventually soared from the hundreds to well over the thousand mark.

"The children revealed a lot about what their concerns are during these early school years. I observed a noticeable pattern emerge in the reports," said Laurie. "The children spoke a lot about their appreciation for being included, their appreciation for having someone to play with, and their relief and appreciation when another student comforted them after a spill."

The response to the new program was astounding and was more than Laurie had hoped for. Participation by the students increased weekly. Subsequently, the load of volunteer work for this one parent increased by leaps and bounds. Students had filed sixty reports of kindness in one week alone.

"It became a challenge to fit everything on the bulletin board, and to keep it sparkling and colorful. The kids loved the glitter of the displays," Laurie said. She devoted hundreds of hours working both at home and at the school to prepare materials and build weekly displays to keep the children engaged.

The elementary school took on a conspicuous change. Kids were sharing lunches and opening doors for one another. Kindness thrived! Even the crossing guard at the crosswalk was reported for her acts of kindness. "The wonderful thing about this," observed Laurie, "was that the report was put in by a youngster who was so shy he had never even spoken to the crossing guard, although the guard had spoken words of encouragement to this particular child many times."

A child who held the reputation for being arrogant was suddenly helping another clean out her desk. One lonely child reported of a classmate: "When I needed a friend to play with, she was there." The reports went up weekly, but not just as ordinary reports. Each weekend Laurie chose a theme. One week she placed the names of the youngsters on lightning bolts, and another week every report was done on teddy bears, and yet another time on little T-shirts, all hanging on a clothesline.

The bulletin board itself was always eye-catching, and crowds gathered so that soon parents, teachers, and other staff were also gathering around to view the theme and designs for the new week.

When the school year drew to a close, Laurie took each and every "good deed" report and attached them to one long continuous roll of paper. Once posted, this was to be the final reminder to all — that little things do make a difference. She chose a time when only teachers were at the school, and she and her young daughter literally wrapped the school walls with over a thousand kindness reports.

Motivated by her concern for her daughter and the other children, one parent found a way to counteract bullying and meanness — by reporting acts of kindness.

"I sincerely believed, and still do, that an act of kindness should receive ten times the attention given to a deed that came about because of wrong choices. I wanted my program to encourage both students and adults to focus on the positive, on what is appreciated, not on what is annoying or hurtful."

On the final school day that year, Laurie asked the principal if the children could leave their classrooms and walk about to view this accumulated list of their good deeds and thoughtfulness. The students were told that any reports that featured their name could be taken home as souvenirs.

Choked with emotion, Laurie felt an overwhelming sense of satisfaction as she watched excited students gather around the reports, first reading them, then commenting and remembering. Students took great pride in how many reports bore their names and raced around the halls to retrieve the reports to take them home as mementos. In recognizing the smallest of gestures, these students made a huge difference in the lives of one another. Just wait until next year!

~Ellie Braun-Haley

How to Build a Sailboat

There's a long, long trail a-winding into the land of my dreams.
~Stoddard King, Jr.

When I was young, a few books were neatly stacked on the end table in our family room. One of those, about how to build a sailboat, always intrigued me. Its glossy photos of sleek craft cutting through turquoise water spoke of adventure. The step-by-step guidelines were written to convince readers like myself that building such a boat was as easy as following the directions on the back of a cake mix box. Yet I always opened that book with the same sense of puzzlement. My mom had given it to my dad for his birthday one year, and I guess the implication was that he wanted to build one. The puzzle was my mom thinking that dad would ever do it.

My dad was handy, no question. But growing up, he and my grandpa owned three department stores in our small town and the surrounding communities, and he worked Monday through Saturday every week that I could remember. On most evenings, he set up his bookkeeping at the kitchen table. Sunday was his only free day, and usually involved yard work or upkeep on our house, the three store buildings, or, as they aged, my grandmothers' houses. He built many practical things over the years—cabinets, shelves, a playhouse — but never a sailboat. I concluded, as I flipped the pages in that book, that though my dad dreamed of building such a master-piece, he just wasn't in a position to act on his dreams.

Dreams, I was sure, were things that one attained in the short term. I dreamed of a new bike, getting my braces off, or making the cheerleading team. My idea of a "long-term" dream back then was getting my ears pierced when I turned fifteen. It didn't occur to me that dreams could, or should, lurk for very long.

As malls and new highways were built in our rural communities and people found it easier to leave town to shop, my father's stores struggled. With my grandfather gone, my dad worked harder to keep it all together. Though Dad never let on, I'm sure his dreams at the time concentrated on just making payroll. Swept up in my own world of proms, graduation and college classes, I barely noticed that his fifty-hour weeks had increased to eighty.

As a married adult, I began to learn that some dreams, like saving for our first house, take time. About this time my dad announced that he was selling the stores and retiring. Looking back, I wonder why I was surprised. Preoccupied with my own life, I guess I hadn't noticed it had gotten that hard. "Dad," I remember asking with concern, "what will you do?" Now it was his turn to be surprised. Didn't I realize, he asked me, that there were so many things he'd just been waiting to do?

Dad dusted off those many dreams, prioritized a list, and never looked back. He's learned to scuba dive, has built local renown for his duck decoy carvings, hammered for Habitat for Humanity and recently ran as the only fifty-year graduate in the 5K Alumni race at his alma mater. He and Mom have traveled the world, taught English as a Second Language to new Americans and welcomed six grandchildren into the world.

It turns out that Dad knew a lot about dreams. He knew that sometimes, like it or not, they are shelved for the rigors of life. He taught me that as long as you have the courage to pull them back out, they can be as glossy and vibrant as ever. Dad never did build that sailboat. He swapped that dream for a more practical option in the landlocked Midwest, and got his pilot's license the year after he retired. He is now putting the finishing touches on a Starduster II biplane he has built from a starter pile of metal. I learned many things from my dad, but one of the most powerful has been the hope and happiness of reaching for life's dreams—even if they take time to build.

~Gail Wilkinson

Love, Mom

A hundred hearts would be too few
To carry all my love for you.
~Author Unknown

can't say I was sad to see my daughter Zoey go to kindergarten.
I love school so much that I have been continuously in school
for three decades as either a student or a teacher. I'd say I was
more excited for her than anything else. Zoey is like me—a rule
follower, a bookworm, and a social butterfly. She entered kindergarten
knowing how to read, and I was confident she'd enjoy every minute of
school.

As I packed her lunch on the first morning, I decided I'd write
a little note. I went to our dining room table, and I dug through the
craft supplies. I found a piece of construction paper and some stick-
ers. I created a very silly little card. I wrote, "Happy 1st Day of School
Lovey Dovey! Have fun. Be good. Remember manners matter! Love,
Mom." I did feel a small twinge as I thought of my little girl in a loud
and chaotic cafeteria. I felt better knowing she'd open her lunchbox
and see my note.

In the midst of telling us the details of her first day, we didn't
think to ask about lunch or the note. However, as the days turned
to weeks, I continued to make little cards—frequently related to the
seasons or a holiday. Some days I cut out a heart. Other days, I wrote
a poem. Occasionally, in the rush of the morning, my notes were me-

diocre, but I felt strongly that I should always include one. The notes became inside jokes with us — or so I thought.

One day, on the drive home from school, I asked Zoey, "Do you like the notes I write you?"

Perhaps I was having some parental insecurity or it was just a random thought. To my surprise, she replied, "We love them!"

What did she mean by "we?" What she said next inspires me to go the extra mile, even if it seems to be a small matter.

"We all read your notes. We take turns. Sophia, Courtney, Piper, and Emilee. One day the lunch lady who walks around had to tell us a word. She couldn't believe I could read!"

"What do all your friends think of your notes?" I asked, immediately worried they were yanking them from her tiny little hands and mocking her. Perhaps in her naïveté, she wouldn't know if they were making fun of her.

"They L-O-V-E my notes!"

"Oh, good," I said, relieved. I was now very thankful that I had always provided a note, albeit a lame one sometimes.

"Want to know something?" she added. .

"What?" I asked, contemplating my new wider audience.

"No matter who reads the note, we always know how it ends. When we get to the end part, we always say 'Love, Mom' together, really loud!"

"That is a very good thing to remember," I told her.

"We know! It is our favorite part," she replied, tugging her backpack out of the car and smiling at me over her shoulder.

~Amber Chandler

Becoming a Second Generation Parent

Life is what happens while you are busy making other plans.
~John Lennon

My husband Paul and I sat across the courtroom from his son Andrew and his girlfriend Tammy. Our lawyer sat beside us, the familiar yellow legal pad and expandable folder in front of her.

Andrew's extremely short hair was dyed black. Small sores and scabs peppered Tammy's arms and face; she'd been scratching at imaginary insects crawling on her skin again.

These sights did not compare though with the smell... their water had been shut off for almost an entire year. How they had lived in those conditions for so long was incomprehensible to Paul and me. The stench slapped us in the face the moment they entered and I stifled a gag as we rose to our feet as the judge entered.

After a small recess, the judge made his ruling. Two and a half million grandparents in this country are raising their grandchildren. Paul and I had just been added to those numbers.

Three years ago, I had my life planned. I was finishing my teaching degree, a dream I had had since I was a child. I had married a wonderful man whose children were already adults, and I had my daughter, Sarah, a high school sophomore. Life wasn't perfect but it was going along at a steady pace.

And then we got the phone call.

Andrew was Paul's older child and since we had been together, Paul had battled with Andrew over his substance abuse. We knew Andrew had a problem, but until he wanted to change, there wasn't anything we could do. It seemed as though he was getting his life on track that year; he had a decent construction job and he and his long-time girlfriend, Tammy, had just had a baby boy.

Unfortunately, we only saw Andrew and Sam a couple of times in the next few months. Andrew would give us excuses as to why we couldn't come by or take Sam for a visit. As new grandparents, Paul and I were hurt but optimistic that we could mend the rift in our family over time.

In February of 2007, I got a call from Child Protective Services. What they told me still makes me shudder, thinking of how Paul and I had been so oblivious to all the signs. The caseworker told us that Sam had tested positive for methamphetamines and THC (the drug in marijuana) at birth and had been taken away from Andrew and Tammy. Andrew hadn't even mentioned that Paul and I existed, and instead signed over temporary custody to Tammy's parents.

That same month everything changed when Tammy's parents tested positive for substance abuse as well. "We can either place Sam with you, or he will go into foster care," the caseworker told me in a matter-of-fact way.

I stood there with the phone clutched tightly in my hand staring at Paul's questioning face. "I understand," I choked out. "Could I call you back after I speak to my husband?" I hung up and turned to Paul. As I explained what she had told me, I could see Paul's heart breaking. "What should we do?" I asked him quietly.

"We really don't have any other choice but to bring him home with us," he answered, echoing my own thoughts.

A week later, we stood outside a small two-story house in the bitter north Texas wind. The yard was strewn with broken toys and trash. Dead weeds scratched against the side of the porch. The door's paint, blistered and peeling, reminded me of a three-day-old sunburn. I had never been to Tammy's parents' home, and its condition shocked me. This is where our grandson had been living?

As we entered the front room, my eyes quickly adjusted to the sight; a full-size bed, two playpens, and a small bassinet cluttered the small area. In the bassinet, shoved up against the television, a small bundle was squirming. I looked down into the crib to see Sam's blue eyes smiling up at me. "Why hello there, little one," I greeted him, and was quickly rewarded with a huge smile. I knew instantly that I would do whatever I could for this precious child.

We couldn't take him with us that day, which tore Paul and me to pieces. Over the next two weeks, along with my class schedule, Paul's work, and Sarah's school activities, we were also meeting with CPS, scheduling our own drug testing to prove we were clean, and trying to remember all the necessary items needed for a baby. At the end of March, just before Paul's birthday, Sam came home with us.

Andrew and Tammy had signed over temporary custody to Paul and me, and our hope was that this crisis would be the shock they needed to get straight. However, by June it was evident that they had no intention of changing their lifestyle or getting clean to get Sam back. Our CPS caseworker suggested we find a lawyer and Paul and I agreed.

In May of 2008, the judge awarded us full custody of Sam. Through research, I discovered that babies born to mothers addicted to meth can seem sluggish and have uncontrollable tremors. I learned that these babies have a higher risk of stroke before being born. Luckily, Sam is relatively healthy, and Paul and I monitor him closely for any signs that his development is lagging behind that of other children his age. While his development was slow in the beginning, he is now an active, happy three-year-old. Unfortunately, not enough research has been done on the long-term effects of methamphetamines on children.

Thankfully, Paul and I managed to weather this storm without any major damage to our marriage, but getting Sam came at a cost. Paul, who had dreams of retiring once I began teaching, had to change jobs to support the costs of a new baby. I had hoped to finish college in 2008, but I wasn't able to take summer classes and care for Sam at the same time. While our life hasn't worked out the way we planned, Paul and I would not have it any other way. We are amazed at how this little guy makes us feel both old and young at the same time. And while we might have to postpone our retirement plans of travel and relaxation, our new adventures with Sam will be priceless.

~Christine Long

Chapter
7

Raising Great Kids

Use the Power of Forgiveness

Midnight Grace

A mom forgives us all our faults, not to mention one or two we
don't even have.
~Robert Brault

om and I stood in the hallway, nose to nose. Her hands were on her hips and her feet peeped out from her long robe. Even her toes looked curled and angry.

"I think you'd better go to bed now," she said. "I'll be talking with your dad when he gets home. He'll be in to give you your consequence."

I spun around and stomped to my bedroom. Then I yanked the curtains shut, flipped the light switch, and plopped down on my bed. 10:15. The green digital numbers reported that my dad would be home from second shift soon. Dad was a gentle man, but I knew that I'd be in trouble. Worst of all, I deserved it.

I'd had the worst day at junior high school. My best friend, Mary Ellen, decided to join forces with cool-girl Regina. So there was no room for me at the lunch table. I ate my turkey-on-wheat alone, in the library, pretending to be immersed in a book. Then we square danced in P.E. class. I was nervous about holding hands with a boy. The boy was unkind, refused to hold my cold, clammy hand, and called me Trout for the rest of the day.

Of course, none of this had anything to do with my mom, except that I'd been terrible to her that afternoon. Years later I'd learn the terminology — misplaced anger — but on that day I'd just been hurt and mad and Mom was the retaliation target.

I watched the numbers morph until 10:30. "Might as well lie down," I muttered. I pulled back the comforter and slid between flannel sheets. As I lay there, I replayed the day's events through my mind.

Mom had baked cookies and they'd been fresh, piled on a plate, when I got home from school. Peanut butter. Sprinkled with sugar and imprinted with the tines of a fork.

"Couldn't you have made chocolate chip?" I said.

Mom looked up from the table where she helped my sister with her homework. "I could have," she said. "But I made peanut butter. Why don't you pour a glass of milk?" Then she smiled.

Later that night, when she pulled chicken from the oven, I balked again. Never mind that Dad was at work and Mom still put a nice meal on the table. I wanted hamburgers. "No one even likes that kind of chicken, Mom. Why didn't you make hamburgers?"

Mom breathed deep and ran her fingers through her long blond hair. "I made chicken and I've never heard anyone complain about it before," she said.

And it went downhill from there. I growled and complained until Mom hit her limit, lost her cool, and we had a shouting match in the hall.

By the time I heard the garage door open, I felt pretty bad about the whole thing.

I lay in bed and listened. The creak of the door. Dad's boots squeaking on the tile. Muffled voices in the kitchen. Then silence.

I wondered what my consequence would be. After soaking in the dark for a while, I didn't really care anymore. I'd hurt my mom. I'd seen it in her green eyes.

Why had I taken my troubles out on Mom? I knew that if I'd come home and shared what had happened, Mom would've listened. She would have offered encouragement and compassion. Then she would've said something funny and we'd have ended up laughing.

But I hadn't done that.

Before long, I heard Dad's quiet, bootless footfalls pass back down the hall. Then I heard the bathroom door shut. Then the rush of water. "Why is he taking his shower first?" I wondered.

The longer I waited, the heavier my heart felt. I considered getting up to apologize, but Mom didn't want to see me. I decided it was better to wait for Dad.

The sounds of the night were exaggerated in the dark. The rumble of the heater. The wind outside my window. Then a strange sound. A whirring from the kitchen. The clank of dishes. "What's going on?" I wondered.

The minutes stretched long, but finally my bedroom door creaked open. A shaft of light stretched across the room and stung my eyes. Soft footsteps to my bedside. Mom's hair slid past my cheek as she leaned over to whisper in my ear. "Why don't you come down to the kitchen?" she said.

I shimmied out of my bed and followed Mom through the bedroom and down the hall. As I passed the bathroom, I noticed the door was open. Dad had gone to bed. I was halfway to the kitchen when I smelled the thick, juicy scent of hamburgers.

I rounded the corner, puzzled, confused, and wondering if I'd fallen asleep and was dreaming. The kitchen table was set for two. "Have a seat," Mom said. She bent to lift a tray of French fries from the oven.

I sat.

Mom scooped the steamy fries to our plates and then poured thick, vanilla shakes into the tall glasses she'd set on the table. Then she slid two burgers from the griddle onto rolls and placed them on our plates. Then she sat down, too.

"Ketchup?" she asked. She tilted the bottle in my direction.

I reached out to grasp the bottle, but I couldn't. My eyes turned to my pajama-clad lap. "Mom, I've been awful to you today. I had a bad day at school and I came home and took it all out on you. You didn't deserve it. And I don't deserve this," I said. "I'm sorry."

I looked up.

Mom put the bottle down. She stretched her hand across the table. "You're in a tough spot, Shawnie. Halfway to being a woman. Halfway from being a girl. I remember those days." She smiled and tears welled in her eyes. "And I forgive you." She stretched her fingers toward me.

I reached out and took her hand, soft and comforting.

"Now," she said. "How about some ketchup for that burger?"

I wiped my own tears and nodded.

Mom and I sat in the kitchen and munched burgers while the night wrapped around our house. We slurped shakes, crunched fries, laughed and cried.

And I learned a lot about grace.

It's now twenty-seven years later, and I'm the mother of five sons. They are good boys, but there are many, many times when a hefty consequence is laid out for one of them. And rightly so.

But then there are the other times. The times when I remember that night. The silence of the dark broken by Mom's laughter. The warmth of her hand around mine. The sizzle of the burgers and the salty, crisp fries.

The night when I should've been served a consequence.

But instead, my precious mom pulled out the griddle, wiped the dust from the blender, and dished up a hearty portion of grace.

~Shawnelle Eliasen

A Few Kind Words

No one rises to low expectations.
~Les Brown

What would it take to reach him? His name was Gary. He was sixteen years old. He had already had several brushes with the law and had done time in several juvenile correctional facilities. Now, he sat in my classroom bored and defiant. What would it take?

He had linked up with another young man in the class who had a background that was strikingly similar to his background. His name was Lee. Lee, like Gary, had committed some offenses and done some time. Both of them had brilliant minds. They both had little respect for authority. Gary and Lee would do whatever they felt they were grown enough to do. Sometimes they would just sit in the back of the room and play around on Lee's laptop, composing beats and making up raps. At other times, they would hold conversations and freely use profane language. Some days, they would get up and walk out of class without permission, and then there were those days when the two of them would not bother to come to class at all. I am ashamed to say that I was grateful for those days. Sometimes, the battlefield called the inner-city classroom can be such a draining place that you are thankful to receive a moment of peace, no matter how it comes to you. I knew I had a job to do, but I wondered what it would take.

When the time came to distribute the first progress report of the year, I did so with a little trepidation. I knew that there would be a confrontation because of what I had written on Gary's report in the teacher's comment section. I started off by saying that Gary was very bright. I then went on to say that he could be rude and disrespectful. I even commented on his open use of profanity in the classroom. I approached him, handed him his report and went on to distribute the rest of the reports to his classmates. I watched out of the corner of my eye as he read his report. I noticed no significant change in his facial expression, so I relaxed just a little bit. As I headed for my desk, Gary called to me. I went toward him determined to stand my ground.

"Did you write this?"

"Yes, I did."

"What do you mean, I'm disrespectful?"

"I mean what I say."

"I don't disrespect you."

"You disrespect me every day. You talk over me while I'm trying to teach class. You…"

"I don't disrespect you."

"Okay, Gary. But I believe you do."

I walked to the front of the room and attempted to begin to teach class. As I spoke, Gary made sure he was speaking. He matched me word for word, sentence for sentence. It got so bad that I had to stop what I was doing to address him. I asked him to leave, and he refused. The situation escalated to the point where the principal had to come and intervene. I went home from school that day with the question looming larger than it ever had before. What would it take?

As I rode to school the next day, I hoped that I would not have to see Gary at all. I was at a loss. I did not know what to do. I felt as though I would never reach him. Though I had pondered the question over and over again, I still did not know what it would take. When I pulled up in front of the school, the very first person that I saw was Gary. I lifted my eyes toward heaven, sighed and asked, "What now?"

A still, small voice responded, "Apologize."

My reaction was, "Apologize? I didn't do anything to him!"

Once again, the still, small voice responded, gently urging me to apologize. I was determined not to apologize but the still, small voice began to give me some much-needed instruction.

"Apologize. He has no one in his life speaking positive things to him. He only gets to hear the negative. He needs someone to speak life to him. Apologize, and speak life."

It was quite a humbling moment, a moment of epiphany, the moment when I finally knew what it would take. It was so simple, yet so profound. All it would take was a kind word.

At first, I didn't know what I had to apologize for, but as I thought about it, it became clear: disrespect. I was to apologize for disrespecting *him*. Though I had started his progress report off with the comments concerning how bright he was, that point never came up in our conversation. Only the negative came up, not the positive. I swallowed my pride and approached the bench where he was sitting munching on a snack cake and drinking a juice.

"Gary?"

"Yeah," he said as he looked up.

"I just wanted to apologize. If you feel I disrespected you, that was never my intention. It's just that you have so much going for you. You are so bright and talented, I would be remiss if I allowed you to sit around and not reach your full potential. Disrespect was never my intent. I am sorry."

He looked at me, and I saw something in his eyes I had never seen before: hope. I walked away from him sensing I had said and done the right thing.

When it came time for me to teach his class, I walked in the classroom and was met by a brand-new Gary. The transformation in him was almost startling. He was attentive. He participated in the class. He asked questions. He answered questions. From that day on, he continued to learn, grow and develop. Our relationship developed to the point where we were able to talk about a lot of things. He came to me often for guidance and direction.

Gary is no longer at our school. He had to leave when his father's military unit was transferred to another state. It happened suddenly — so suddenly that I didn't get to say good-bye. I was hurt when I heard he had left us, but I know he didn't leave us without having received what he needed.

What would it take to reach him? His name was Gary. He was sixteen years old. He had already had several brushes with the law and had done time in several juvenile correctional facilities. Now, he had sat in my classroom bored and defiant. What would it take? All that it took was a few kind words.

~Nancy Gilliam

Father Forgets

*We never realize ourselves so vividly as when we are in the
full glow of love for others.*
~Author Unknown

Listen, son. I am saying this as you lie asleep, one little paw crumpled under your cheek and the blond curls sticky wet on your damp forehead. I have stolen into your room alone. Just a few minutes ago, as I sat reading my paper in the library, a stifling wave of remorse swept over me. Guiltily, I came to your bedside.

These are the things I was thinking, son. I had been cross to you. I scolded you as you were dressing for school because you gave your face merely a dab with a towel. I took you to task for not cleaning your shoes. I called out angrily when you threw some of your things on the floor.

At breakfast, I found fault, too. You spilled things. You gulped down your food. You put your elbows on the table. You spread butter too thick on your bread. And as you started off to play and I made for my train, you turned and waved a hand and called, "Good-bye, Daddy!" and I frowned and said in reply, "Hold your shoulders back!"

Then it began all over again in the late afternoon. As I came up the road, I spied you, down on your knees playing marbles. There were holes in your socks. I humiliated you before your friends by marching you ahead of me to the house. Socks were expensive — and if you had to buy them, you would be more careful! Imagine that, son, from a father!

Do you remember, later, when I was reading in the library, how you came in, timidly, with a sort of hurt look in your eyes? When I glanced up over my paper, impatient at the interruption, you hesitated at the door. "What is it you want?" I snapped.

You said nothing, but ran across in one tempestuous plunge, and threw your arms around my neck and kissed me, and your small arms tightened with affection that God had set blooming in your heart and that even neglect could not wither. And then you were gone, pattering up the stairs.

Well, son, it was shortly afterwards that my paper slipped from my hands and a terrible sickening fear came over me. What has habit been doing to me? The habit of finding fault, of reprimanding — this was my reward to you for being a boy. It was not that I did not love you; it was that I expected too much of you. I was measuring you by the yardstick of my years.

And there was so much that was good and fine and true in your character. The little heart of you was as big as the dawn itself over the wide hills. This was shown by your spontaneous impulse to rush in and kiss me goodnight. Nothing else matters tonight, son. I have come to your bedside in the darkness, and I have knelt here, ashamed!

It is a feeble moment; I know you would not understand these things if I told them to you during your waking hours. But tomorrow, I will be a real daddy! I will chum with you and suffer when you suffer, and laugh when you laugh. I will bite my tongue when impatient words come. I will keep saying as if it were a ritual: "He is a little boy — let him be a little boy!"

I am afraid I have visualized you as a man. Yet as I see you now, son, crumpled and weary in your bed, I see that you are still a baby. Yesterday you were in your mother's arms, your head on her shoulder. I have asked too much of you, yet given too little of myself. Promise me, as I teach you to have the manners of a man, that you will remind me how to have the loving spirit of a child.

~W. Livingston Larned

Stranger than Fiction

In Israel, in order to be a realist, one must believe in miracles.
~David Ben-Gurion

W hen the Old and New Cities of Jerusalem were reunited in 1967, a recently widowed Arab woman, who had been living in Old Jerusalem since 1948, wanted to see once more the house in which she formerly lived. Now that the city was one, she searched for and found her old home. She knocked on the door of the apartment, and a Jewish widow came to the door and greeted her. The Arab woman explained that she had lived there until 1948 and wanted to look around. She was invited in and offered coffee. The Arab woman said, "When I lived here, I hid some valuables. If they are still here, I will share them with you half and half."

The Jewish woman refused. "If they belonged to you and are still here, they are yours." After much discussion back and forth, they entered the bathroom, loosened the floor planks, and found a hoard of gold coins. The Jewish woman said, "I shall ask the government to let you keep them." She did and permission was granted.

The two widows visited each other again and again, and one day the Arab woman told her, "You know, in the 1948 fighting here, my husband and I were so frightened that we ran away to escape. We grabbed our belongings, took the children, and each fled separately. We had a three-month-old son. I thought my husband had taken him, and he thought I had. Imagine our grief when we were reunited in Old Jerusalem to find that neither of us had taken the child."

The Jewish woman turned pale, and asked the exact date. The Arab woman named the date and the hour, and the Jewish widow told her: "My husband was one of the Israeli troops that entered Jerusalem. He came into this house and found a baby on the floor. He asked if he could keep the house and the baby, too. Permission was granted."

At that moment, a twenty-year-old Israeli soldier in uniform walked into the room, and the Jewish woman broke down in tears. "This is your son," she cried.

This is one of those incredible tales we hear. And the aftermath? The two women liked each other so much that the Jewish widow asked the Arab mother: "Look, we are both widows living alone. Our children are grown up. This house has brought you luck. You have found your son, or our son. Why don't we live together?" And they do.

~Rabbi Hillel E. Silverman

That's What Friends Do

No matter who we are, no matter how successful, no matter what our situation, compassion is something we all need to receive and give.
~Catherine Pulsifer

ack tossed the papers on my desk, his eyebrows knit into a straight line as he glared at me.

"What's wrong?" I asked.

He jabbed a finger at the proposal. "Next time you want to change anything, ask me first," he said, turning on his heels, leaving me stewing in anger.

How dare he treat me like that, I thought. I had changed one long sentence and corrected grammar, something I thought I was paid to do.

It's not that I hadn't been warned. Other women who had worked my job before me called Jack names I couldn't repeat. One coworker took me aside the first day. "He's personally responsible for two different secretaries leaving the firm," she whispered.

As the weeks went by, I grew to despise Jack. His actions made me question much that I believed in, such as turning the other cheek and loving your enemies. Jack quickly slapped a verbal insult on any cheek turned his way. I prayed about the situation, but to be honest,

I wanted to put Jack in his place, not love him.

One day another of his episodes left me in tears. I stormed into his office, prepared to lose my job if needed, but not before I let the man know how I felt. I opened the door and Jack glanced up. "What?" he asked abruptly.

Suddenly I knew what I had to do. After all, he deserved it.

I sat across from him and said calmly, "Jack, the way you've been treating me is wrong. I've never had anyone speak to me that way. As a professional, it's wrong, and I can't allow it to continue."

Jack snickered nervously and leaned back in his chair. I closed my eyes briefly. *God help me,* I prayed.

"I want to make you a promise. I will be a friend," I said. "I will treat you as you deserve to be treated, with respect and kindness. You deserve that. Everybody does." I slipped out of the chair and closed the door behind me.

Jack avoided me the rest of the week. Proposals, specs and letters appeared on my desk while I was at lunch, and my corrected versions were not seen again. I brought cookies to the office one day and left a batch on his desk. Another day I left a note. "Hope your day is going great," it read.

Over the next few weeks, Jack reappeared. He was reserved, but there were no other episodes. Coworkers cornered me in the break room. "Guess you got to Jack," they said. "You must have told him off good."

I shook my head. "Jack and I are becoming friends," I said in faith. I refused to talk about him. Every time I saw Jack in the hall, I smiled at him. After all, that's what friends do.

One year after our "talk," I discovered I had breast cancer. I was thirty-two, the mother of three beautiful young children, and scared. The cancer had metastasized to my lymph nodes and the statistics were not great for long-term survival. After my surgery, friends and loved ones visited and tried to find the right words. No one knew what to say, and many said the wrong things. Others wept, and I tried to encourage them. I clung to hope myself.

One day, Jack stood awkwardly in the doorway of my small, darkened hospital room. I waved him in with a smile. He walked over to my bed and without a word placed a bundle beside me. Inside the package lay several bulbs.

"Tulips," he said.

I grinned, not understanding.

He shuffled his feet, then cleared his throat. "If you plant them when you get home, they'll come up next spring. I just wanted you to know that I think you'll be there to see them when they come up."

Tears clouded my eyes, and I reached out my hand. "Thank you," I whispered. Jack grasped my hand and gruffly replied, "You're welcome. You can't see them now, but next spring you'll see the colors I picked out for you. I think you'll like them." He turned and left without another word.

For ten years, I have watched those red-and-white striped tulips push their way through the soil every spring.

In a moment when I prayed for just the right word, a man with very few words said all the right things.

After all, that's what friends do.

~T. Suzanne Eller

Secret Smiles

*We should all have one person who knows how to bless us despite
the evidence. Grandmother was that person to me.*
~Phyllis Theroux

Crash! I stop sweeping the back patio. "Cody, what happened?"

"Nothin', Grandma."

"Are you bouncing that ball in my living room?"

Silence.

"Well?"

"I'm not now."

Cody is my first grandchild. He's a perpetual motion six-year-old. He's adorable and I love him from his sweaty head to his grubby toes. He makes me laugh and allows me to look at the world through his young, curious eyes. His gap-toothed grin melts my heart. Just when I think my old, exhausted body can't take another minute, he does something so sweet and caring that tears form in my eyes.

I pick up my leaf piles, toss them into the garbage can, and put the broom and dustpan away. I slide open the patio door and look for a first grader who is supposedly doing his homework. Silence is alleged to be golden, but this is too quiet. What's that kid done now? Where is he? What do I smell? Faint whiffs of peppermint linger in the air.

Hurrying into the living room, I glance at the glass shelves holding my treasures. Everything appears unscathed. All the porcelain figurines are in place. My eyes land on my favorite. The dancing girl's head sits at a jaunty angle and she looks quite sticky. Hidden behind a chair I spy an open jar of peppermint-scented paste.

Cody tiptoes into the room and throws his arms around my waist. "That girl's head sort of fell off, but I fixed it," he whispers. "Can this be our secret? And we won't tell my mom, okay? I'm really, really, really sorry, Grandma."

Cody's apology corrects my priorities. Treasures don't sit on shelves; they sneak up behind you and throw their arms around your waist. I can super-glue my dancing girl later. Right now it's hugging time.

* * *

Years later my daughter looks at my porcelain figurines on the shelves. "I've always liked this one best." She picks up the dancing girl. "Did you know there's a crack line around her neck?" Nineteen-year-old Cody and I share a smile.

~Sharon Landeen

Forgiveness Is Possible

*Do all things with love... keep your love in your heart. Being
deeply loved by someone gives you strength, while loving someone
deeply gives you courage.*
~Jackielou Camacho

t was November 2011 and I was driving home from a very long
day at the office. When a call from my ex-husband interrupted
the blissful silence of my drive, I wondered if I was ready for one
of his raging phone calls. We had divorced six years earlier, and
unfortunately his anger toward me for the divorce had not softened. We
only spoke to each other if absolutely necessary. I hesitantly answered
the phone. I hoped my chipper attitude would help set the tone for our
exchange.

His words took my breath away. He had stage IV esophageal and
stomach cancer.

All I was able to whisper was, "I am sorry, so sorry."

Tears stung my eyes as I thought of our children who were seventeen and fifteen, too young to lose a father. My head swam with questions as I pulled into my driveway. How would the children handle
the loss of their father? Who would take care of him? I ran into the
house as I retched up my lunch. My head hung over the toilet bowel
as tears streamed down my face.

My phone rang again; it was my real estate agent. I was numb
from my ex-husband's news when she excitedly told me there was an

offer on my home.

"That's great," I mumbled.

As I hung up the phone, I wondered about the statistical probability that I would receive an offer on my home the same night that my ex-husband was diagnosed with terminal cancer? My house had been on the market for three years. Clearly the universe had spoken to me. In that moment I knew what I needed to do.

I resolved to move the children and myself in with him. I had faith that this would be a turning point for my ex-husband, and he would embrace spending quality time with our children. They would have the opportunity to know their father. I worried the caretaker role would fall on my daughter otherwise. If we moved in together, I could assume this role so my children would not be burdened with the responsibility.

Despite my resolve, I was concerned. I had worked so hard to divorce my husband and the process had been scary. How could I live with him again? Everyone thought my idea was crazy, even our children.

We moved in just before Christmas and began a sophisticated dance of living as a family unit once again. The children had spent very little time with their father in the years since our divorce, with infrequent visitation. My hope was that they would have the opportunity to get to know their father and reconnect. We would live together for the next ten months. It was not easy. We had our share of tender moments and we had our share of meltdowns.

A few months into living together, the stress began to take a toll on me. Each day his actions and behavior brought up old hurts and wounds from the past. The anxiety-related anger and hostility created irregular heart rhythms. I was reliving our history each day. I knew I must do something to break the cycle. I had to find forgiveness.

Over the next few weeks, I searched for answers on the Internet and in bookstores, but nothing resonated with me. I was desperate to block the pain of the past. I wanted to stop replaying the old movies from years ago that were triggering my emotions. While I could not control his actions, I could control my emotions. I could chose to feel like a victim or embrace happiness and separate myself from his behavior.

We are a product of our lifetime of experiences, and his shaped his choices. He grew up angry, defensive and afraid. Every bad choice he made was driven by his fear. The minute I stopped judging my ex-husband's actions, I broke the link between his behaviors and my emotions. When I could view his actions without judging them, I no longer felt any emotion toward his conduct. By separating his actions from my emotions, I created space in my heart where I planted the seeds of empathy and compassion, and forgiveness began to grow.

My days became happier and calmer. Peace filled the house as forgiveness took root. I often felt as though my energy was reverberating at a higher, more harmonious level, which gave me strength.

It is easy to say the words, "I forgive," but they have no impact if your actions are not aligned with your thoughts. So I began to place the intention of forgiveness into every daily chore and interaction. Cooking has always been the way I demonstrated love for my family and friends. As the end approached, I hosted many lunches and dinners for friends and family in our home so they could say their goodbyes.

The payoff came one bright sunny morning just a few weeks before he passed. We were preparing for the last set of guests to arrive. Only family would be allowed to visit after this day. He thanked me for entertaining the multitude of friends over the last week. As he left the room, he turned and said he loved me and without thinking I responded, "I love you too."

I was stunned as the reality of my words sunk in. It was an honest moment, and I did love him. Not as my husband, but as the father of our children. I loved him for just being a human being, a child of God. Forgiveness had given me the ability to stop judging him and accept him for who he was. I was finally at peace with our past. It was time to let go of our history, so we could both move on. A warm glow washed over me, filled with the power of grace and forgiveness.

Just three weeks later, he passed peacefully at home early one morning in his bedroom with our family dog by his side.

Today both our children are in college and embracing life without their father. The time we spent together building positive memories as a family has helped to soften the grief process for them. Most importantly, we have experienced the power of forgiveness.

~Karen Todd Scarpulla

My Finest Teachers

Remember, we all stumble, every one of us. That's why it's a comfort to go hand in hand.
~Emily Kimbrough

I was five years old when I first learned how cruel kids could be. My friend and I were riding the bus to school, and a little girl with blond hair was sitting behind us. We didn't know her, but we knew her name was Sue.

As Sue sat there, my friend and I began to hurt her. We pushed her and scratched at her arm. We said mean things to her. *What had prompted this most hurtful and cruel behavior? What had she done?* Nothing.

Her only "crime" was that she looked different. Her mouth was different than ours, and when she spoke, it sounded different. She sat silently and endured our cruelty. She could have called to the bus driver or told us to stop, but she chose not to.

After arriving at school, I was called to the principal's office. I can still remember the look on Mrs. Barto's face and the sadness in her eyes as she asked me why I had done this. I hung my head and said I didn't know, and I honestly didn't. That was the sad part. That was the last day Sue ever came to our school.

Years later, in high school, I met Sue again. She was nice to me. Although she didn't recognize me, I knew it was Sue. I could still see the mild trace of a scar on her upper lip. I wanted to tell her how sorry I was, that I was the mean little kid who had taunted her that day, but instead I hid in the anonymity of being a teenager. She never knew it was me, and I never had the courage to tell her.

In a hospital room some twenty-six years after kindergarten, my fifth baby was born. The words they used to describe him were hard for me to hear, "Down syndrome."

As I looked at my newborn son, my heart ached. All I could think about was Sue. *Had her mother held her and loved her, just as I did with my David?* Of course, she had. Though David looked different to the doctors, he looked beautiful to me. All of a sudden, I realized that, someday, others might be as cruel to David as I had been to Sue — all because he was different.

It felt like my life was shattering. I felt like God had made a mistake in sending David to me. I was sure some other mother could love him more and be a better mom. I knew I didn't have what it took to be the mother of a child with a disability. This was more than I could bear.

Then a phone call came to the hospital. It was my friend Kris. With her usual enthusiasm, she greeted me with, "I heard you have a beautiful baby boy!" My mind raced. Surely, no one had told her about my baby because they didn't want to hurt her. They knew that her daughter Kari was profoundly mentally and physically disabled and was not expected to live very long.

I never quite understood Kris. She treated Kari as you would any baby. I never once saw that look of disappointment that I thought the mother of a child with a severe disability should have. Secretly, I wondered if she really understood how bad off Kari was.

I didn't know the words to say, but I knew I had to tell her the truth. Through my tears, I replied, "I do, Kris, but he's handicapped."

Immediately, and with excitement in her voice, she said, "I know. Isn't that wonderful?"

I was so taken aback. When she said that, it was almost as if she were sharing a delightful secret that only she and I knew. *How could she, of all people, be happy for me?* Something in her voice gave me hope.

Yet, even with that hope, I struggled. I have never grieved so much for anything or anyone as I did for my David.

Are there still unkind children left in this world? Perhaps, but my experience has been that most kids are good and kind.

Sue taught me forgiveness. It is because of her that I can forgive myself for how I once treated her, as well as for my uninformed thoughts regarding my son.

Kris taught me acceptance. She taught me to be able to see what others could not — the worth of a child.

I remembered how Kris had told me that when Kari was born, the doctors had told her to take her baby home and just love her because she would not live through the weekend. Kris told me that when she got home, she made a list of the things she wanted to do before her baby died. She wanted to kiss her and sing to her. She wanted to rub baby lotion on her and put a pink bow in her hair. She wanted to cut a locket of her hair and tell her how much she loved her. Kris told me she considered each day after completing the items on that list a Bonus Day. God gave Kris 3,779 bonus days.

But it has been my son, David, who has become my finest teacher. He has taught me that the only sadness I should feel at the birth of a child with a disability is for those who have not learned how to love him yet.

~Gina Johnson

Just a Little Phone Call

A man cannot free himself from the past more easily than he can
from his own body.
~André Maurois

The backs of my thighs were beginning to feel cold from the linoleum. I had been sitting there for twenty minutes trying to make a phone call, but had only managed to push three of the numbers. This wasn't the first time I had attempted to call him. But something deep inside said this was the day.

I inhaled deeply, dialed the phone number and exhaled. Through the pictures that had been torn and tossed, the memories that had been forgotten and the stories that had been left untold, that phone number was etched in my mind. It stayed there despite my attempts to forget. It was as if my mind knew I might want it someday.

"Hello." It was him, I was certain. The voice was so familiar — a combination of Yonkers and a rough life of sixty-five years. Although I was calling from my kitchen thirteen states away, his voice overwhelmed the space as if he were in the same room. For a moment I couldn't breathe. I thought about hanging up.

"Hello," he repeated.

"Hey, Dad, it's me, Kierstan."

Without missing a beat he responded. "Well hello stranger, what's new?"

Did he really just ask me "what's new?" What an absolutely complicated question, yet so expected. Where could I start? I could share how the weather had turned really cold and my herbs are starting to die. I've never been able to keep anything alive. Perhaps I could brag for a few minutes about installing a light dimmer. Maybe he would like to hear about my successful Thanksgiving dinner that I cooked entirely by myself for my boyfriend and me. I'd even admit the turkey was slightly dry. This sounded like typical father/daughter subject matter. The only problem was, we weren't typical. It had been fourteen years since we'd last spoken. Yet the comfort in his voice bid me on and I was desperate to keep that connection.

How do you sum up half of your life? In fourteen years I went through middle school, high school, college, a year of law school and eventually earned a master's degree. I had lived with my grandma and grandpa. I had lived with my aunt and uncle. I had lived with a roommate. I had lived alone. I was with my mother, his wife, before she died. I had been to four continents. I had lived in five different states. I had been married. I was divorced. All of this would be news to him.

The last time I had seen my dad I was in sixth grade. I thought about starting there. I ended up winning that science fair, thanks for the help. I broke up with Tom a few days later. I wore braces most of middle school, although the gap between my two front teeth was never corrected. I joined the middle school cross-country team. I loved running though I've never been very good. When I looked back I realized the moments that make up everyday life are experienced with wholeness from using all your senses. Despite the desire to share my past, pieces would be missed in its retelling.

Part of me thought I'd really like to take this slowly, just tell him a little at a time, bite-size pieces. He would understand that, he's a chef. But another part of me had this impulse to tell him everything as fast as I could. I couldn't be sure if he would answer again should I call another day. I needed to tell him who I was, just so he would know. But how do you tell someone who you are when you aren't absolutely certain yourself?

For years I would say to myself, "If I ever talk to my dad again,

I'm going to tell him…." I wished now I had written some of those things down. I wished now I hadn't waited so long to call. But I felt fragile beneath the strength of his words, or rather, his silence. I had woken up this morning with the realization that if my dad chose to hang up the phone or talk to me, either way I would manage. I would heal. I was prepared for that. From the initial hello, I felt complete in spaces I had not realized were empty. I am so glad he did not hang up.

"What's new, Dad?" I said. "Well, everything's new and so much is exactly as you'd remember. I made it; or rather I'm making it every day. I'm not perfect but I just recently decided that I am pretty proud of the woman I'm becoming, and I think, should you choose to get to know me, you might be proud of me, too. I miss mom. I became a social worker and I'm certain she influenced that decision. By God's sense of humor I look just like you, Dad. I'm creative like you, though in different ways. I'm not particularly religious, though I think God's been looking out for me. Most importantly, I'm not angry anymore. I guess what I am trying to say is, if you call me I'll answer."

He gave me the score of the Cub's game, recited to me a lamb recipe I will never make and told me he had a box of pictures. Would I like it if he sent them? He wasn't overly sentimental but he was exactly as I remembered, and that seemed enough. The conversation flowed easily. We laughed a lot. So much of my sense of humor comes from him. After about an hour, we decided to hang up, but before we did he surprised me.

"I love you," he said.

And just like that, I felt like someone's daughter.

~Kierstan Gilmore

Hello, My Name Is Claire and I'm an Alcoholic

A desire to be in charge of our own lives, a need for control, is born in each of us. It is essential to our mental health, and our success, that we take control.

~Robert F. Bennett

am an alcoholic. It took half my lifetime to admit it. I kept thinking that if I did, it would give me a label I wasn't ready to wear. I am so many other things first: a wife, a writer, a ballet teacher, a child of God.

I have no blatant, dramatic war stories, I didn't suffer any losses and I never hit rock bottom, which is typically the thing that leads to the undeniable admission of alcoholism. What I had instead was suspicion and a psychological dependency that grew until it took over completely.

Alcohol is in the very fabric of the culture in which I was raised. In the Deep South, very little is done without it. It stands sentry at the center of every social gathering from the cradle to the grave, and I never questioned it or considered it unusual in the least because it was always just there. Outside of the house I grew up in, alcohol was everywhere, and within the walls of the house, varying bottles held pride of place on a large, silver serving tray upon a marble console in the living room. Every night, when the grandfather clock in the entrance hall approached five o'clock, I could find my mother in the living room, seated elegantly across from my father, holding what would be the first of three Scotch and sodas. This was how my parents reviewed the happenings of the day and it left me with an implied template of civility, which I carried outside of my childhood, and into the life I would create.

Because alcohol was in my life, because I was someone who used it socially, I formed many friendships with women who did the same. It gave us a reason to get together after work; it dictated the venue and gave us something to bond over. We'd talk about our work, our relationships and our lives expansively, and boy, we had some good times. The men we were attracted to did the same, so suffice it to say, alcohol was also at the heart of our romantic relationships. The two-year courtship I had with my husband was fueled by champagne, and our wedding wasn't any different. When the honeymoon was over, we settled into the rhythm of our lives. After we set up home and hearth, I had my own silver serving tray of liquor bottles on a marble console.

And, I was indiscriminate. I drank when I felt celebratory and I drank when I was stressed or sad. I had many different justifications. I was indiscriminate in the blind way that one foot unthinkingly follows the other, until a distance has been covered and you turn around and recognize how you arrived at the very place you are standing. When I finally turned and looked behind me, it was three in the morning, I was holding a wine glass in my hand, and my husband had retreated to the master bedroom in anger hours before. I was outside on the patio praying to God for my life to change.

"Please, God," I begged. "I'll do anything you want, just please, please, change my life."

I had this vision that one day I was going to be whole, one day I was going to be fulfilled, one day I was going to be the person I always suspected I could be. I could almost feel the best-case scenario of myself living and breathing but I couldn't fathom what it would take to usher in the change until a thought occurred to me: "Why don't you start by putting down that glass you're holding?"

When I did put down the wine glass, I woke up my husband with these words, "I need to go to treatment and I need to go today."

I pressed pause on my life and went to treatment for thirty days. While there, I became a voracious student of the disease of alcoholism. I wanted to know everything there is to know about it. I became the focus of my own case study, sponging up all the information until I was saturated. Admitting that I am an alcoholic wasn't enough for me; I wanted to know why I am one. I wanted to know what got me there. I wanted to know why I was anesthetizing myself.

If you're reading this and saying to yourself that you can relate to any point within whatsoever; if there is a nagging similarity to your relationship with alcohol and mine, then there is a good chance that you have someone in your bloodline who can say the same. That's what I learned in treatment. It didn't take the onus off me but it did help alleviate my self-judgment. I am after all, a nice girl from a nice background; it's just that I had this genetic time bomb that lay dormant until I set it off like an atom blast whose fallout will go on forever. It doesn't make me a bad person; it just makes me an alcoholic.

The hardest part of all of this was admitting that I have a problem with alcohol. But now that I have, the self-exploratory work that has ensued has been liberating and my life has turned drastically in a positive direction. It must have something to do with the adage of when you see your enemy, call it by name and the truth is, I can't hear myself say it often enough:

"Hello, my name is Claire and I am an alcoholic."

~Claire Fullerton

Chapter
8

Raising Great Kids

Think Outside the Box

Pizza Night

A grandmother is a little bit parent, a little bit teacher, and a little bit best friend.
~Author Unknown

My first week at college was rough. I already had two quizzes to study for, a project to begin, and a pile of lecture notes to review. My financial aid was a mess, and my roommate wouldn't speak to me. Everything was unfamiliar, and I didn't know anyone. This was not how I had planned things.

While I was only three hours from home, it seemed much farther. I couldn't wait until the weekend.

Finally, it was Friday. I told my roommate I was going home. He actually acknowledged me by nodding his head once. If Western had a degree in video games, this guy would get an A. As I drove home, I prayed and asked the Lord to please take my mess and take control over it.

I got home and no one was there. "Great," I thought. "Just when I need them the most." Then, out of the blue, it occurred to me that I hadn't seen my grandmother in weeks even though she only lived ten minutes away.

Expecting no company, Grandma's porch light was out. I could see the light of the TV flickering in the window. I knocked at the door and heard Grandma coming to the door. Suddenly, I was blinded by the porch light and the door swung open. "Well, hello there! I sure didn't expect to see you," she exclaimed.

Pictures of all the grandkids crowded the mantle and every available space on every shelf in the living room. The ceramic pig that had given Grandpa the last smile I saw him smile sat on a shelf across the room from me. I still remembered giving it to him for Christmas more than fifteen years ago. The wooden duck our last pastor had carved for Grandma and Grandpa sat on yet another shelf. I could see into the kitchen from where I sat and noticed the door to the stairwell. That stairwell led to an upstairs adventure paradise for us grandkids for so many years.

I was already glad I had come to see Grandma. We talked about my week. I had so much to tell. I had been there for over an hour when Grandma asked me something I never thought I'd hear her ask. "I have a pizza in the freezer. You in the mood for pizza?" she asked.

"You like pizza, Grandma?"

"I love pizza, especially after I doctor it up!"

Grandma is well known for her cooking. I couldn't imagine what doctoring up a pizza meant to her.

As we added extra cheese, pepperoni, and peppers to the pizza, I realized I had never really had a conversation with Grandma until that night. My grandfather had passed away nearly fifteen years earlier, and I always regretted that I never really got to talk to Grandpa. I suddenly felt so blessed to have this evening with Grandma. The pizza turned out awesome. The best pizza I had ever had, in fact.

The thing I noticed about Grandma was that she really listened to me. Often, I find myself interrupting people to give advice. I realized that sometimes we just need to listen. Grandma would only occasionally say, "Just pray about it."

So I prayed about my situation all weekend. The next week was so much better. I didn't even go home that next weekend. I hadn't even realized that Western had such a beautiful campus. I had been blinded by my troubles but Jesus had removed the trouble. Now I could see.

I started making a point to get to Grandma's at least once a month for pizza. We still have those pizza nights four years later. I'm just thankful that the Lord led me to Grandma when I needed an ear. As the ways of the Lord often turn out, I got so much more.

~William Mark Baldwin

Rest in Peace:
The "I Can't" Funeral

Optimism is the foundation of courage.
~Nicholas Murray Butler

Donna's fourth-grade classroom looked like many others I had seen in the past. Students sat in five rows of six desks. The teacher's desk was in the front and faced the students. The bulletin board featured student work. In most respects it appeared to be a traditional elementary classroom. Yet something seemed different that day I entered it for the first time. There seemed to be an undercurrent of excitement.

Donna was a veteran small-town Michigan schoolteacher only two years away from retirement. In addition she was a volunteer participant in a county-wide staff development project I had organized and facilitated. The training focused on language arts ideas that would empower students to feel good about themselves and take charge of their lives. Donna's job was to attend training sessions and implement the concepts being presented. My job was to make classroom visitations and encourage implementation.

I took an empty seat in the back of the room and watched. All the students were working on a task, filling a sheet of notebook paper with thoughts and ideas. The 10-year-old student closest to me was filling her page with "I Can'ts."

"I can't kick the soccer ball past second base."

"I can't do long division with more than three numerals."

"I can't get Debbie to like me."

Her page was half full and she showed no signs of letting up. She worked on with determination and persistence.

I walked down the row glancing at students' papers. Everyone was writing sentences, describing things they couldn't do.

"I can't do 10 push-ups."

"I can't hit one over the left-field fence."

"I can't eat only one cookie."

By this time, the activity engaged my curiosity, so I decided to check with the teacher to see what was going on. As I approached her, I noticed that she too was busy writing. I felt it best not to interrupt.

"I can't get John's mother to come in for a teacher conference."

"I can't get my daughter to put gas in the car."

"I can't get Alan to use words instead of fists."

Thwarted in my efforts to determine why students and teacher were dwelling on the negative instead of writing the more positive "I Can" statements, I returned to my seat and continued my observations. Students wrote for another 10 minutes. Most filled their page. Some started another.

"Finish the one you're on and don't start a new one," were the instructions Donna used to signal the end of the activity. Students were then instructed to fold their papers in half and bring them to the front. When students reached the teacher's desk, they placed their "I Can't" statements into an empty shoebox.

When all of the student papers were collected, Donna added hers. She put the lid on the box, tucked it under her arm and headed out the door and down the hall. Students followed the teacher. I followed the students.

Halfway down the hall the procession stopped. Donna entered the custodian's room, rummaged around and came out with a shovel. Shovel in one hand, shoebox in the other, Donna marched the students out of the school to the farthest corner of the playground.

There they began to dig.

They were going to bury their "I Can'ts"! The digging took over 10 minutes because most of the fourth-graders wanted a turn. When the hole approached three feet deep, the digging ended. The box of "I Can'ts" was placed in position at the bottom of the hole and quickly covered with dirt.

Thirty-one 10- and 11-year-olds stood around the freshly dug gravesite. Each had at least one page full of "I Can'ts" in the shoebox, four feet under. So did their teacher.

At this point Donna announced, "Boys and girls, please join hands and bow your heads." The students complied. They quickly formed a circle around the grave, creating a bond with their hands. They lowered their heads and waited. Donna delivered the eulogy.

"Friends, we gather today to honor the memory of 'I Can't.' While he was with us on earth, he touched the lives of everyone, some more than others. His name, unfortunately, has been spoken in every public building — schools, city halls, state capitols and yes, even The White House.

"We have provided 'I Can't' with a final resting place and a headstone that contains his epitaph. He is survived by his brothers and sister, 'I Can', 'I Will' and 'I'm Going to Right Away.' They are not as well known as their famous relative and are certainly not as strong and powerful yet.

"Perhaps some day, with your help, they will make an even bigger mark on the world.

"May 'I Can't' rest in peace and may everyone present pick up their lives and move forward in his absence. Amen." As I listened to the eulogy I realized that these students would never forget this day. The activity was symbolic, a metaphor for life. It was a right-brain experience that would stick in the unconscious and conscious mind forever. Writing "I Can'ts," burying them and hearing the eulogy. That was a major effort on the part of this teacher. And she wasn't done yet. At the conclusion of the eulogy she turned the students around, marched them back into the classroom and held a wake.

They celebrated the passing of "I Can't" with cookies, popcorn and fruit juices. As part of the celebration, Donna cut out a large tombstone from butcher paper. She wrote the words "I Can't" at the top and put RIP in the middle. The date was added at the bottom.

The paper tombstone hung in Donna's classroom for the remainder of the year. On those rare occasions when a student forgot and said, "I Can't," Donna simply pointed to the RIP sign. The student then remembered that "I Can't" was dead and chose to rephrase the statement.

I wasn't one of Donna's students. She was one of mine. Yet that day I learned an enduring lesson from her.

Now, years later, whenever I hear the phrase, "I Can't," I see images of that fourth-grade funeral. Like the students, I remember that "I Can't" is dead.

~Chick Moorman

Granny's Bible

*A single conversation with a wise man
is better than ten years of study.*
~Chinese Proverb

I will never forget the first time I heard my granny quote the Bible. No, not the King James version. You know which one I'm talking about. The one that you actually live by every day of your life.

I was about eight years old at the time and a real brat. I had been fighting with the little girl next door and she was almost as mean as I was. We were pretty deep into battle when she threw a rock and hit me square between the eyes. Clutching my head and sobbing, I ran straight into the house to tattle. Granny met me at the door after seeing me come running across the lawn and hearing my screams.

"What's wrong?" she asked in her usual gruff way.

"That little girl threw a rock and hit me in the head," I managed through the tears.

"Well," said Granny smugly, "you just go pick up the biggest rock you can find and hit her back!"

I stopped crying immediately. "But Granny," I stammered. "I don't think..."

"Listen," she interrupted. "The Bible says feed them out of the same spoon." I happily obeyed. I never realized it then, but that was only the beginning of a lifetime of "Bible quotes" that would help me through life's biggest obstacles.

Several years later, and before I had enough sense to realize it, I was engaged to be married. My fiancé left it up to me to pick our wedding date. I unknowingly picked the date on which his mother had died many years ago. Instead of telling me that he didn't want to get married on this particular day, he told me he didn't want to marry me at all! I was simply heartbroken. I wandered through the house until I found Granny sewing in the den. I fell on my knees, laid my head in her lap, and started to cry.

"Granny, my fiancé doesn't love me. He doesn't want to marry me," I said.

"Well, that no good punk," she said angrily. "You just go tell him that the Bible says what goes around comes around. Someday he'll want to marry a girl and she'll do him the way he's doing you."

"But Granny," I said, "I don't think that the..."

"Listen," she interrupted. "You just go tell him what I said. You'll get your feller back." I married him in two months.

After our first three months of marriage bliss, we had our first fight. Oh, how that broke my heart. Packing my bags, I decided to go back home. When Granny saw me coming up the walk, she met me at the door.

"Well, what's wrong?" she asked. I was already clenching my jaw to keep from crying.

"We had a huge fight and he called me a spoiled brat," I told her.

"Come here," she said wearily. Putting her arm around my shoulder, she guided me into the kitchen where she put water on for tea. "So he called you a spoiled brat," she said over the whistle of the kettle. She looked very thoughtful as she poured water into waiting cups. "Okay," she said. "You just go right back home and tell him that the Bible says it takes one to know one."

"But Granny," I started to say, "I don't think..."

"Listen," she interrupted, "I was reading the Bible before you were even a twinkle in your daddy's eye." I did as she said and that was our last fight for a long time.

Before long I was expecting my first baby. Granny put me right to work crocheting a baby blanket. I could crochet fairly well, but let's just say Martha Stewart would never hire me to make anything for her. I became extremely flustered and did a double loop when I should have done a single.

"Oh gosh," I wailed. "I'll never learn this." I showed her what I had done. "Granny, I'm just going to do another double and no one will ever know the difference." That was the wrong thing to say.

"Yes it will make a difference," she said sternly. "Besides, the Bible says that two wrongs don't make a right."

My mouth dropped to the floor. "But Granny," I said. "I don't think the Bible..."

"Listen," she interrupted, "do you want your baby bundled in a blanket that wasn't made properly?" I unraveled the whole thing and started over.

I took my son to see Granny a while ago. She was sitting on her front porch crocheting and drinking tea. She was getting old but her usual spunk was still there. I sat down in the chair beside her and poured myself some tea. My son toddled off into the house to find the treat that Granny always had for him. After a while, we got to talking and forgot all about him. "Oh no," I gasped at the realization. "I forgot all about that kid."

As I started to get up, Granny reached for my arm and gently pushed me back down into my chair.

"You think he's going to keep meddling when he hears you coming? No, he's smarter than that," she added, with pride in her eyes. "Besides, the Bible says that you have to lay over to catch a meddler."

"But Granny," I said, "I don't think," and then I stopped. All through my years Granny had been quoting me the Bible. Her Bible, and it had always solved whatever problems had been thrown in my path. Smiling and shaking my head, I went into the house to get my son. Carrying him out on the porch, I placed him in the chair beside Granny. "Well Granny," I said, "I think I'm going to run to the store and get us all some ice cream." Pointing to my son, I asked, "Do you mind if he stays here? I'll only be a minute."

"Sure," she nodded. As I turned the car around and headed down the drive, I stopped and looked in my rear view mirror. There they were, two of the most precious people in my life. She, leaning over and quoting her Bible and he, hanging on to every precious word. I knew how he felt. He'll question it someday, but when he grows up he'll realize everything he holds dear is because of the Bible — Granny's Unforgettable Bible.

~Robin Rylee Harderson

When Darth Vader Attacks

If you want children to keep their feet on the ground, put some responsibility on their shoulders.
~Abigail Van Buren

Getting my eight-year-old son to clean his room should have been a five-minute chore, but in reality it was always the longest hour of my day. Yes, it would have been so much easier for me to just tidy it up myself, but that wouldn't teach him responsibility. It was the same thing every evening. He would whine and complain, and I would try not to lose my mind. So here it was, 8:00 p.m. again. I opened the door to his room and looked around at the oh-so-familiar scene. The towel from his morning shower was on the floor. The sheet and blanket from his bed were halfway off. His books were never on his end table where they were supposed to be; they were usually somewhere on the floor among litters of *Star Wars* toys and dinosaurs. As I looked at the mess, I said to myself, "I'm a creative type. There must be a better way...." Then it hit me.

"Scott!" I sounded alarmed. "Quick, Darth Vader is on his way here, and he's going to aim his death ray on all your men. They're not protected; they're all out on the planet surface." At first, he just looked at me, uncertain if I'd finally lost my mind. "Come on," I said. "You're their commander. Get in there and get them back in the Millennium Falcon."

"What do I do?" he asked with a smile.

"Open the hatch to the Millennium Falcon," I said, pointing to his toy box. "Order your men to pick up all their equipment and weapons, and herd all the dinosaurs inside where they'll be safe."

He rushed as fast as he could to pick up each toy.

"Now you've got to pick up the books with the secret formula in them and put them on the stand with the magic light. It protects them so Darth Vader won't be able to touch them."

"Yeah," he joined me. "'Cause if he does try to touch them, this laser light comes on, and it burns a hole right through his hand." He turned on his lamp to show me how it would work.

When he was done with the floor, I adjusted his shower water and called out to him from the bathroom. "Hurry, he's almost here! You've got to get protected with the invisibility shower so he can't find you. Make sure to throw your clothes in the hamper because if he sees them on the floor, he'll know where you are." No child ever ran so fast to take a shower.

"Make sure you use the invisibility soap and get it all over every part of you. If you leave any skin uncovered, he'll be able to find you."

I put his pajamas on his bed. "I left your 'uniform' on your 'escape pod.' Dry off and put it on." I couldn't believe this was working. While he showered, I went into the kitchen to put away the dishes.

When I heard the shower water stop, I returned to his room and noticed that he had dropped his towel next to the one from the day before. "You better pick up both those towels and put them in the hamper so I can wash them tonight." He hesitated. "If you leave them out, Darth Vader will smell your scent on them and find you." Now he rushed to pick up both towels, tossing them in the hamper.

"Make sure you brush your teeth with invisibility toothpaste, too. That way he won't see your teeth when you open your mouth."

Grabbing his toothpaste and toothbrush, he quickly brushed his teeth and, surprisingly, even put away the toothpaste and toothbrush without being told. This was catching on.

"Only one thing left so he won't get you," I warned.

"What's that, Mom?" He was so excited. "Get into your escape pod and pull the invisible sheet and blanket up over you so you won't be seen." He jumped into bed, smoothing out his sheet and blanket.

"Goodnight, Commander." I turned out his light. "You should be safe... this time."

"Wait!" he called out. "He'll see my head. I can't keep my head under the covers or I can't breathe."

"You're right, Commander," I answered. "You need some invisibility dust on your head and even your arms, just in case they come out of the covers."

"We don't have any invisibility dust," he replied.

"The Rebel Force smuggled out some for you just today. I'll go get it," I said as I walked into my bathroom and grabbed the talcum powder. Returning to his room, I held it over his head and arms, sprinkling it down on his arm and a little in his hair.

"I'm good now, Mom," he said, rubbing it all over his head and arms.

"May the force be with you," I said as I left.

"What is the force anyway?" he asked.

"The force is God," I answered. "We almost forgot; you have to say your prayers. Ask that the force of God is with you always."

"For real, right?" he asked. "Not just when the pretend Darth Vader comes?"

"Roger that, Commander. The force is always with you. Good night."

~Diana Perry

It's in the Little Things

One thing I had learned from watching chimpanzees with their
infants is that having a child should be fun.
~Jane Goodall

t was one of those days when there was way too much to do. I had fallen behind in most of my household chores. I hadn't been to the grocery store in nearly forever and we were out of pretty much everything. The laundry was piled up well above the tops of the hampers and the house was stretching even my reasonably loose standards of cleanliness. And besides all that, I had two article deadlines and needed to spend some serious time at my computer.

All of that, and my four children were on a break from school. They were thrilled to be home and asked me repeatedly how we would spend their day off.

They were going to be disappointed with my plans for the day. There was absolutely nothing fun about them. Nothing special, nothing school break-worthy at all.

The kids woke up that morning, expecting their usual bowls of cold cereal. But we were out of milk, and my kids hate dry cereal. There were no eggs and no bread, which left few breakfast options. I searched through the freezer, hoping for a box of frozen waffles. No such luck. I rooted around in the fridge, finally finding a tube of buttermilk biscuits. I sprinkled them with cinnamon and sugar, baked them, and gave them to the kids.

"I'm sorry that I can't offer you anything better this morning, but I haven't had time to go shopping," I said. The kids didn't bother responding. They were too busy shoving my makeshift cinnamon rolls into their mouths.

After breakfast, I started a load of laundry and sat down at the computer. My youngest daughter, Julia, walked toward me, wearing her I'm-about-to-whine face. "But, Mommy, I thought we were going to do something fun today," she said. "Since it's our day off from school."

"I know it's your day off, but it's not Mommy's day off," I explained. "I have work to do."

"Can you play a game with me?" she begged. "Like *Candy Land*? Or beauty shop?"

I sighed. I really didn't have time to play. I desperately needed to get some work done. But then I had an idea. "Can we play beauty shop while I work?"

So I got my article done, and my toenails painted at the same time.

My oldest, Austin, volunteered to fix lunch so I could keep working. The younger kids were thrilled with his selections. Not exactly the choices the food pyramid people advise, but the kids had fun and I met my writing deadlines.

Shortly after lunch, we made the trek to the grocery store. Austin pushed the cart, while the younger kids collected coupons from the little dispensers scattered throughout the store. I got what I needed—with a few additions from my entourage, of course.

Back at home, the kids decided to play "grocery store" with the coupons they had collected during our trip. They lined up the canned goods on the kitchen counters and the snacks on the island and pretended to re-buy our groceries.

For the remainder of the afternoon, I cleaned house, folded laundry, and started dinner. The kids continued with their game until my husband, Eric, walked through the door.

He spotted me and grinned. "So how was the kids' big day off today?"

I began to explain that we hadn't done anything special because I'd been too busy with chores. But the kids interrupted me.

"Daddy, did you see Mommy's toenails? She let me sit under her computer desk and paint them while she typed!" Julia said. "It was so much fun!"

"And, Dad, we had the best breakfast today," said Austin. "Have you ever made those special biscuits for Dad? They were awesome!"

Eric gave me a questioning look and all I could do was shrug. My two middle kids, Jordan and Lea, piped up to tell their dad about the coupon game and Austin's special lunch. "We had such a great day today, Dad! It was a blast!"

I looked at my children's faces. They were lit up with excitement. Excitement about makeshift cinnamon rolls, a most unhealthy lunch, coupons from the grocery store, and painted toenails.

"You guys really had a good day? You're not disappointed that we didn't do something fun?" I asked.

Austin shrugged and said, "Life is only as fun as you make it, Mom."

I nodded, realizing how right he was. Happiness is far more about our attitude than our circumstances.

I hugged my kids and thanked them for reminding me to look for happiness in the little things.

Julia smiled and said, "And the little things that make you the happiest are us, right, Mommy?"

Wow, my kids sure are smart.

~Diane Stark

Special Hour

Lost time is never found again.
~Benjamin Franklin

ven though I was a stay-at-home mom, there were never enough hours in a day to accomplish everything I set out to do. My husband helped me around the house, my three-year-old son was unusually well behaved, and yet I constantly felt pressed for time.

It seemed like we had a revolving door in our home. Our social life was active. People dropped in knowing they'd be welcome. There was always a pot of coffee going, along with an abundance of home-baked goodies. I was always available for friends with problems who wanted to talk. If someone visited at mealtimes, there was plenty to fill an extra plate.

I prided myself on being a friend whenever needed, but while I was accessible to everyone else, I began to notice I was becoming less available to my own family.

One afternoon in particular opened my eyes. It was a gorgeous summer day, but I hardly noticed. I was intent on getting my groceries home before the ice cream melted. My son was dawdling like most three-year-olds, inspecting every flower, blade of grass and crack in the sidewalk. I barked for him to hurry, yanking his arm less gently than I normally would. He reluctantly toddled behind me, his little legs pumping to keep up with my impatient pace.

As we approached the park at the corner of our street, he stared longingly at the swings. He resisted my hold on his wrist, and I took a deep breath.

"Not today, honey," I informed him, making an effort to soften my voice. I was expecting three friends for dinner, not counting last-minute drop-ins, and I still had a lot to do. There simply wasn't time to stop at the park, even for a few minutes.

I tried to ignore the pleading look in my son's eyes, feeling even guiltier when his little shoulders slumped in quiet, resigned acceptance. It occurred to me that I'd seen him do that far too often lately. I cringed inwardly, remembering all the times I'd shooed him away when he asked me to play with a new toy or watch a cartoon with him. Lately, we'd even stopped reading bedtime stories, too. Instead I'd rush through our bathtime ritual, get him into pajamas and tap my foot anxiously while he brushed his teeth, ushering him off to bed so I could return phone calls or get back to a card game with company.

When we got home, I sent my son to play in our back yard while I quickly unpacked the groceries and put them away. I hurriedly tidied up and was about to put the roast in the oven when I noticed I didn't hear him babbling to himself the way he always did. I hurried out the back door, my heart in my throat, breathing a sigh of relief when I saw him sitting quietly on the top step hugging himself.

"Are you okay, honey?" I asked, checking his forehead to see if he had a fever. It was unusual for him to be so quiet. Satisfied that his brow was cool, I spun around to get back to my preparations, not even waiting for him to answer my question.

"Mummy, sit with me?" he pleaded.

"Not now, David," I told him. "I'm very —"

"Busy," he finished for me. "I know." His sad, wistful tone pierced through me, and I turned to look at him as he stared blankly ahead.

That's when I noticed the changes in him. He was losing that baby look. His little face seemed longer and leaner. The pudginess of his soft arms and knees was almost completely gone. When had that happened? When did I last pick him up to nestle my nose in his clean hair or inhale the sweetness of him?

I raced back into the house. Popping the roast into the refrigerator, I checked quickly to make sure I had what I needed to make my son's beloved hot dogs instead. Then I picked up the phone to cancel dinner plans, not caring if my friends would be upset.

Grabbing juice boxes, a few cookies and some fresh fruit, I called my son.

"Let's go," I told him, smiling widely.

"To the store again?" he asked, and I was overcome with shame. It was about the only place I had taken him lately.

"No, we're going to the park," I announced, squirming guiltily when I saw his expression of pure joy over such a small outing. "Get your bucket and shovels and some trucks, okay?" I added, handing him a bag for his toys.

He scurried back less than three minutes later, his bag bulging with assorted treasures from his room. I spotted his white stuffed frog peeking out and ignored my voice of reason. Dirt washes out, I reminded myself cheerfully, grabbing my house key and taking his hand.

My son talked non-stop all the way to the park, and I listened to his chatter with renewed loving interest. For two hours, we played together, digging in the sandbox, swinging, seesawing and climbing on the park equipment. Then we sat on the grass with our snacks while we looked for animals in the clouds.

When we got home, I put him down for a nap, not even bothering to scrub his face or hands. I watched him doze off with a tired but blissful smile and swore to myself that things would change.

The next day, I implemented Special Hour. At least four times a week, I hung a Do Not Disturb sign that David helped me make on our front door. We ceremoniously took the phone off the hook, turned off the TV and set the oven timer for sixty minutes. Then my son decided what he wanted to do with that time — his time. We would read stories, color, draw, build a lopsided castle with blocks, or just talk. But no matter what he chose, he had my undivided attention.

If the doorbell rang, I would ask the caller to return later. As the answering machine collected messages, I lost myself in my son's little world of fantasy, imagination and fun. Depending on what shift my husband worked, he would join us when he could. Many times, we were so engrossed in what we were doing that we ignored the timer going off to finish whatever project we were immersed in.

Special Hour lasted for many years until my son, an only child, began school and had a social life of his own, becoming too active to "amuse Mom and Dad." I often think back on those days, grateful that I discovered the importance of making time for what was most precious in my life — before being a busy mom made me too busy to be a mom.

~Marya Morin

Juggler Extraordinaire

Our greatest danger in life is permitting the urgent things to
crowd out the important.
~Charles E. Hummel

"Play with me, Mom! Please! Come play *Memory* with me!" my daughter, Alicia, would plead.

When the kids were young and the house in a state of chaos, I would feel the pressure of divided loyalties—clearly both the house and my children needed my attention. When I made the choice to sit on the floor and play the *Memory* game with my daughter, I would comfort myself by saying, "No one is going to remember if on (fill in the date) your house was clean or not, but your kids will remember if you had time for them."

In those years when the kids were young I decided to go back to college and finish my degree. I became a juggler extraordinaire. We would pick a favorite park and, in between rescuing a child dangling from the monkey bars, I would work on my statistics homework. We would spend an afternoon at Chuck E. Cheese, a pizza parlor filled with noisy arcade games, where I would dole out tokens while grappling with a calculus problem. I would cheer my son around the baseball bases after a big hit and at the same time crack the books to cram for an exam.

Finishing my degree led to a corporate job, and more juggling. Over the years I did my best to divide my loyalties wisely. I wish I could say I always prioritized in favor of my children, but sometimes it wasn't possible. But I can say that I have never regretted the times I chose my children over other demands. It was a juggling act that I continued to practice even as the children grew into adulthood.

When Alicia graduated from college she took a job that required her to move across the country. "Mom, will you come out to D.C. with me? Could you stay with me that first week, Mom? I have so much to do!" Life was busy at home with our own business, but I knew when I looked back on that week in July of 2006 no one would remember what work I did, but my daughter would remember the time we spent together. How could we forget the drive from the airport in D.C. in the convertible rental car? It was so small that we had to drive with the top down and sit the luggage, the bulk of her belongings, upright in the back seat like two large, lifeless hitchhikers. Or the hours spent picking out work clothes to get her started in her new career with confidence. The week went by fast. She settled into her new job and soon weeks became a couple of years, and then I got the call.

"I think he's the one, Mom." I could tell from the sound of her voice that he was. I thought back over the years, the beaus that had come and gone. The drop-everything-I-need-your-help talks on the phone about heartache and healing. I thought about the juggling, the prioritizing, the wisdom, the growth and the love.

It was decided that the wedding would be in Georgia, where my daughter's fiancé was from. It was hard to be of much help planning a wedding from so far away. At a time when mother and daughter would normally tackle the task together, we were many miles apart.

"Mom, I'm going to e-mail you a link. I think we have found the place. It's absolutely beautiful! I wish you could see it!" She was right; it looked gorgeous. A Tuscan-themed winery, with the Georgia mountains as a backdrop, would make the perfect place for a wedding. Her words, "Mom, I wish you could see it..." echoed in my mind.

"I know you're busy, Mom, but what would you think about going with me to Georgia? You could meet Drew's folks and we could get stuff done for the wedding." You couldn't keep me away.

It was a week spent meeting new family and taking walks with the mother of the groom, who became a new friend. There was cake tasting and flower viewing. And then there was the drive to Dahlonega, a quaint town and home to Montaluce, the winery location for the big day. I was charmed the minute we drove onto the property. A gently winding road wove its way through what looked like a little Tuscan village. Villas dotted the hills and a congregation of homes in a little valley had me imagining that people lived there who spoke Italian with a southern twang.

At the end of the road stood the winery itself, and we walked inside to the balcony overlooking the vineyards.

"Down there is where they would do the ceremony, Mom." My eyes filled with tears. It was beautiful, almost as beautiful as my precious daughter standing next to me. I had to juggle things to be there that week, but it was all worth it. And I knew that as the wedding date drew near I would juggle some more to be there for her.

The wedding was a magical day, made even more memorable by the time spent with my daughter in preparation for the big event. In hindsight, I don't remember the things that didn't get done or the money that I didn't make during that time. I don't regret juggling some things so I could spend that special time with my daughter. In fact, I think the art of proper juggling has served me well. I expect to use it often when I hear my future grandchildren say, "Nana, will you play with me? Please?"

~Lynne Leite

Putting Down Roots

It takes hands to build a house, but only hearts can build a home.
~Author Unknown

It's not easy to be a stay-at-home mom. It's even more difficult to be a stay-at-home military mom. I know, because I've been both. From military bases to apartments to mobile home communities, the one thing we could always count on was moving. Goodbye to old friends, hello to new ones. So long to the old school and on to the new. From climate to climate and town to town, I found myself wondering if my children would ever be able to put down roots.

It's true that I would be there for them, but money was always short, and sometimes my husband's pay record would be lost for months. Pinching pennies became an art form. Have you ever gone grocery shopping with a bag full of small change? Well, I have. From dusk to dawn, I made my children's clothing, often redesigning hand-me-downs. I became their nutritionist and gourmet chef. I was once asked what made me so creative. My answer was both brief and honest: desperation. It was hard, but it was also a joyful experience that was both rich and rewarding.

My children adjusted with courage and humor. Their strength amazed me. But with no extended family, I often wondered if they would ever feel that they had roots. Oh, how I had wanted those roots when I was a child. Would my children be harmed in the long run by moving from place to place? What could I do? Then one day, when they were very small, I had a revelation.

Jenny was about five years old and Helen was little more than a baby. That was when I began the gardens. Tiny things, at first. Just a child's garden, filled with baby carrots, herbs, and annual flowers. To hear Jenny and Helen tell about it nearly thirty years later, one would think we had owned a farm. Adults now, they often talk about what it felt like to fill little baskets with their own growing things.

From tiny vegetables and flowers we moved on to flowering shrubs and garden design. I made it up as I went along. To tell you the truth, I hadn't a clue. Finally, in Charleston, South Carolina, we planted the apple tree. I think that we harvested one apple and split it four ways. South Carolina is not exactly the perfect apple state. But that was never the point.

We lived in Charleston for nearly eight years and our garden grew larger each year. With each new plant, I learned more, and my girls and I would discuss just what those fibrous roots signified. What about the roots that we planted, only to leave them behind for someone else? Not long ago, we did a search on Google Earth, and we found the duplex that had contained the laughter and dreams that we shared for eight years in Charleston Navy housing. We scanned closer and closer — down, down, and down — and there it was, our little apple tree, alive and well.

Bittersweet tears spilled down my cheeks as I remembered the day we planted that tree. It had survived hurricanes, drought, and much sorrow, and so had we. At that moment, I finally understood. The apple tree's roots, growing deep in South Carolina soil, were much like our family. Deep in the soil of shared joys and sorrows, our roots are strong in one another, in faith and in love.

~Jaye Lewis

Letters to Mamaw

To send a letter is a good way to go somewhere without moving
anything but your heart.
~Phyllis Theroux

My grandmother's eightieth birthday was approaching and I was at a loss as to what to give her. She had recently moved into a nursing home and didn't have room for extra "stuff." She insisted that she didn't need a thing.

Finally, I came up with an idea. In her birthday card, I sent her a gift certificate for "A letter a week for the next year!" It was a big commitment. I've never been much of a letter writer, but now I was living far from home, and should be able to find plenty of news. Growing up just a mile from my grandparents, we'd always been close. I knew that she'd love to hear what was going on in my life.

The letter gift certificate was a huge hit. She got fifty-two letters that first year. Some were long and filled with homesickness. Others were short and newsy. More than once what she received was just a funny card with a few short lines. All showed her that I was thinking of her regularly.

As her next birthday rolled around, she asked for another letter gift certificate for her birthday. In fact, that's also what she wanted for her next eight birthdays.

For nine and a half years I wrote her. She was rarely able to write back. So much happened in those nine years! At first I wrote about the cold Michigan winters and working on my graduate degree. Then I wrote about my pregnancy, which turned out to be twins! We lived in four different places during those years and I described them all. During the boys' preschool years I shared every funny thing they did and said, and as they grew they started adding "picture letters" to the envelope. I sent postcard letters from vacations.

I flew home annually to visit and soon realized that the entire nursing home staff knew all the details of my life, as more and more often they were reading the letters to her.

My last letter arrived the day after her death. I've always wanted relationships with no regrets. None of that "I wish I had told her I loved her" for me! I felt I had given her the best gift I could.

What I hadn't counted on was how her gift would come back full-circle to me.

Months later, while going through her things, my dad found a box full of her correspondence. It was filled with letters from me. Those letters are a journal of my life. Some were unremarkable. Others were filled with moments and pictures I had completely forgotten. Such as on May 22, 1997, when I told her that the twins were having Western day at preschool and that when I explained to three-year-old Ben that the boys would be dressing up as cowboys he asked, "Will the girls be dressing up as cows?" Funny, I don't remember that. In some ways it seems I missed those years due to motherly exhaustion. She saved those memories for me in my letters.

Life really does fly by. Loved ones come and go. But sometimes our gifts to others come back to us in unexpected ways. This is one of those times.

~Lisa Kulka

ttyl

Computing is not about computers any more. It is about living.
~Nicholas Negroponte

"We threw a bash at LEGOLAND for my granddaughter's birthday," my girlfriend said and then passed a picture around. "Look at that sweet face." I glanced at it, then zipped up my jacket against the chill I felt inside. I played golf with three girlfriends and their chatter about grandchildren shouldn't have bothered me. But it did.

More pictures were passed around. "My Heather snuggles on my lap while we watch movies." "I had Tyler for a sleepover last weekend."

I swallowed the lump in my throat. My grandsons live in Wisconsin, 2,000 miles away from me in Southern California.

Phone calls often went like this: "How are you?" I'd ask.

"Fine," they'd say.

"What are you doing in school that's fun?"

"Nothing."

"How are your grades? What's your favorite class?" I'd ask, trying to keep them on the phone for a few more minutes.

I loved seeing them and flew there as often as I could. We baked cookies, visited Chuck E. Cheese, and played video games. I showered them with love, and them to me when we were together, but each passing year brought changes to their lives, and each trip ended much too soon. I'd ache to know who their current friends were, what movies they liked while they were still out in the theaters, whether they won or lost their latest baseball game.

Shortly after the new year began, I went to lunch with a different friend. She asked about Nick, fifteen, and Colton, ten.

"If you want to be part of their world, you have to use their technology," she said.

"Like what? I call them all the time," I protested. "And I visit as often as I can."

"What about e-mail? You can do that every day. My grandson lives on it. I'll bet your older grandson does too."

Driving home, I mulled it over. Questions popped into my head — did Nick have access to a computer? Would he think it dorky and weird to talk to his grandmother online? Would he even want to?

I called my daughter-in-law. "Nick's on my computer all the time," she said, "and has his own e-mail address. Colton isn't into the computer yet, but I'll tell Nick you called."

I hung up the phone and tried to put it out of my mind. After all, Nick was fifteen years old, with more important things to do than converse with his grandmother.

The next morning I sat down at my computer. There was an unusual address in my e-mail account with a subject line of "Hey." Could that be Nick? I clicked it open and devoured every word.

Hey its Nick,

My mom told me that you wanted to keep in touch with me or something like that i cant exactly remember what she said. But ya im doing pretty good here accept they wont let me wrestle because I failed 1 class which was math and I was very surprised at that cause I thought I was good at math. But it is like 12:44 am here and I don't feel like going to sleep lol but ya e-mail me back

Love ya lots,
Nick

I shot one right back, trying hard not to sound desperate for contact with him. I wanted to be cool. And I didn't correct his grammar, though I could have. I wanted to accept him for who he was, spelling mistakes and all.

Yo, Grandma B here,

Nice to hear from you. Sad to hear that you can't wrestle cause you failed 1 class. Bummer. I was never very good at math. But if you thought you were, it's too bad that you didn't get a passing grade. How come you can't sleep at 12:44 a.m.? I'm snoring by that time.

Love you double lots,

Grandma B

Pressing "send," I noticed the time. He was two hours ahead of me, so I pictured him roaming the halls in school, putting books in his locker, or poring over a textbook in study hall. How I wished I lived near enough to see his football games or wrestling matches. Now all I could do was wonder if he'd e-mail back. Did I dare to have even a sliver of hope that we could bridge the miles between us?

Later that day, a little ping sounded. I had mail.

Hey,

Ya I hate that I cant wrestle. that camera you sent me is pretty sweet if you want to see the videos I took go to this... [link] Colton is the recorder lol i will be making tons more once summer comes and i can bike and skateboard and stuff like that.

Love ya triple lots,

Nick

I clicked on the link. There he was skateboarding, flying high into the air and landing with a thud. It was awesome to see.

Nick e-mailed again.

Last night I went bowling and got 5 strikes in a row when they had good music and then a song I didn't like came on and I got a gutter ball.

Often, his e-mails had weird letters in them, like ttyl or idk. It took me a while to figure out those meant "talk to you later," and "I don't know."

Months went by. Sometimes days passed before he responded to an e-mail, often apologizing for being so busy with schoolwork and sports. One day he attached photographs that I eagerly devoured. I felt like I was right there with him whenever I'd read an e-mail, watch a video, or see a picture.

Last week I saw my golfing friends again. One of them brought a picture of her granddaughter at a dance recital. I had one to share too. "Hey, look at the picture of Nick in his football uniform that he attached to his latest e-mail. Doesn't he look cool?"

It's been fun to learn the ways to stay connected in a teenager's world. Thanks to being open to a friend's suggestion and the willingness to change, this grandmother has learned a whole new way of relating to her grandsons.

~B.J. Taylor

Tell Them You Can Do It

Confidence is a habit that can be developed by acting as if you already had the confidence you desire to have.
~Brian Tracy

f I had to choose the one piece of motherly advice that has made the biggest difference in my life, it would be "Tell them you can do it." The funny thing is, Mother didn't actually give this advice to me. It was meant for someone else entirely. I'm just lucky she happened to repeat the story to me.

My family lived in the same town that was home to the state's oldest university, the University of Florida. Students from the College of Education frequently sought internships with teachers in the local public schools. Mother took on an intern from time to time, even though it usually meant extra work for her.

Mother's interns often sought her help with applications, references and the like because they hoped to find full-time teaching jobs when they graduated. A counseling session with one of them prior to a job interview led to the advice that has stuck with me ever since.

I don't know whether the intern actually asked for Mother's advice — probably, she just mentioned the upcoming interview. For some reason, Mother told me about it the same day, after she got home from work. "I told her, if they ask you if you can teach math, or geography, or even home economics, you tell them you can do it. Whatever they want you to do, you tell them you can do it."

Mother wasn't an overly confident person. Yes, she had two college degrees and yes, she had years of teaching experience, but she never expected any special recognition or praise. She didn't seek it, and she usually didn't get it. When I was young, I didn't fully comprehend all that my mother had accomplished.

The first in her family to graduate from college, Mother told me she had been terrified when she left her small hometown. Headed for Florida State College for Women, she was afraid of having to return home because she couldn't cut it. But she didn't fail. She graduated at age nineteen, taught for several years, and then landed a job as administrative assistant to the College of Education dean at the University of Florida.

While Mother was working at the university, she took graduate courses and continued her education, eventually earning a master's degree. It was there she met her one and only, the man she eventually married. Mother and Daddy were devoted to each other, sharing a lifelong love and mutual respect.

My mother was an accomplished lady in her own right, but she often took a back seat to my father, who, as the primary breadwinner, had a more exciting job as principal of our local high school. Although he was a quiet and humble man, Daddy was recognized for his leadership skills and frequently served in highly visible roles in church and civic organizations. Daddy was in the limelight, and Mother pretty much stayed in the background.

Unlike Mother and her intern, I never applied for a teaching job. I earned a law degree and then went to work for a law firm. For the first five years of my career, I felt woefully ill-equipped to handle just about everything that crossed my desk. I found transaction work painstaking and confusing, courtroom appearances scary and intimidating. But I kept that to myself. I told the big guys I could do it. And I did, even though I was quaking inside.

Later, when I went to work at a corporation, I became an expert in a number of fields I had previously known nothing about. The job demanded it; there was no one else to do it, so I did. Ultimately, I was asked to add management of the company's internal audit department, including the top audit job, to my responsibilities, despite the fact that I was not an auditor and did not have a financial background. I told them I could do it, and I did.

The biggest rewards in my career, and the most gratifying experiences of my life, have come as a result of stretching beyond my comfort zone. I've seen the same principle at work in the lives of younger people I have mentored. No one gets ahead by underestimating what she can do.

Years after Mother advised her intern on how to handle that critical first job interview, I told her how much her wise counsel had inspired me, even though I was not its intended recipient. I asked her why she had given that particular piece of advice to her protégé.

"I knew how much she needed that job," Mother said.

Mother wasn't into fakery or boasting or dissimulation. She just knew that deep down beyond the nattering voices that tell us we can't do the things we'd like to do, there is a boundless well of ability and grit. It will bubble up to the surface if we just let it.

I'm glad I had the opportunity to thank Mother for the advice that has been so helpful to me over the years. Even so, I am not sure she understood the extent of its impact. It is with me still, encouraging me when I'm tired, intimidated or overwhelmed.

"Tell them you can do it." Mother's words ring in my ears, firm resolve underscoring each one.

Echoing her voice, I whisper to myself, "I can do it."

And then, I do.

~Mary Wood Bridgman

Nothin' Says Lovin' Like...

The torch of love is lit in the kitchen.
~Author Unknown

hristmas was coming, and I didn't have one ounce of spirit or energy. I couldn't even muster a half-hearted "ho-ho." I was a gray heap of sorrow, enmeshed in my own pity party.

I had taken a last walk with my closest friend that year and still grieved her passing. Neither of my away-from-home daughters would be able to get back for the holidays. My recently retired husband, grappling with his own identity, didn't or couldn't see that I was a mess. My joints ached; I felt old, looked old and was losing my grip on things that had always been so sure and steady in my life. I slogged through my days, unable to even recognize myself.

I mourned for the past when everything ran smoothly: The girls were growing; I was busy and involved in their lives; my husband was working. My grief had reached crisis proportions after our move across town a few months earlier. Even my neighbors had been replaced with strangers.

I tried walking the new neighborhood. I tried holiday shopping. I even saw a movie or two. But I felt like I had lost my way. Then the phone rang one afternoon.

"Isabel," a voice chirped. "It's Julie. Nicholas is wondering if you're planning your annual cookie-baking day. Are you?"

Ever since Nicholas was able to toddle across my kitchen in the old neighborhood, we'd had tea together and baked cookies. This year, his younger brother Zachary was old enough to join the activities.

"Oh Julie, I don't think…" I paused and mustered some false enthusiasm. "Of course I'm going to bake with Nicholas. And send Zachary along, too. It'll be great!"

I set the date and hung up the phone with a weight sitting in the bottom of my stomach like a wad of raw cookie dough. This was the last thing in the world I wanted — two little boys racing all over my house, my kitchen and my life. Still, it *would* be nice to carry on an old tradition.

Down the block lived another child, a quiet little thing, sometimes peeking out at me from behind a large ash tree in her front yard. One day I saw her sitting idly on the curb and, recognizing a kindred spirit, joined her.

"Hi. I'm Isabel. I moved in over there," I pointed, "and I'm lonesome because I don't know anybody. What's your name?"

"Kelsey," she answered. "I don't have anything to do."

"Hmm. Well, I've got just the thing," I heard myself saying. "Tomorrow my friends Nicholas and Zachary are coming to bake cookies. Would you like to come?"

Kelsey's mother eagerly brought her over the next morning. Standing on my doorstep were three grinning kids and two parents. I told the grown-ups that it would take about three hours, but I'd call when everybody was ready to go home.

And the four of us got started.

We measured.

We mixed.

We laughed when flour powdered our faces and hair.

The dough was over-rolled and over-handled, but it didn't seem to matter. Nor did anyone care when the cookie-cutter shapes were crooked or lopsided. And there were no tears shed over the burned sheet of Christmas trees that set off the smoke alarm. Instead, we discovered they made splendid Frisbees to bulls-eye the frozen birdbath out back.

Amid singing and conversations both long and short, I hauled out the frosting: red and green pastry tubes that oozed both top and bottom. After a mini-lesson in rosette making, the three little ones practiced squeezing the sugar concoction onto the countertop. Did you know that red and green icing turns mouth, teeth and tongue an awful purple? Even my own!

Tiny fingers pressed raisin eyes and red cinnamon buttons onto gingerbread fronts. The kids ate two for every one they used. Colored sugar sprinkled the table, the Santa cookies and the floor.

Secrets were whispered, little hurts mended and problems solved while we downed three refills of beyond-sugary sugarplum tea in real china cups.

And — miracle of miracles — frosted holiday cookies, divided by lacy paper doilies, were all neatly packed in white boxes decorated with "Merry-Christmas-I-love-you" tags when the doorbell rang. *Six hours later.*

"I thought you came here to decorate cookies, not yourselves," Kelsey's mother teased. All three kids grinned back with purple teeth. I kept my own mouth closed.

"I miss you, Isabel." Nicholas grabbed me around the waist before he left. "The lady in your old house doesn't make us cookies or tea."

"Yeah," chimed in Zachary.

"One day," I smiled, holding Nick's rosy cheeks in both my hands, "you're going to grow up, and you won't want to bake Christmas cookies anymore. And I'll understand."

"Oh no, Isabel! I will never, never be too old for you. I love you."

"I love you, too," said Zachary.

"Me, too," whispered Kelsey.

And suddenly they were stuck to me like Velcro.

Christmas came. I invited all the old neighbors and a few of the new ones. My daughters phoned, bereft and homesick, and, of course, we all cried. I still missed my friend. And my husband didn't change at all. But the most important thing I learned that year was:

When life seems sorrowful — reach out.

Find children.

Bake cookies.

~Isabel Bearman Bucher

The Good Mom

Deep summer is when laziness finds respectability.
~Sam Keen

My alarm clock blasted music way too lively for my early-morning mood. I crawled out of bed with a groan, stumbling over a basket overflowing with dirty laundry. Whatever happened to our lazy days of summer? My mind drifted back to when my girls were younger — back when we slept late during summer vacations. Now, activities like gymnastics, band and volleyball camps, softball games and a number of other commitments had turned our lazy days into crazy days.

I maneuvered my way toward the kitchen through a path of flip-flops. Last night's dinner dishes greeted me at the sink. Oh yes, I thought, remembering our hectic evening the night before. We had scarfed down frozen pizza, grabbed our lawn chairs and rushed out the door for my daughter's six o'clock softball game.

Something is wrong with this picture, I thought, scraping dried pepperoni off a dinner plate. As much as I enjoyed watching and supporting my girls' activities, our busy schedule left little time for housework. Somehow we had plenty of time to make messes, but never enough to clean them up.

Whenever I complained, my husband always gave me the same advice: "Get those girls to help you."

"I know," I said, feeling a twinge of guilt, "but that's easier said than done." They always seemed to have an excuse.

"How about folding some laundry?"

"Okay, Mom, this TV show is almost over."

"Girls, I need you to unload the dishwasher."

"Sure, Mom, but can I do it in a couple of minutes? I'm so close to the next level on this game."

Truth be told, it probably was my fault. I wanted to be a good mom—and good moms didn't follow their kids around nagging them all day. But I didn't feel like a good mom. I was a tired mom. A grumpy mom. I was a mom who needed help, and I knew the perfect way to motivate my girls.

"Okay, guys," I said one morning during breakfast, "today we're starting something new." Three pairs of eyes gazed up at me from their bowls of cereal. "From now on, each of you must complete a chore each day before getting on a screen."

"A screen?" my youngest asked, tilting her head to the side.

"Yes, a screen," I said. "You know, TVs, computers, Wii games, iPhones…"

One by one, each girl's mouth dropped open. They weren't excited, but I was eager to set my plan into action.

I'll admit the first few days were a challenge. Like most kids, they tested me, seeing if I would stand my ground. But within a couple of weeks, doing chores became our daily routine. My plan worked great—and no nagging was needed.

I used to think being a good mom meant self-sacrifice and being able to do it all. Now I have a new definition. A good mom builds a team and teaches responsibility. She is more able to enjoy her kids because she's no longer stressed out, sleep-deprived and exhausted. Once I learned how to share the load, I think I became a pretty good mom.

~Sheri Zeck

What Lurks Behind the Trees

Tell me a fact and I'll learn. Tell me a truth and I'll believe. But tell me a story and it will live in my heart forever.
~Indian Proverb

A large oil landscape, featuring a mountainside covered with spruce and pine trees, hung above the sofa in our living room for several years. It is a decent enough painting, one of my earlier ones, and I enjoyed looking at it, but never without seeing what I could have done to make it better.

One day, Nicholas, my three-year-old grandson, climbed onto my lap and burrowed his head into my shoulder. It was nearing his naptime, and we both liked cuddling before he went to sleep.

"What's behind the trees, Grandma?" he asked me, drowsiness in his voice.

"What trees, sweetie?"

"In that picture." He pointed to the painting. Quickly, my imagination kicked into third gear.

"Oh, I think there's a small, spotted fawn, a baby deer, frolicking along a path that's shaded by the tall trees," I told him. "He's chasing a butterfly! There he goes, running and skipping up the mountain, around bushes, through the trees, having a wonderful time. Uh, oh!" I gasped.

"What?" Nick looked up at me.

"The baby deer ran right into a baby elk! They stood and looked at each other, and then the little elk started to chase the baby deer back down the mountainside! They ran and ran and then... Uh, oh! They ran right into the Daddy Deer! He's really big! Baby deer hides behind his Daddy, and the little elk stops so fast, his hooves skid."

"Then what?" Nick was no longer drowsy. He sat up, staring at the painting.

"Well, there they go, Daddy and Baby Deer, chasing Baby Elk! They run right back up the mountain. Uh, oh! Standing in the path, glaring down at Daddy Deer, is Daddy Elk! He is huge! Much, much bigger than Daddy Deer! Baby Elk runs behind his daddy and peeks around his legs. He sticks his tongue out at the deer family, and then the elk begin to chase the deer. Back down the mountain they go, faster and faster!"

I continued with the story, building it animal by animal, until there was a parade of imaginary creatures, each bigger than the last one, chasing each other up and down the mountain. The elk is vanquished by a larger moose and calf, who, in turn are dispatched by a ferocious grizzly bear and cub. I ended the story with a moral: Never bully or tease someone who is smaller or weaker, for there will always be someone bigger and stronger to bring down the bully.

The telephone rang, and Nicholas slipped from my lap. I went into the kitchen to take the call, leaving the little boy happily playing with some toys on the floor. He was no longer sleepy. My conversation took only a few minutes; and when I quietly returned to the living room, I had to completely stop in my tracks at the sight of my grandson.

He had climbed onto the back of the sofa. Cautiously, he was pulling the painting away from the wall. I watched as he slowly peeked around the edge of the frame, his little body trembling with suspense and a hint of fear at what he might discover "behind the trees." He pulled the painting away from the wall just a bit more, until he could get a clear view. Then he carefully allowed it to resettle to its original position.

I slipped quietly back into the kitchen, but stood where I could watch him. Nick sat on the sofa, his eyes glued to the painting, and watched it for several seconds before he went back to his toys. I resumed my position in the rocker-recliner, and it wasn't long before my little grandson was back in my lap.

He looked up at my face, his big brown eyes filled with wonder. "Tell me again, Grandma. Tell me about what's behind the trees."

It became his favorite "Grandma" story, and I repeated it, with embellishments, over and over to him and a few years later to his little sister, Jessica, and to their younger cousins, Scott and Stephanie, all of whom were born during the next five years. But it was Nick who first told his sister and his cousins "what lurked behind the trees" in Grandma's painting.

I remain in awe of the power in a child's imagination. Imagination. That's what really resides behind the trees, behind creativity, and, eventually, behind invention and production.

~Barbara Elliott Carpenter

Chapter 9

Raising Great Kids

Learn from the Next Generation

The Honors Class

Don't live down to expectations. Go out there and do something remarkable.
~Wendy Wasserstein

The motley looking group of eleventh graders didn't look like any "honors" U.S. History class I'd ever imagined. They shuffled into my classroom, which I'd painstakingly decorated with Presidential portraits and colorful maps and framed copies of the Declaration of Independence and the Constitution, with an "attitude" that was apparent even to a rookie teacher.

Which is exactly what I was. Fresh out of college with a degree in history, a teaching certificate, and not a lick of experience. I was grateful to have a job, even if it was in one of the rougher high schools in the city where I lived.

"Good morning," I said brightly. I was greeted with vacant stares. "I'm so excited to have been selected to teach this honors class," I continued. "They usually don't let first-year teachers do that."

Several of the students sat up straighter and cut their eyes at each other. Too late, I wondered if I should have tried to hide the fact that I had zero teaching experience. Oh, well. "We're going to do things a little differently in this class because I know that all of you want a challenge."

By now, every student was staring at me with a puzzled expression.

"First off, let's rearrange these desks," I said. "I like lots of class discussion, so let's put them in a big circle so we can all see each other's faces." Several of the kids rolled their eyes, but they all got up and began scooting the desks out of the traditional straight rows. "Perfect! Thanks. Now, everybody choose a seat and let's play a game. When I point to you, tell me your name. Then tell me what you hate most about history."

Finally, some smiles. And lots more as our game progressed.

Amanda hated how history seemed to be all about war. Jose didn't like memorizing names and dates. Gerald was convinced that nothing that had happened in the past was relevant to his life. "Why should I care about a bunch of dead white guys?" was how he put it. Caitlyn hated tricky true-false questions. Miranda despised fill-in-the-blank tests.

We had just made our way around the circle when the bell rang. Who knew fifty minutes could pass so quickly?

Armed with the feedback my students had given me, I began formulating a plan. No teaching straight from the textbook for this group. No "read the chapter and answer the questions at the end" homework. These kids were bright. They were motivated. My honors class deserved to be taught in a way that would speak to them.

We'd study social and economic history, not just battles and generals. We'd tie current events into events from the past. We'd read novels to bring home the humanity of history. *Across Five Aprils* when studying the Civil War. *The Grapes of Wrath* to learn about the Great Depression. *The Things They Carried* when talking about Vietnam.

Tests would cover the facts, but also require higher level thinking skills. No tricky true-false questions. No fill-in-the-blank.

At first, I was surprised by how many of my students used poor grammar and lacked writing skills. And some seemed to falter when reading out loud. But we worked on those skills while we were learning history. I found that many of the kids were not only willing, but eager to attend the after-school study sessions I offered and to accept the help of peer tutors.

Four of my students came to love the subject matter so much that they formed their own "History Bowl" team and entered a countywide contest. Though they didn't take first place, they were ecstatic over the Honorable Mention trophy they brought home to our classroom.

The school year came to an end more quickly than I could have imagined. Though I had grown fond of many of my students, the ones in the honors class held a special place in my heart. Most had earned A's and B's. No one had averaged lower than a C.

During our final teacher workday before summer break, the principal called me into her office for my end-of-the-year evaluation.

"I want to congratulate you on a great rookie season," she said with a smile. "Especially on how well you did with your remedial kids."

"Remedial kids? I don't understand. I didn't have any remedial classes."

Mrs. Anderson looked at me in a strange way. "Your first period class was remedial. Surely you saw that indicated at the top of the roll." She pulled a file folder from a drawer and handed it to me. "And you must have suspected the students in that class were below average by the way they dressed and the way they carried themselves. Not to mention their terrible grammar and poor reading and writing skills."

I opened the file folder and removed a copy of the roll from my first period class. There at the top, plain as day, was the word HONORS. I showed it to Mrs. Anderson.

"Oh, dear," she said. "What a huge mistake! How did you ever manage, treating slow students as though they were…"

I couldn't help but finish the sentence for her. "As though they were bright?"

She nodded, looking more than a little sheepish.

"You know what, Mrs. Anderson? I think we've both learned a lesson from this. One they didn't teach in any of the education courses I took. But one I'll never forget."

"Nor will I," she said, circling the word HONORS with a red marker before placing the paper back in the folder. "Next year, I may just have this printed at the top of all the class rolls."

~Jennie Ivey

We Make Our Own Choices

The trouble with learning to parent on the job is that your child is the teacher.
~Robert Brault

Many years ago, I had a busy health care practice and was commuting two hours a day. I didn't get to spend much time with my family. At the time, our son Gabriel was almost three, and our other son Noah was nine months old. In addition to the practice and the young family, I was president of my professional association. Life was very busy.

Colleagues looked upon me with respect, asking, "How do you do it all?" Well, "it all" was about to collapse around me. My wife had suffered postpartum depression after Gabriel's birth and after Noah's it was even more severe. I ignored the clues that things weren't going well for her. I was busy, so I encouraged her to stay positive, read inspirational books, eat well, and exercise. I was so committed to my work that I dismissed her concerns, expecting her to make do.

When my wife admitted herself to hospital, the medical staff suggested she stay over the weekend for further evaluation. I didn't voice my protest, but I was thinking about the professional work I had to do.

After the weekend, I met with the medical staff and my wife. I listened quietly as they described that my wife needed to be admitted for several weeks. I defiantly told the psychiatrist that "you do not know my wife... she's not depressed!" Somehow I remained oblivious to my own observations and concerns regarding what I had seen and heard at home over many months.

I encouraged my wife to resist, believing the psychiatrist "crazy" for wanting to institutionalize her. I secretly panicked over missing my work and not meeting my financial obligations. The psychiatrist persisted, and stated my wife would not be free to leave until she was feeling better.

I remember the long walk down the overpass to the hospital parking lot. The children were with me and were quite fatigued from being at the hospital during their naptime. I still couldn't believe what was happening. I tried to remain calm for my older son, Gabriel, stating that Mommy had to stay with the doctors for a little while.

Later, when my mother joined us, I broke down. I cried for days—unusual because all my life I had concealed my emotions. I had developed great defiance towards a bullying father and refused to show vulnerability. Now, I couldn't hold back my feelings.

I arranged for all my appointments to be cancelled until further notice, and I made arrangements to take a leave of absence from the board of directors. I felt very alone for several days, crying whenever I had a short break from the all-encompassing duties of caring for our children. We visited my wife in hospital and I felt a deep ache in my gut every time we had to say goodbye.

My good friend Scott listened to my shock and despair. "How will I get through this?" I asked. "You have to... you have no choice," he compassionately replied.

Before this incident, I'd never been alone with the children for more than eight hours at a time. Now, I was their primary caretaker. Noah had still been breastfeeding, so we had to wean him onto a formula during my wife's hospitalization. This meant I had to awake in the night to feed him, change him, and care for both of them... all things my wife had done before.

I struggled to learn new skills, but over time I gained confidence as I realized I could care for my children. I actually enjoyed being home and spending time with them. My mother was a great help, and afforded me time here and there to go for walks to ruminate on my situation and process my feelings. I was beginning to understand and appreciate how challenging my wife's role had been.

The hospital visits were rough. My wife expressed anger over my former absences due to my professional pursuits. I was angry over the upheaval of my life. The social worker and hospital staff helped us to express our emotions and heal as we experienced many painful feelings.

I remember the day that was the turning point, when my hope was renewed. I realized that life had not stopped, but was in fact evolving for us. My wife had been in the hospital for about three weeks at this point, and I was playing outside with my older son. As we climbed atop a huge rock, Gabriel said "Daddy…"

"Yes, Gabriel." I turned to look at him, and was absolutely captivated by the young brown eyes that seemed far older and experienced than the boy that held them. As I gazed into these brown eyes, Gabriel said, "Daddy… we make our own choices."

I stared in disbelief. How could a boy so young say something so profound? I responded, "What… what did you say, Gabriel?" He realized my surprise and laughed with glee. He said again, "We make our own choices!"

The full impact of this message did not resonate within me at the time. I was not expecting to hear such words from a boy not yet three. But as I relayed the story to friends and family, I understood the clear message.

I was justifying my long hours and professional position as being best for the family. I realized my family had not been my first priority, but instead my status, prestige and desire for more material things were. I would have to change if I wanted to experience the home life I desired, and that my family deserved.

My new experience showed me I could be a competent and loving father and husband, and that I could miss several weeks of work without financial disaster. I made the decision to choose balance and happiness. I learned to let go of things that seemed important, but in the final analysis were not.

My life has far greater integrity now, and people no longer ask me "How do you do it all?" My wife is strong and vibrant, and the happiest I've ever seen her in our marriage together. The boys recognize the stability in our family, and are confident, healthy, and loving. I am aware that every day I make my own choices.

It may be interesting to note that the name Gabriel translates into "messenger of God." And on that sunny day in February many years ago, for me... he was.

~Donald Quinn Dillon

Same Agenda

Grandchildren are loving reminders of what we're really here for.
~Janet Lanese

W e were sitting in the crowded auditorium waiting for the program to view the performance of our seven-year-old grandson, Tanner, in his school's annual Christmas pageant.

It was difficult to say who was more excited — the children or the audience. I looked around and spotted my son and his wife, with their four-month-old baby boy, and Tanner's maternal grandparents seated several rows behind us. We acknowledged each other with a smile and a wave.

Then I saw them — Tanner's "biological" paternal grandparents. My son and Tanner's mother had dated briefly as sixteen-year-olds, split up, then became reacquainted shortly after their high-school graduation when Tanner was just six months old. Even though my daughter-in-law never married Tanner's father, his parents had fought for grandparents' rights and won. Tanner may call my son "Daddy," but Tanner is bound by court order to go every other weekend for visitation with the parents of his "biological" father.

We had taken Tanner into our hearts as our own, and we weren't very willing to share him.

This had always been a particular sore spot for me. We did not know them well, and I feared the worst when he went with them on their weekend. In retrospect, we should have viewed it as commendable that they were interested enough in Tanner to pay a lawyer and go through the complicated legal system.

So there we were, separated by a few rows of folding chairs. There were only a few instances where we had been thrown together, and each of these meetings had been uncomfortable. I saw the woman look at us, nudge her husband and whisper in his ear. He immediately looked back at us as well.

My ears were burning as if on fire. I attempted to remember why we were here — our common bond, a child that meant so much to us.

Shortly thereafter the program started, and for the next hour we were enthralled. Before we knew it, the lights were on, and we were gathering our things to leave. We followed the crowd into the hall and searched for our grandson.

We soon found him, and suddenly three sets of grandparents were thrown together, each waiting to take our turn in congratulating Tanner on a fine performance. We eyed each other and spoke a brief "hello."

Finally, it was our turn to hug Tanner and discuss his job well done. His eyes were shining brightly, and he was obviously proud to be the object of so much adoration.

I leaned down to hear what he was saying. "Grandma, I'm so lucky!" Tanner exclaimed, clapping his hands together.

"Because you did such a fine job?" I innocently asked.

"No, because all my favorite people are here! My Mom, Dad, little brother, and *all* my grandmas and grandpas are here together, just to see *me!*"

I looked up, stunned at his remark.

My eyes met those of the "other" grandma, and I could see she was feeling the same shame as I was. I was horrified at my thoughts and feelings over all these years.

What had given only me the right to love this little boy? They obviously loved him as much as we did, and he obviously loved each of us. They also no doubt had their own fears about us. How could we have been so blind?

As I looked around, I could see we were all ashamed of our previous feelings on this subject. We visited briefly, said our good-byes and went our separate ways.

I've thought a lot about our encounter since that night, and I admit I feel that a weight has been lifted off my shoulders. I don't fear Tanner's weekend visits like I used to.

I discovered that we all have the same agenda — to love a little boy who truly belongs to all of us.

~Patricia Pinney

Running Home

I would not waste my life in friction when it could be turned into momentum.
~Frances Willard

Shortly after my son turned ten, we moved to a new school district. Weeks passed and it seemed as though everyone in the family had made the transition well. After school, my son's only goal was to play outside with the neighbor kids. They all seemed to get along and have fun together. I found some comfort in knowing that he felt that he belonged. His new friends helped him blossom in a way that I had never noticed before. I told him one day that I thought his calling was to be a comedian. His eyes brightened and he beamed.

A few months after our move, my son walked in the door after school looking upset. I asked what was going on and he replied, "Nothing." I noticed as he passed that his brow was sweaty and his face looked a little flushed. With the cool weather outside, it seemed strange that he would build up a sweat walking from the bus stop to the house. I followed him into his room and asked him again if everything was all right. He seemed a little aggravated and said that he was fine, just tired. For a moment he seemed so mature for a ten-year-old. Still something seemed odd, but I decided to let it go.

The next afternoon I noticed the neighbor kids got home fifteen minutes before my son. I was beginning to get worried when he came in the door. He avoided my eyes as he passed and again I could see the sweat on his brow. I followed him into his room and tried to help him lift his backpack from his shoulder. He quickly pulled away. "What's going on?" I asked. I didn't know if he was fighting tears or trying to think up a story to tell me but he paused a few moments before answering.

Suddenly he stood up as tall as he could, looked me straight in the eye and said, "It's nothing, Mom. I can handle it." His maturity caught me by surprise, although my mother's intuition made me hesitate. I decided to back off and let him handle it for the time being.

The following afternoon I confronted the neighbor kids. Corralling the girl who professed to be his best friend, I asked if she knew where he was. She looked at her feet and managed to mumble something to the effect that I better ask him. I ran to the house to get my car keys and look for him. As I raced back to the car, keys in hand, I nearly stumbled over the neighbor girl. She was ready to confess and told me that my son had been getting off at the first bus stop eight blocks away. He would run home. She added that he wasn't doing anything wrong.

Then I saw my son walking slowly towards me. His head hung low and his shoulders where hunched. As he approached I could see tears on his cheeks. As soon as he saw me, he reached up quickly and wiped his eyes. I tried to act as though nothing were wrong. "Hey, did you decide to walk home?" I asked. He brushed past me and headed towards the house.

"What's going on?" I asked, when we were inside. He turned to me and dropped his backpack to the floor in a gesture of defiance.

"I didn't want to move here," he said quietly.

"Is there a problem at school?" I asked. "Is there something I need to know about?"

He let out a sigh of frustration, looked me straight in the eye and blurted out, "There's nothing you can do about this, Mom!"

"I could try," I offered.

"What could you do?" he cried. "This kid wants to beat me up and waits for me at the bus stop. If you call the school or anyone else he will just get even madder."

"Someone has to do something about a bully like that," I said. "I could talk to his parents."

"Mom, his parents don't care what he does. They cheer him on when he hits someone."

I was exasperated. I was devastated. I had taught my son never to hit anyone, to always try to talk things out, to resolve things peacefully. I felt completely useless as a parent. I sat down beside him. With a sigh of surrender, I said, "We can call the police."

Suddenly he sat up, turned to me and said, "Mom, I can take care of this. I'm not going to fight him. I can get off at the first bus stop and walk from there. It's no problem."

I was so angry at this bully and even more so at his parents. I wondered what kind of people would incite their son to bully other kids. I wanted to go to them and threaten them and give them a little of their own medicine. I just wanted to inflict the same fear and pain on them that their bullying son had inflicted on mine. But when I looked at my son, he actually looked sort of relaxed. His mouth turned up in his old familiar grin and he said, "Mom, it's going to be okay."

A few days later, my son was back to riding the bus home to the stop near our house. The bully had realized that my son was a comedian and had the ability to make even a bully laugh. Or maybe the kid realized that he needed fewer enemies; whatever the case, my son had reconciled their differences and resolved the problem peacefully.

It is amazing to me, as a parent, that my son was able to find a solution to such a big problem. He brings peace to situations where I would only create more chaos. Being a parent doesn't give us all the answers. Sometime the answers come in a simple form that only a kid can understand.

~Kim Ozment-Gold

Our "Family"

True generosity is an offering; given freely and out of pure love.
No strings attached. No expectations.
~Suze Orman

My daughter Gina was in Mrs. Melton's fourth-grade class. After only a month in school, she began to come home on a regular basis asking for pencils, crayons, paper, etc. At first I just dutifully provided whatever she needed, never questioning her.

After ongoing requests for items that should have easily lasted a mere six weeks of fourth grade, I became concerned and asked her, "Gina, what are you doing with your school supplies?" She would always respond with an answer that satisfied me.

One day, after supplying the same thing only a week earlier, I became irritated with her pleading for more and sternly asked her once more, "Gina! what is going on with your school supplies?" Knowing her excuses would no longer work, she bent her head and began to cry. I lifted her tiny chin and looked into those big brown eyes, filled now with tears. "What?! What is wrong?" My mind was racing with all sorts of ideas. Had she been bullied by another child? Was she giving her supplies to him or her to keep from being hurt, or to gain their approval? I couldn't imagine what was going on, but I knew it was something serious for her to cry. I waited for what seemed like an eternity for her to answer.

"Mom," she began, "there is a boy in my class; he doesn't have any of the supplies he needs to do his work. The other kids make fun of him because his papers are messy and he only has two crayons to color with. I have been putting the new supplies you bought me in his desk before the others come in, so he doesn't know it's me. Please don't get mad at me, Mom. I didn't mean to tell you a lie, but I didn't want anyone to know it was me."

My heart sank as I stood there in disbelief. She had taken on the role of an adult and tried to hide it like a child. I knelt down and hugged her to me, not wanting her to see my own tears. When I pulled myself together, I stood up and said, "Gina, I would never get mad at you for wanting to help someone, but why didn't you just come and tell me?" I didn't have to wait for her to answer.

The next day I visited Mrs. Melton. I told her what Gina had said. She knew John's situation all too well. The oldest of four boys, their parents had just moved here and when the school presented them with the school supply list for all four grades they were overwhelmed. When the boys came to school the next week, they barely had the necessities — a few sheets of paper and a pencil each.

I asked Mrs. Melton for the list from all four grades and told her I would take care of it the next day. She smiled and gave me the lists.

The next day, we brought the supplies in and gave them to the office with instructions to give them to the boys.

As Christmas neared, the thought of John, his brothers and family weighed heavily on my mind. What would they do? Surely they would not have money for gifts.

I asked Mrs. Melton if she could get me their address. At first she refused, reminding me that there was a policy that protected the privacy of the students, but because she knew me from my work at the school and involvement on the PTA board, she slipped a piece of paper into my hand and whispered, "Don't tell anyone I gave it to you."

When my family began to set the stage for our traditional Christmas Eve, which was usually held at my house, I simply told them all that my husband, the kids and I did not want gifts, but instead we would prefer to have groceries and gifts for our "family."

As the girls and I shopped throughout the holiday season, they delighted in picking things out for the four boys. Gina was especially interested in things for John.

Christmas Eve came and my family began to arrive. Each of them had bags of food and gifts wrapped for the children. My living room was full and the excitement was contagious.

Finally at 9:00 we decided it was time to take our treasures to them. My brothers, dad, uncles and nephews loaded up their trucks and set out for the apartment complex address that Mrs. Melton gave us.

They knocked on the door and a little boy appeared. They asked for his mother or dad and he ran away. The guys waited until a young man, hardly more than a child himself, came to the door. He looked at the men standing there, with arms full of gifts and bags full of groceries, and couldn't say a word. The men pushed past him and went straight to the kitchen counter to set the bags down.

There was no furniture. It was an empty one-bedroom apartment with a few blankets on the floor and a small TV where they obviously spent their time. A Christmas tree was the result of the kids bringing in a bush they had found in the field behind the complex. A few paper decorations made in their classrooms made it look like a real Christmas tree. Nothing was underneath.

The boys and their parents stood without speaking as the men sat down bag after bag. They finally asked who had sent them, how did they know them and so on. But the men just left them with shouts of "Merry Christmas!"

When the guys got back to my house they didn't say a word. They couldn't.

To break the silence, my aunt stood up and began to sing "Silent Night," and we all joined in.

When school resumed, Gina came home daily telling of John's new clothes and how the other children now played with him and treated him like the rest of the children.

She never told a soul at school about what we did, but every

Christmas since that one she will say to me, "Mom, I wonder what happened to John and his family? While I'm not quite sure of the answer, I'd like to think that John and his family were somehow helped by my daughter's gift.

~Linda Snelson

I Found My Son Again

Every day is an opportunity to make a new happy ending.
~Author Unknown

Let me share with you a story to illustrate the power of gratitude and mutual understanding that emerged through empathic listening.

I have a dear friend who once shared with me his deep concern over a son he described as being "rebellious," "disturbing," and "an ingrate."

"Stephen, I don't know what to do," he said. "It's gotten to the point where if I come into the room to watch television with my son, he turns it off and walks out. I've tried my best to reach him, but it's just beyond me."

At the time I was teaching some university classes around the 7 Habits. I said, "Why don't you come with me to my class right now? We're going to be talking about Habit 5 — how to listen empathically to another person before you attempt to explain yourself. My guess is that your son may not feel understood."

"I already understand him," he replied. "And I can see problems he's going to have if he doesn't listen to me."

"Let me suggest that you assume you know nothing about your son. Just start with a clean slate. Listen to him without any moral evaluation or judgment. Come to class and learn how to do this and how to listen within his frame of reference."

So he came. Thinking he understood after just one class, he went to his son and said, "I need to listen to you. I probably don't understand you, and I want to."

His son replied, "You have never understood me — ever!" And with that, he walked out.

The following day my friend said, "Stephen, it didn't work. I made such an effort, and this is how he treated me! I felt like saying, 'You idiot! Aren't you grateful for what I've done and what I'm trying to do now?' I really don't know if there's any hope."

I said, "He's testing your sincerity. And what did he find out? He found out you don't really want to understand him. You want him to shape up."

"He should, the little whippersnapper!" he replied. "He knows full well what he's doing to mess things up."

I replied, "Look at the spirit inside you now. You're angry and frustrated and full of judgments. Do you think you can use some surface-level listening technique with your son and get him to open up? Do you think it's possible for you to talk to him or even look at him without somehow communicating all those negative things you're feeling deep inside? You've got to do much more private work inside your own mind and heart. You'll eventually learn to appreciate him and to love him unconditionally just the way he is rather than withholding your love until he shapes up. On the way, you'll learn to listen within his frame of reference and, if necessary, apologize for your judgments and past mistakes or do whatever it takes."

My friend caught the message. He could see that he had been trying to practice the technique at the surface but was not dealing with what would produce the power to practice it sincerely and consistently, regardless of the outcome.

So he returned to class for more learning and began to work on his feelings and motives, particularly the need to appreciate, respect and empathize. He soon started to sense a new attitude within himself. His feelings about his son turned more tender and sensitive and open. He became profoundly grateful for his son, simply because he sincerely wanted to understood and appreciate his son.

He finally said, "I'm ready. I'm going to try it again."

I said, "He'll test your sincerity again."

"It's all right, Stephen," he replied. "At this point I feel as if he could reject every overture I make, and it would be all right. I would just keep making them because it's the right thing to do, and he's worth it. I feel so grateful for him and for the hard learning."

That night he sat down with his son and said, "I know you feel as though I haven't tried to understand and appreciate you, but I want you to know that I am trying and will continue to try."

Again, the boy coldly replied, "you have never understood me." He stood up and started to walk out, but just as he reached the door, my friend said to his son, "Before you leave, I want to say that I'm really sorry for the way I embarrassed you in front of your friends the other night."

His son whipped around and said, "You have no idea how much that embarrassed me!" His eyes began to fill with tears.

"Stephen," he said to me later, "all the training and encouragement you gave me did not even begin to have the impact of that moment when I saw my son begin to tear up. I had no idea that he even cared, that he was that vulnerable. For the first time I *really* wanted to listen. My gratitude grew immensely."

And listen he did. The boy gradually began to open up. They talked until midnight, and when his wife came in and said, "It's time for bed," his son quickly replied, "We want to talk, don't we, Dad?" They continued to talk into the early morning hours.

The next day in the hallway of my office building, my friend, with tears in his eyes, said, "Stephen, I found my son again."

As my friend discovered, there are certain fundamental principles that govern in all human interactions, and living in harmony with those principles or natural laws is absolutely essential for quality family life. In this situation, for example, the principles my friend had been violating were the basic principles of gratitude, empathy and respect. The son also violated them. But this father's choice to live in harmony with that principle — to try to genuinely and empathically listen to and understand his son — dramatically changed the entire situation. The son also felt so grateful for his father and for the understanding they achieved. You change one element in any chemical formula and everything changes.

Exercising the principles of gratitude, empathy and respect and being to able to genuinely and empathically listen to another human being are among the habits of highly effective people in any walk of life. Can you imagine a truly effective individual who would not respect and appreciate others or who would not deeply listen and understand?

~Stephen R. Covey

Defending Our Children

*When you are a mother, you are never really alone in your
thoughts. A mother always has to think twice, once for herself
and once for her child.*
~Sophia Loren

My husband and I had finally decided to be licensed
for foster care. Our children were young at the time,
and they were excited to get involved in caring for
a little brother or sister. The children we cared for
were never much older than three months, almost exclusively female,
and African American.

Providing foster care was a fun, rewarding and exhausting ministry. Everyone in the family was involved, pitching in where they could.
It truly was an enjoyable experience. There was only one big issue. My
father-in-law.

Our first long-term placement was three-month-old Evelyn, who
lived with us for two years. She was an even-tempered, fun-loving
little girl.

My husband's father was an eighty-year-old immigrant from the
"old country." Having suffered a stroke before my husband was born,
his body was paralyzed on the left side. My father-in-law didn't like
Evelyn because she was African American.

When taking a family picture, he'd make sure she was positioned behind someone. While she sat uncomprehendingly in her high chair, he would point his finger at her and request that she "Go back to Africa."

Mercifully, my children were too young to know what he was saying. My mother-in-law would glare and tell him to stop. But that only worked for a while. It would start all over again at the next visit.

I would leave those weekly dinners with a mix of anger and sadness. This was my child he was talking to. How could he do that? My husband wouldn't address the issue. "That's just him," he'd say. "He doesn't know any better."

After living with us for two years, Evelyn was adopted by her maternal grandmother.

Time passed, and we were ready to accept another long-term placement. I told my husband that I'd have to call his father first. His remarks and attitude would no longer be tolerated. The words were bad enough, but now my children were older, and they would understand his hurtful comments.

If he couldn't change, we would stop visiting. He wasn't going to be a reason to stop fostering, but he'd sure be a reason to stop putting a helpless child in his line of fire. I had to speak up.

I practiced my lines for days. It felt like weeks. The day of the call, I paced around the house waiting for more courage. I muttered to myself, "Come on now! It's just a phone call. What's the worst that can happen? What if he gets so mad, he refuses to speak to me again?"

All of this internal chatter wasn't helping. I was getting short of breath, which happens when I get nervous. Shaking my hands, trying in vain to flip away those nerves, I finally called.

My mother-in-law answered the phone, and we exchanged pleasantries. I asked to speak to my father-in-law. "Oh!" she responded. I never called to talk exclusively to him, so I knew she'd be surprised. Now he was on the phone.

Oh boy. My words came out very slowly at first. My stomach was flipping. "Hi!" I started out brightly. I should get an Academy Award for acting. I was feeling anything but bright.

"Remember how we were foster parents a few years ago?" No response. I plunged ahead. "I know how you treated our daughter last time. You said some mean things, and it really upset me."

It felt like I'd popped the cork from a shaken bottle of champagne. Finally released from my mind, the words now tumbled over each other in the race to be expressed.

"We are going to be taking another placement soon, and I wanted you to know that I can't accept that kind of attitude toward any child we are caring for."

Continued silence on the other end of the phone. Now for the really scary part. "If you feel that you can't change, we won't be visiting you while we are caring for this child."

And I was done. I felt like I was suspended in midair. Or waiting for the ax to fall. Now what?

Silence.

After a few seconds, which felt like years, he told me he didn't understand what I was talking about. While he did have a thick accent, I knew he had heard and understood me. I asked for my mother-in-law, and I explained the situation to her. I was a complete sweaty mess at this point.

She told me that she would speak to him as soon as we got off the phone.

Click.

Oh my Lord, call the paramedics. How I hated this. I try to avoid confrontation, and apparently my father-in-law does too. We never spoke of it again. We never had to.

I don't think he had ever been approached this way by any of his immediate family, and the experience probably shocked him. Maybe he was as surprised as my husband that he was capable of changing his behavior.

He accepted our next daughter. Not with open arms, but with tolerance. He would offer her little treats at the dinner table, and praise her block-building skills. It was a transforming moment for me to see him change so radically. Actually, it was probably more transforming for him.

We went on to care for ten more children, and with each one, he became more and more at ease. Seeing him finally singing "Happy Birthday" to our foster children, I knew his heart had changed.

This whole episode showed me how important it is to stand up for what is right, with or without fear. It taught me that sometimes you just have to take the lead, bite the bullet, grab the bull by the horns… pick your favorite cliché.

In spite of my anxiety, I had to do the right thing and speak up. You know what else I learned? That words can change the world, one person at a time.

~Ceil Ryan

Broken Shells

Wisdom is ofttimes nearer when we stoop than when we soar.
~William Wordsworth

t was a warm summer afternoon in mid-July at the Jersey shore. My four-year-old son and I just loved venturing off to the beach just before dinner when the rest of the vacationers seemed to be leaving for the day. The sun was still hot and shining bright. With bucket in hand, we'd hit the sand and start our adventure. Will would run so quickly to the edge of the water and be soaked before I got there, laughing as the waves crashed and nearly knocked him down. I remember the days not so long ago when a trip to the beach was just unbearable for my little boy. His sensitivities to sights, sounds, and touches would prevent us from enjoying everyday activities, such as a walk by the shore. My son, Will, was diagnosed with autism spectrum disorder (ASD), and despite the fact that he is high-functioning, he has spent many hours in therapy, helping him to overcome the many challenges he faces. The beach is now one of his favorite places to visit. I am thrilled, because it is a place where I feel at home and filled with peace, and I wanted to be able to share that with Will.

Presently, we are able to walk along the edge of the water almost daily in the summer months, looking for seashells to fill our red sand-castle-shaped bucket. Some days, the bucket is full, and other days just a few shells make it into the bucket. On this particular day, there didn't seem to be too many shells washed up on the shore. Will began picking up whatever shells he saw lying in the sand. After a while, I peered into the bucket and saw nothing but broken shells. "Will," I said, "all of these shells are broken and no good. You need to find shells like this," I continued, as I held up a perfectly shaped clamshell. Will gave me a puzzled look and continued on his way, gathering whatever shells he came upon and dropping them into the bucket.

I continued my search for some time, and then stopped to watch him drop more broken shells into the bucket. Again I stopped, but this time I asked in a more stern voice, "Will, why do you insist on filling our bucket with shells that are broken?" He looked up at me through his glasses with his big blue eyes and replied, "Mom, there are way more shells on the beach that are broken than there are perfect ones that you are searching for. We'll get the bucket filled faster with the broken ones." *True,* I thought, *but who wants a bucketful of broken shells?* Will stared at me as if he knew what I was thinking. "Mom, these shells are broken, but they are still beautiful," he chimed. Just then he reached his little hand into the bucket and began pulling out the different shells and commenting on their uniqueness. "This one is broken, but look, it has the color purple on it. Mom, none of yours have purple on them," he said with such pride.

"You're right, Will," I agreed.

"And, Mom, this one looks like a smile when you hold it this way," he said as he reached for another broken shell. "It reminds me of a clown. This one is round like the sun, and these ones are stuck together like butterfly wings."

My eyes filled with tears as I realized my son was teaching me a most valuable lesson. I reached my hand into the bucket and began to take out the few perfect shells I had collected and placed them back on the beach. Will and I walked along the beach, collecting only broken shells in our bucket and admiring their beauty.

When we arrived back at our beach home, we rinsed off our bucket of shells and proudly displayed our "broken shell garden" next to our patio. It is a constant reminder of how none of us are perfect. We are all broken in some way, but we still possess beauty and uniqueness beyond belief. Now, whenever we go to the beach, we gather only broken shells. Yes, it's true, while the perfect shells are few and far between, there are many more broken shells left lying on the beach that go unnoticed. If we take the time to look more closely at the broken shells, we can find beauty in their imperfections, and maybe even learn something about ourselves.

~Debbie Jaskot

A New Home

Bringing up a family should be an adventure, not an anxious discipline in which everybody is constantly graded for performance.
~Milton R. Saperstein

"Mom, watch out!" my daughter Melissa screamed as a drenched brown pooch charged under our van. Slamming my foot on the brakes, we jerked to a stop. Stepping out into the freezing rain, we hunched down on opposite sides of the van, making kissing noises to coax the little dog — who, miraculously, I hadn't hit — to us. The shivering pup jumped into Melissa's arms and then onto her lap once she sat down again in the heated van.

We were on our way home from Melissa's sixth-grade basketball game. Her once-white shirt with the red number 7 was now covered in dirty black paw prints. I stared at the mess as she wrapped her shirt around the small dog.

"That shirt will never come clean!"

"Well, at least we saved his life," she frowned as she cuddled him. "Running through all those cars he could have been killed."

She continued petting him. "He's so cute. And he doesn't have a collar. Can we keep him?"

I knew how she felt. I loved animals myself — especially dogs. But I also knew the mess they made. Dogs dig through the garbage. They chew up paper, shoes and anything else they can fit in their mouths. Not to mention the little piles and puddles they make when you're trying to housebreak them. I didn't need a dog. I loved the clean, bright house we had recently moved into, and I wanted to keep my new house looking just that — new.

I glanced at the ball of brown fur and the black mask outlining his wide, wondering eyes. *She's right. He is cute.*

The smell of wet dog escalated with the burst of heat coming out of the vents, bringing me to my senses. I turned the heat down and shook my head. "Melissa, we've been through this before. I told all four of you kids when we moved into the new house: absolutely no pets."

As we pulled into the drive, she said, "But Mom, it's the middle of February. He'll freeze out here."

I glanced at the pup licking Melissa's fingers. "Okay," I decided. "We'll give him a bath, keep him for the night and call the animal shelter tomorrow."

Still frowning, Melissa nodded and slid out of the van. Carrying the dog in her arms, she entered the house. By the time I reached the door, the news was already out.

"We've got a new puppy!" Robert, Brian and Jeremiah chorused.

"I'm afraid not," I said, as I took off my shoes. "We're only keeping him overnight."

Wiggling out of Melissa's arms, the pup scampered across the room and jumped up on my couch.

"Get down!" I shouted, pointing my finger at him and toward the floor.

He licked his nose remorsefully and sat there shaking.

"Mom, you're scaring him." Melissa scooped him into her arms. "C'mon, boy, I'll take you to my room."

"Ah-ah," I corrected, "bath first."

All four kids crowded around the puppy in the bathroom. I listened over the running water as each became excited over every splash the dog made. Their giggles brought a smile to my face. *Maybe it wouldn't be such a bad idea to have a dog.*

I glanced around the kitchen with its shiny black-and-white tile floor. Picturing a dog dish, with food and water heaping into a sloshing puddle of goo, I turned toward the living room. With this messy weather, I envisioned my pale-blue carpeting "decorated" with tiny black paw prints. Not to mention the shedding, fleas and all the other things a dog can bring. I shook my head. *A dog will ruin this place.*

After his bath, Melissa brought him out wrapped in one of our good white towels. He looked like a drowned rat, except for his big, brown puppy-dog eyes. The boys raced around the kitchen getting food and water.

The water sloshed back and forth in the bowl. "Be careful, Jeremiah," I warned. "You're gonna spill—" When Jeremiah heard my voice he stopped with a sudden jerk. Water splashed onto his face and down the front of shirt and blue jeans, soaking the floor.

I ran to get towels. When I returned, I watched in horror as the pup tramped through the water. Even after his bath, his feet were still dirty and left muddy little prints all over my kitchen floor. "Wipe his feet and put him in your room, Melissa. *Now!*"

Melissa snatched the dog up, with the boys traipsing at her heels. I sighed as I wiped up the mud and water. After a few minutes, the floor shined like new, and laughter erupted from Melissa's bedroom.

My husband, John, came in from work moments later. "What's so funny?" he asked after he kissed me on the cheek.

"A dog."

"A dog?" he asked, surprised. "We have a dog?"

"Not by choice," I explained. "It ran under the van. And of course I couldn't just leave him in the middle of the street."

John smiled. "What happened to no pets?"

"I told them he's going tomorrow."

After John joined the kids he came back out. "You know, he is really cute."

"Yeah, I know." He didn't have to convince me; my resolve was already slipping.

The next morning, the kids mauled the dog with hugs and tears. "Can't we keep him?" they sobbed. I watched how he gently and tenderly licked each one as if to comfort them.

"I promise we'll take care of him," Melissa said.

"Yeah, and I'll water him," Jeremiah added. I smiled, remembering the incident the night before. "But I won't fill his dish so full next time."

How could I say no? *He's housebroken. He's cute. And he's great with the kids.*

"We'll see," I said, as they scooted out the door for school. "But first, I'll have to call the dog pound to make sure no one is looking for him."

Their faces lit up as they trotted down the drive. With John already at work, the pup and I watched from the door as the four kids skipped down the street. Once they turned the corner, I grabbed the phone book and found the number for the animal shelter.

The lady at the shelter informed me that no one had reported a brown dog missing. However, she instructed me to put an ad in the local paper about him for three days, and if no one responded, we could legally keep him for our own. I called the newspaper and placed the ad. Although I had mixed feelings, mostly I hoped his owners would claim him.

Each day, the kids would ask the same question, "Did anyone call?" And each day it was always the same answer: "Nope."

By the third day, the dog and I had spent so much time together that he followed me around the house. If I sat on the couch, he'd jump in my lap. If I folded clothes, he'd lie by the dryer. If I made dinner, he'd sit by the refrigerator. Even when I went to bed, he'd follow, wanting to cuddle up with me.

"Looks like we have to come up with a name," I said Sunday morning at breakfast.

The kids cheered and threw out some names. When we returned from church, I played the messages on our answering machine, my heart sinking when I heard: "I think you may have my dog."

After speaking with the lady, I realized that Snickers was indeed her dog. She explained she'd be over to get him within the hour. As we sat around the table, picking at the pot roast, tears flooded our plates like a river. Even I had grown attached to this sweet little dog.

When the lady arrived, I met her at the door. I clenched a wet tissue in my hands and invited her in. She took in the scene: four mournful children sitting in a huddle around the little dog and petting him, while Snickers, perched on Melissa's lap, licked her tears away.

After a long moment, she said, "I want you to have him. I can see you love him and we already have another dog."

I gave her a hug while the kids cheered in the background.

Snickers has definitely left his mark on our house. Still, I wouldn't trade his muddy paw prints for anything—not even the nicest-looking house in the world! For, although he makes little messes sometimes, he has filled our hearts with love. Before Snickers came into our lives, we had a new house. Now we have a new home.

~Elisabeth A. Freeman

More

We worry about what a child will become tomorrow, yet we forget that he is someone today.
~Stacia Tauscher

Her tiny, delicate features drew me closer for another look. With my very first glance I thought her to be perfectly angelic. A halo of soft auburn hair framed the pretty little face that ever-so-shyly curved in a smile. Her tongue was reaching for something it couldn't find... a taste, a touch... just reaching, reaching.

"She's beautiful," I said to my son's girlfriend Amanda. Lilly was her daughter from a previous marriage. She and Jim had been dating for a few months, and this was the first time I had met them.

Jim had told me that Lilly had Down syndrome. I really had no idea what to expect. I'd known very few people with disabilities, and honestly was uncertain about what having Down syndrome entailed.

"Would it be okay to hold her?" I asked.

Amanda took Lilly out of her car seat and handed her to me. Her little head leaned softly on my shoulder as though she had known me forever. She smelled of baby shampoo and milk, the way my own babies smelled so many years ago. It broke my heart to think of her father and how he couldn't accept the fact that his daughter had a disability. The marriage ended in part because of his intolerance.

I spent the next few weeks getting to know Amanda and Lilly, and in those weeks came to understand the passion this mother had for her child.

"Lilly was born with a heart condition," Amanda explained. Apparently most Downs children are born with heart defects. "Lilly was one of the lucky ones. Hers was able to be fixed." This meant Lilly wouldn't endure the subsequent surgeries so many Downs children face during their childhoods.

Amanda's days were packed with work, doctor's appointments, and therapies for Lilly. While Lilly's heart was strong, her immune system was weak, and she had developed skin conditions and allergies to some foods. Still Amanda persevered with a smile and strong determination, never allowing her life's circumstances to get her down. She astonished our family with her amazingly upbeat attitude. The more we got to know Lilly, the more we understood how and why Amanda's outlook stayed so positive.

We started seeing Amanda mirrored in Lilly's eyes, Lilly's attitude, and Lilly's ever-changing and developing personality. We had initially met a small, rather shy peanut of a girl, and within months knew an active, happy little girl with the ability to melt hearts wherever she went.

In time we watched Lilly learn a few words, crawl in her offbeat way, and show favoritism for toys, foods, and people. Lilly's therapist was teaching her American Sign Language so we all tried to learn. Lilly and Amanda of course outshined us all, but we tried hard to keep up with the basics and signed to Lilly things like "fish," "all done," "I love you," and Lilly's favorite word — "more."

"More" is the word Lilly uses now to indicate she'd like another cookie. It means she likes her dinner and will eat a few more bites. It means she wants to play "this little piggy went to market…" for the umpteenth time, or sing "Twinkle Twinkle Little Star" yet again.

"More" took on a brand new meaning for all of us, too. It meant we could spend more time singing, laughing, tickling and teaching Lilly the things she seemed so eager to learn; and while she may not learn them as quickly as "normal" children, we all delight in the little steps of progress — the little things in life.

"More" means we sit a while longer at the dinner table and chat with one another about the day's events, while Lilly has another dish of fruit or another ginger snap, or while she tries drinking water from a sippy cup like the big kids do.

Above all else, "more" signifies the way Lilly and Amanda have enriched our lives since meeting them three years ago. By not judging and freely accepting this little wonder and her beautiful mom, we've learned love doesn't come in perfect packages. We've learned there's a lot to do to improve upon life's little bumps in the road, but that such improvements make us all better people in the end.

We've learned to love more freely. We've learned to hug more often. We've learned that wet and sloppy kisses on our cheek or on our eyebrow are sometimes the very best ones we can receive.

We've learned that life doesn't come with guarantees, but gives us incredible gifts we'd never expected. And we've learned just how precious those gifts can be when wrapped in the package of a sweet little girl with Down syndrome.

Jim, Amanda, and Lilly will soon be a family. A wedding is in the very near future, and that will make me Lilly's "Nana." In the meantime we're blessed to see them several times each week. When I hear my front door open, followed by the pitter-patter of uneven — sometimes clumsy — little steps coming down the hallway toward my home office, I smile. Joy seeps in and fills me up, as a little girl named Lilly walks through the doorway and smiles a big crooked smile, with arms outstretched, and calls me "Nana."

I look at Amanda, trailing swiftly behind, and my heart fills with love and gratitude for the precious gift she's nurtured and shared with us here. And it is then that I truly know I've been offered, as has my son Jim — and we've all freely accepted so very, very much "more!"

~Kimberly Ripley

Grandmother's Gift

Books are the quietest and most constant of friends; they are the most accessible and wisest of counselors, and the most patient of teachers.
~Charles W. Eliot

My grandmother has been gone for many years now and while she was alive, we were not particularly close. We saw each other infrequently and each conversation was strained. How is it possible that a woman whose life only briefly intersected with mine would influence me in such a profound way? This is a story of a grandmother who loved a little girl and bestowed upon her a gift. She did not know if she would ever receive a thank you. This grandmother knew that what she had to give was one of the greatest gifts a child could receive.

My grandmother lived alone, far away in an apartment in a big imposing building my brother, sister and I called "the castle." She was well educated, spoke several languages, traveled through Europe alone, collected antiques, and listened to opera. Her apartment was decorated with antiques and filled with hundreds of books she read and spoke of often.

I lived in suburban Long Island and only saw her once each year or so. My father would call her on Sunday nights and ask me to speak on the phone with her. I would wail at the thought. My father would always make eyes at me, which told me I didn't have a choice. He would always insist that she missed me and loved me but I didn't really ever believe him. I knew she would ask me about school, about what I was reading and what I was learning about. I was a horrible student who could never pay attention and squirmed in my classroom seat. I wanted to be outside playing and talking with my friends.

I would begrudgingly take the phone and speak to her for a few long moments. "I wish this lady would get a clue to what life is really about," I would think as I hung up the phone. Her inability to know what was important was never more evident than at gift-giving time.

Each year, on Christmas morning, my brother, sister and I would run down the stairs and see a beautiful tree surrounded by brightly wrapped packages. We would dive into the pile with great delight, ripping the paper and revealing all the latest toys. Eventually, I would see an odd-looking package deep under the tree that I knew could only be from Grandmother. She never used traditional Christmas paper and her presents always had brightly colored ribbons in yellows, oranges or lavender. Each year I would take that package, feel the weight of it in my hand, knock on it with my fist and hear a sharp tap. "Another book, just like every year!" I would think and then promptly toss it aside without even opening it. I would gleefully play with my toys on Christmas morning and for days and even weeks after. Eventually, I would open Grandmother's gift and glance through the pages of the book she had chosen. My grandmother, in her distinctive, beautiful handwriting, would inscribe each book: "To Elizabeth Rose, with love, from Grandmother." I would read the book and sometimes memorize the text. I still didn't count this as playing, or having fun. I certainly knew in my heart that reading a book or talking about school was no fun for a child.

As the years passed, my interest in school remained minimal. It was all too boring and formal for me. I was more resistant than ever to speaking to Grandmother on Sunday evenings. School, books and what "interesting things I had learned lately" were boring topics for old people to discuss. Didn't Grandmother know that all I cared about was friends, clothes and boys? Each Christmas, more books were under the tree, reinforcing my belief that she really didn't care.

Although I was not interested in school, I had enormous patience with younger children. Our neighbor across the street asked me to help her daughter with her homework after school. I was able to teach her in the way I wish I were able to learn. I made up songs and stories to help her memorize facts and we played games to test what she had learned. Her mom remarked, "You should become a teacher when you grow up Liz; you are so good at helping children." At first, the idea seemed ridiculous to me. I was a terrible student. How could it ever happen?

Slowly the idea took root and I decided to give college a try. Having a goal made things easier for me and I began to apply myself. Selecting courses and having different teachers suited me as well. My second semester, I sat in my first required education class — Children's Literature. The professor spoke about making children's books come alive, filling children's worlds with rich vocabulary, and the characteristics of a classic children's book. It was my favorite class and I was always eager to get there and participate in each discussion. About midway into the class our teacher discussed the differences between a children's book that is here for the moment and those that are enduring classics. She flashed a list of books on her overhead projector that included titles that had been awarded a Newbery Medal or were Caldecott winners. It was then a lump began to form in my throat.

Armed with a handwritten copy of my teacher's list of classics, I raced home, dropped my schoolbooks and ran to the basement. There in the corner on a dusty shelf sat the most amazing collection of children's books any teacher could hope to have. As I ran my fingers across the bindings of *Frederick*, *Tales from the Ballet*, *The Trumpet of the Swan* and *Stuart Little* memories came flooding back. Memories of receiving these books, staring at those pages late at night curled up in my bed and gazing at beautiful pictures. I remembered my grandmother reading Leo Lionni's *Frederick* to me when she came to visit one spring. I was so sure I had figured out the ending, and finding out I was wrong delighted me.

It was then I realized I didn't remember most of the toys I had gotten all those Christmases and with the exception of one old doll, all of the mounds of presents did not make it to my adulthood. Most, in fact, were discarded soon after they were played with or were broken or sold at garage sales. Now I stood before a treasure that I would not trade for anything. As I bent back the cover of *Make Way for Ducklings*, I saw my grandmother's familiar and stylish handwriting that read, "To Elizabeth Rose, with love, from Grandmother." Love was exactly what my grandmother had been giving me all of my years. She resisted the happiness of a beaming child opening an expensive toy and replaced it with a gift that was a part of her. She didn't give me what I wanted in my little girl mind, but what she knew I needed — a gift for the soul that would last a lifetime. Now I saw how wise she had been and how each book was so carefully selected at different times of my life.

I sat down that day and wrote my grandmother a letter. I expressed as well as I could how much I was enjoying school and how my collection of children's books was a treasure. I wrote about my happy memories reading them and about how much I knew I was loved. I placed my letter in a box with a pillow that had a mallard duck on the front. It looks like the duck in the book, *Make Way for Ducklings*, I wrote. This letter was as much for me as it was for her and I planned on telling her more about school and hearing more about her favorite books each time we spoke. Sometimes, what we plan never happens. Shortly after she received my letter, my grandmother died. My aunt who lives nearby told me how much my words had meant to her in her final days.

I continued to water the seed she planted so long ago. I graduated college with honors and received my master's degree in remedial reading. I became a teacher and I try my best to plant those tiny seeds in all my students. Sometimes I can see the world of words opening up right before their eyes. Some students squirm and do not pay attention, but I do not lose faith or feel as if all my efforts won't someday change their lives and that seed won't take root. I know now that I don't have to see the finished product to believe that a work I have started may take many years to reach completion.

I find that I am most happy now only when I am stealing moments in my busy day to read a good book. Although my own children can now read independently, I still take delight in reading aloud to them. This summer I read them *Island of the Blue Dolphins* and they would groan when I called them over to listen. Undaunted, I would read, and by the close of each session they would always ask for more. Now, I consider my time reading peaceful, a world of possibilities, second only to church. As I open the cover to a new book, I feel the shadow of my grandmother beside me and it is almost as if the inside cover of every book reads, "To Elizabeth Rose, with love, from Grandmother."

~Elizabeth Rose Reardon Farella

Meet Amy Newmark

Amy Newmark was a writer, speaker, Wall Street analyst and business executive in the worlds of finance and telecommunications for thirty years. Today she is publisher, editor-in-chief and coauthor of the *Chicken Soup for the Soul* book series. By curating and editing inspirational true stories from ordinary people who have had extraordinary experiences, Amy has kept the twenty-two-year-old Chicken Soup for the Soul brand fresh and relevant, and still part of the social zeitgeist.

Amy graduated *magna cum laude* from Harvard University where she majored in Portuguese and minored in French. She wrote her thesis about popular, spoken-word poetry in Brazil, which involved traveling throughout Brazil and meeting with poets and writers to collect their stories. She is delighted to have come full circle in her writing career — from collecting poetry "from the people" in Brazil as a twenty-year-old to, three decades later, collecting stories and poems "from the people" for Chicken Soup for the Soul.

Amy has a national syndicated newspaper column and is a frequent radio and TV guest, passing along the real-life lessons and useful tips she has picked up from reading and editing thousands of Chicken Soup for the Soul stories.

She and her husband are the proud parents of four grown children. Follow her on Twitter @amynewmark and @chickensoupsoul.

Meet Dr. Milton Boniuk

Dr. Milton Boniuk has practiced ophthalmology for nearly sixty years, and is The Caroline F. Elles Chair of Ophthalmology and Professor of Ophthalmology at Baylor College of Medicine in Houston, Texas. A native of Nova Scotia, Dr. Boniuk attended medical school at Dalhousie University in Halifax, Nova Scotia before moving to the United States for his residency at Wills Eye Hospital in Philadelphia, followed by a fellowship at the Armed Forces Institute of Pathology in Washington, D.C.

Dr. Boniuk and his wife Laurie live near their children and grandchildren in Houston. The Boniuk family has a strong commitment to philanthropy and a vision for change. Their belief that the world can be made a better place guides the work of The Boniuk Foundation, which sponsored this collection of Chicken Soup for the Soul stories. The Foundation believes that all religions, cultures, and ethnicities have a unique contribution to share with the world, and that differences among individuals are to be celebrated and not feared. Thus, the values of compassion, tolerance, and respect must be instilled in our young people, and this volume is designed to do that in an entertaining and accessible way.

Dr. Boniuk and his wife Laurie have also funded The Boniuk Institute for the Study and Advancement of Religious Tolerance at

Rice University, with the mission of promoting research, education, outreach, and better parenting to foster religious tolerance by using innovative methods to reach young people, their parents, and their grandparents. The Institute's logo is seen on the cover of this book, with its three key words—Tolerance, Respect, and Compassion—surrounded by the symbols of many of the world's major religions.

Sharing Happiness, Inspiration, and Wellness

Real people sharing real stories, every day, all over the world. In 2007, *USA Today* named *Chicken Soup for the Soul* one of the five most memorable books in the last quarter-century. With over 100 million books sold to date in the U.S. and Canada alone, more than 200 titles in print, and translations into more than forty languages, "chicken soup for the soul" is one of the world's best-known phrases.

Today, twenty-two years after we first began sharing happiness, inspiration and wellness through our books, we continue to delight our readers with new titles, but have also evolved beyond the bookstore, with wholesome and balanced pet food, delicious nutritious comfort food, and a major motion picture in development. As a socially conscious company, we use the sales of our products to give back, supporting numerous non-profits in the U.S. and across the globe. Whatever you're doing, wherever you are, Chicken Soup for the Soul is "always there for you™." Thanks for reading!

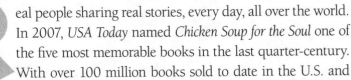

Share with Us

We all have had Chicken Soup for the Soul moments in our lives. If you would like to share your story or poem with millions of people around the world, go to chickensoup.com and click on "Submit Your Story." You may be able to help another reader, and become a published author at the same time. Some of our past contributors have launched writing and speaking careers from the publication of their stories in our books!

We only accept story submissions via our website. They are no longer accepted via mail or fax.

To contact us regarding other matters, please send us an e-mail through webmaster@chickensoupforthesoul.com, or fax or write us at:

Chicken Soup for the Soul
P.O. Box 700
Cos Cob, CT 06807-0700
Fax: 203-861-7194

One more note from your friends at Chicken Soup for the Soul: Occasionally, we receive an unsolicited book manuscript from one of our readers, and we would like to respectfully inform you that we do not accept unsolicited manuscripts and we must discard the ones that appear.

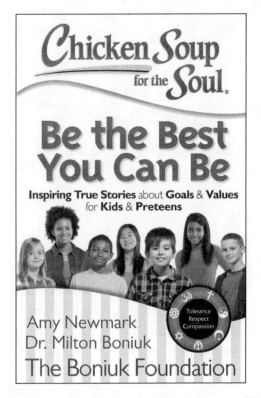

Chicken Soup for the Soul.

Be the Best You Can Be

Inspiring True Stories about **Goals** & **Values** for **Kids** & **Preteens**

Amy Newmark
Dr. Milton Boniuk
The Boniuk Foundation

Tolerance
Respect
Compassion

Self-esteem, tolerance, good values — these are gifts that will last children a lifetime and help them become successful adults. This book, a joint project of Chicken Soup for the Soul and The Boniuk Foundation, harnesses the power of storytelling to inspire and teach kids about working together to promote tolerance, respect, and compassion. The stories, about embracing differences, rejecting stereotypes, and making good choices, are great for kids to discuss with each other and the adults in their lives. It's part of a larger effort that includes additional books for teens, college students, parents, and grandparents, as well as a family television show every Saturday morning starting in October.

978-1-942649-00-7

More great advice

To be a success in life it's important to get along with other people at home, at school, at work and at play. These stories—addressing topics as diverse as embracing differences, rejecting stereotypes, making good life choices and exhibiting self-esteem—have been specially selected from Chicken Soup for the Soul's vast library of bestselling books. Both entertaining and inspirational, each personal account is a way to show tomorrow's leaders not just what a role model looks like, but how they too can be role models. The values that young adults learn today will stay with them for the rest of their lives, whether it's showing maturity and understanding about bullying; religious, ethnic, and lifestyle tolerance; or sticking up for what's right. These stories will help them see how to become the best adults they can be, and how to create their best futures.

978-1-942649-02-1

and inspiration!

The Boniuk Foundation

www.theboniukfoundation.org

For moments that become stories™
www.chickensoup.com